BLOOD
&
THUNDER

BLOOD
&
THUNDER

INSIDE AN ULSTER PROTESTANT BAND

DARACH MACDONALD

MERCIER PRESS
IRISH PUBLISHER – IRISH STORY

MERCIER PRESS
Cork
www.mercierpress.ie

Trade enquiries to CMD BookSource,
55a Spruce Avenue, Stillorgan Industrial Park,
Blackrock, County Dublin

ISBN: 978 1 85635 672 5

10 9 8 7 6 5 4 3 2 1

A CIP record for this title is available from the British Library

Acknowledgement

The author would like to acknowledge the grant received from the Arts
Council of Northern Ireland, for the research and writing of this book.

Printed and bound in the EU.

CONTENTS

INTRODUCTION

KINGS OF THE WILD FRONTIER

Our flags in front fly proudly o'er us,
Next the drummers go thundering by;
Then the flutes playing tunes of glory
'No Surrender' is the Castlederg cry.

Chorus of 'The Castlederg Song'

Thursday, 18 December 2008

Derek Hussey looks me in the eye as I perch on the edge of a bar stool opposite him. We are in the otherwise deserted Davy Crockett Lounge at the back of his pub, The Castle Inn, on Main Street, Castlederg. 'I think there's a great story to be told about Ulster Loyalist culture through the Blood and Thunder bands,' he remarks. 'Pity it's a Taig who'll be telling it.' I return his steady gaze with a look of surprise. He pauses momentarily, then smiles. The Ulster Unionist councillor, former member for West Tyrone in the Northern Ireland Assembly and founding bandmaster of the

7

Castlederg Young Loyalists Flute Band, is taking the sting out of his observation with that smile; but we both know he means what he says. For here I am, an outsider from an Irish Catholic background and the editor, until recently, of the local newspaper that traditionally served the Nationalist population, poking my nose into a fundamental aspect of modern Ulster Loyalist culture and aiming to present it to the scrutiny of a public which, if it is familiar with the sound and spectacle of what are widely known as 'Kick the Pope' bands, has probably made up its mind about them already.

Yet the former bandmaster, whose credentials as a tough-talking Loyalist proved crucial to David Trimble's Ulster Unionist Party in the transition to the devolved power-sharing government of Northern Ireland, is still prepared to take a risk. Indeed, he is immensely proud of the Blood and Thunder band he led from its beginning and of the values and traditions it represents. He believes that if there is to be full reconciliation of Northern Ireland's divided society, then there has to be respect for Ulster Loyalist culture and absolute acceptance of its celebration of Protestant identity and history. Crucial to the understanding and acceptance of this is the need for fair appraisal and equal treatment of the core aspects of a vibrant culture that revolves around parades, rituals and musical celebration of what are regarded as the great events that combined to create the Ulster Protestant identity. The role of marching bands is at least as central now to all that celebration as the more formal and widely known loyal institutions (Orange Order, Royal Black Preceptory and the Apprentice Boys of Derry) they accompany on parades for the big public occasions of the traditional marching season. For it is widely acknowledged that the huge crowds would not turn out to watch parading lines of men in suits and sashes without the accompanying bands; and of the bands, it is the loud Blood and Thunder flute bands that rule the roost.[1]

The ascendancy of the Blood and Thunder bands – and their steady evolution as more accomplished marching bands – should not be a surprise. For although they are virtually shunned as of little or no consequence by the mass media and politely ignored by much of 'respectable Unionism', many of these bands have been in existence for thirty years or more. Besides the huge numbers of young band members and adult organisers involved today, countless thousands have passed through their ranks. The Loyalist youth has long been drawn to the muscular music of the Blood and Thunder bands and the military tradition they represent when marching along in formation and in uniform. Indeed, most Unionist leaders have had more than a passing relationship with the Blood and Thunder bands at some point in their lives. So while their critics dismiss them as peripheral, urban manifestations of hard-line attitudes, they are much more representative of Ulster Loyalist culture than other institutions that are in perennial decline. Furthermore, the bands, and the huge, popular Ulster Loyalist movement they represent, are now at a crucial stage of development and the outcome of that will determine in large part the capacity for change across the entire spectrum of the Unionist community in Northern Ireland.

Yet attitudes are slow to change on both sides of the divide. Invariably today, the trenchant objections of Nationalist resident groups to parades by Loyalist organisations have focused on the role of the Blood and Thunder bands. Nationalist groups claim that the bands are openly provocative in their choice of music, choosing what they consider 'sectarian songs' and playing them in a manner that is solely designed to offend. Yet in a year of parades that encompasses almost 4,000 events, of which some 3,000 are organised exclusively on the Unionist side of the community, a mere handful are now regarded as flashpoints. The best known of these are the Drumcree church parade in Portadown, County Armagh, and the Cock of the North parade in the Springfield Road/ Ardoyne area of Belfast. Others that have flared occasionally in recent years are scattered throughout the six counties – in places such as Derry city, Rasharkin in County Antrim, Newry in County Down, Newtownbutler in County Fermanagh and Castlederg in County Tyrone. Invariably the flashpoints have been sparked by a reaction of those who say they have been offended by the Blood and Thunder bands. Yet the simple truth is that thousands of parades in Northern Ireland each year pass off peaceably without any media attention, good or bad, and while some might object to the bands, many more choose to be entertained by them.

In large part, the antipathy of Nationalists to the marching tradition of Ulster Loyalists resides in a refusal to accept the fundamental tradition and culture of the other side of the community. Since the Plantation of Ulster 400 years ago, Protestants have been recruited into exclusive militias for their own protection. From the muster rolls of the seventeenth century through the militias, yeomanry and volunteer armies, to the special constabulary and the part-time regiments of the British army, Ulster Loyalists have participated and revelled in a martial tradition that is largely alien to their Catholic neighbours. The military discipline of parades is written into their genetic code. Yet this generation of young males aged between fourteen and twenty-five is the first generation of Ulster Loyalists not to be recruited into a militia for defence of their community and its political tenets. Instead, young Protestant men and boys find expression of that compulsion in the marching ranks of uniformed Blood and Thunder bands with their military trappings and martial airs. But reflex reactions across the sectarian divide are difficult to change and in an appraisal of the most vibrant aspect of Ulster Protestant culture in the twenty-first century, it is probable that the pace of acceptance will be dictated by the most difficult situations.

Nowhere, perhaps, is the interface of Northern Ireland's divided society more pronounced than in Castlederg, a small rural community centred on a market town in west Tyrone.

With a population of just over 2,500 (of which sixty per cent was identified as Catholic/Nationalist in the 2001 Census), its rural community of thousands more is divided along an even more evenly balanced ratio. The town of Castlederg presides over a landlocked salient of Northern Ireland, with Donegal in the Republic of Ireland to the north and west. Its name derives from the River Derg which flows from the lough surrounding St Patrick's legendary penitential island, Station Island, in nearby County Donegal. Indeed, in medieval times, the town and its valley provided access to Lough Derg, only fifteen miles away, for pilgrims travelling through the Irish realm of the O'Neill clan. Hence, the town was formed around a castle that at one point fell under the control of the rival O'Donnell clan. That early stronghold was replaced by the Planters' castle, the remains of which survive on the banks of the fast-flowing River Derg as it rushes to combine with others in forming the majestic River Foyle that flows through Derry city about twenty-five miles to the north. The ruins of Derg Castle have been preserved and packaged for tourism, despite the worst efforts of small-town vandals, even though there is a continuing absence of tourism, reflected by the fact that the local Tourist Information Office remained 'closed for renovations' right through the 2009 summer season.

Yet tourism is a minor economic consideration in Castlederg. The small town is near the head of a rich river valley that has provided a prosperous farm-based settlement of rural Protestantism on the outer reaches of Northern Ireland. Among its proudest boasts is that it was the ancestral home of Davy Crockett, America's pioneering frontiersman and defender to the last of the Alamo fort in Texas. Although Crockett's family had long since emigrated across the Atlantic Ocean to settle in the Tennessee Mountains, his birthright as a frontiersman is attributed locally in Castlederg to his genetic links to this modern-day frontier town where a local housing estate is named in his honour and where the Crockett family name survived until quite recently. (Possibly for the requisite community balance demanded by political correctness in Northern Ireland, the Protestant Davy Crockett association is usually linked in references with another proud Castlederg boast, that the Tyrone town is the birthplace of Foynes [and later Shannon] Airport chef Joe Sheridan, a Catholic, who invented Irish coffee!)

Yet while 'The Derg' – as it is fondly known by both sides of the community – boasts a long history as a settlement on the upper reaches of an important river valley that forms part of the Foyle river system, in Jonathan Bardon's sweeping work, *A History of Ulster*, it is noted solely – and infamously – for having two Christmas trees, one for the Catholics and one for the Protestants.[2] More ominously, perhaps, in travelogues and official websites it is noted that Castlederg also rivals neighbouring (and bigger) Strabane for the title of the 'most bombed town' in Northern Ireland during the three recent decades of conflict. In the 2005 survey of 'multiple deprivation' carried out by the Northern Ireland Statistics and Research Agency, Castlederg featured with only three other Tyrone communities in the 'top 100' most deprived communities – two of the four were urban wards of Strabane and the other was Coalisland town in the east of the county.[3] The categories of deprivation used as indicators were income, employment, health and disability, education skills and training, proximity to services, living environment, and crime and disorder.

Even so, the town today presents no more visible evidence of its recent troubled past than the occasional derelict façade of former shops that are increasingly familiar in the economic downturn everywhere. Yet it bears deep and lasting wounds in the remarkably large death toll on both sides of the community during the Troubles. Some of those deaths stand out for their almost unspeakable and calculated cruelty given the small community context in which they happened. The local cemetery on the Drumquin Road has an entire section dominated by the graves of those killed by the IRA – most of them serving members in the crown forces, notably the Ulster Defence Regiment. Four of the twenty-four Unionists killed in the Castlederg area during the Troubles were members of the Castlederg Young Loyalists Flute Band and their murders occurred in each of the decades of the band's existence, thereby ensuring that nearly all former, and many serving, band members have played alongside somebody killed by Republicans. On the reverse side of the coin, there are tales of terror and bloodshed to match from the local Nationalist community. These are the bitter grievances that run deep through the fault-lines of a community that seems on the surface to be not much different from similar small towns in other parts of Ireland. Yet even a mention of those grievances has sparked trouble in the past.

Throughout Tyrone and further afield, therefore, Castlederg carries with it the reputation of being a deeply divided community, even if that division is not readily apparent to outsiders other than through the story of the two Christmas trees. Little wonder, therefore, that this small rural town now has two Blood and Thunder bands, the Castlederg Young Loyalists Flute Band which has been 'marching along the border since 1977', and the Pride of the Derg band, which was formed by some disaffected Castlederg Young Loyalists members in 2004 when the parent band formally decided to change its image and discipline by concentrating on the cultural and musical, rather than the more 'recreational', aspects of marching band activities. However, the 'split' could also be seen as part of a general proliferation and realignment of bands as a cultural phenomenon in modern Northern Ireland. While those involved deny political connotations, Castlederg's bands represent the considerable gulf between those Blood and Thunder bands that wish to maintain their provocative 'Kick the Pope' image in high-decibel renditions of a limited number of familiar tunes and those that have decided to concentrate on music and the best possible performance of their cultural heritage, and showcase it for the world if possible.

This shift in emphasis by most of the more accomplished marching bands has been made necessary by changed circumstances. Each year, the public displays of the hundreds of Loyalist bands in Northern Ireland have been the subject of scrutiny by the Parades Commission. Its deliberations are often an opportunity for protest and accusations by political and business representatives on both sides of the community. Nationalists regard band parades as a mere excuse to incite a reaction in peaceful neighbours, and the open provocation and taunting of the past lives on in the popular image. In Castlederg, the Nationalist protests and objections have been aimed primarily at the Castlederg Young Loyalists Flute Band and resulted in the band's parades being prohibited for some time from entering the Ferguson Crescent area of the town centre, which is invariably described as Nationalist, a claim stoutly disputed by local Loyalists. While parades now pass through Ferguson Crescent, they are timed specifically and subjected to major restrictions to reduce their impact on the locals. Still, the annual tit-for-tat representations and appeals to the Parades Commission and the consequent fall-out of trouble during the parades up to 2006, has earned the band a reputation for provocation among Nationalists who are very slow, and even unwilling, to concede that the band has made huge progress in reinventing itself for the new, shared future.

Yet that reputation as 'hard-line' also boosts the attraction of Blood and Thunder bands among the local young Loyalist population. So while the new band, Pride of the Derg, may lay claim to the archetypal no-compromise Blood and Thunder tradition of marching bands whose musical range is restricted to the standard Loyalist tunes, the Castlederg Young Loyalists Flute Band can draw confidently on its continuity as it blends its performance into a mixture of Blood and Thunder and melody flute. It can also draw with confidence on its wide network of friendships, on the admiration of other marching bands for its 'tight style' and its undoubted legacy of sacrifice for the cause of Ulster Loyalism, clearly illustrated by the violent deaths of four of its serving band members. However, this background of lasting admiration for its 'quality over quantity' from others in the marching band movement throughout Northern Ireland, Scotland and parts of England, must be set against the years of open antipathy from Nationalist neighbours in Castlederg. For them, the history of the Castlederg Young Loyalists has been marked by a series of parades that have been described as openly provocative and it may take a long time to show that the tenor of the band's activities has changed radically under the new obligations.

For its part, the Castlederg Young Loyalists Flute Band is immensely proud of its three decades of existence and in an Omagh hotel in 2007, members, past members and a host of supporters and friends from other bands celebrated '30 years of marching along the border'. Since that anniversary year, the band has also had an active alumnus organisation in the CYL Old Boys band, organised and led by founding bandmaster Derek Hussey. The Old Boys parade and perform with the current band on significant major occasions, although it does not take part in the competitive events that make up the bulk of the calendar of Ulster's marching bands.

Meanwhile, back in the Davy Crockett Lounge, the current Castlederg Young Loyalists bandmaster, Trevor Donnell, and Kenny Sproule, a younger member of the band, join us at Councillor Hussey's request. With the freely offered assurance that I am not setting out to 'do a number' on the band, but to explore the Ulster Loyalist cultural phenomenon that has sprung from the Blood and Thunder marching bands using the example of the Castlederg Young Loyalists, they offer to convey my proposal to write a book to band members, and can foresee no problem in an honest portrayal of the band and its musical genre.

So (drum roll please …) this is their story!

CHAPTER 1

DAYS OF BLOOD AND THUNDER

Unlike the Orange Order and other loyal institutions, the Blood and Thunder flute bands make no claims of middle-class respectability and they are certainly not incorporated into the global context of a Masonic and benevolent society tradition. Instead, their image is stridently urban and working-class, proudly and provocatively Loyalist, and one of a quintessentially modern Ulster. Although often shunned and disparaged by polite Unionism, and at best neglected by most commentators on Northern Irish affairs, these bands, the culture they represent and the social networks that surround them are the most vibrant and energetic aspect of Ulster Loyalism in the early twenty-first century. In cities, towns and remote villages, they are the prime focus for Loyalist celebration during an annual marching season that now lasts almost the entire year. They are self-regenerating social and cultural clubs with overwhelmingly young, single and almost exclusively male memberships. They organise and host the Eleventh Night bonfires, as well as most parades and other community social events that bring together huge numbers of supporters in loud, raucous and often alcohol-fuelled rallies; and, invariably, they are a focus of fear and protest for their Nationalist neighbours.

Yet in a society of two sides that remain locked in endless accusations, as well as emulations of each other (Protestants form the Orange Order, Catholics form the Ancient Order of Hibernians, Protestants form bands, Catholics follow suit), the community role of the Blood and Thunder bands most closely corresponds to GAA clubs on the opposite side of the sectarian divide. Throughout Loyalist Ulster, the bands bind their local communities through a common cultural focus while instilling discipline, teamwork and skill in their young recruits. Just like GAA clubs, the life of the Blood and Thunder marching bands revolves around proclaiming local identity and pride, and proving it in competition. Indeed, the energy of Loyalist flute bands is more often spent in scoring points against their competitive rivals than it is in 'marking their territory'. For just as Gaelic games inculcate a deep and abiding sense of Irish cultural identity, along with fervent local and national pride, so the Blood and Thunder bands fuel pride in the identity of Ulster Loyalism with constant reminders of its historical legitimacy and a zealous attachment to a particular place. The very names of these bands usually hark back to a glorious past and also to a specific geographical affinity – Cormeen Rising Sons of

William, Pride of Ballinran, Giant's Causeway Protestant Boys, Castlederg Young Loyalists etc. – and emphasise their role in crystallising that strong sense of communal identity among themselves and amongst their large bands of followers. For that reason, the anticipation which grips the local Blood and Thunder bands at the start of each marching season is more akin to a sports club looking forward to a new championship season than to a group of young musicians sharing a collective interest in an aspect of their cultural heritage.

The sounds and street performances of these Blood and Thunder bands did not really feature in the pantheon of Loyalist culture before the very darkest days of the Troubles during the 1970s. Indeed, while their repertoire of music includes all the traditional tunes, martial airs and hymns that are integral to the celebration of Orange culture, a major catalyst of the Blood and Thunder bands was certainly in the local variation of the youth culture of the 1970s as it manifested itself in Northern Ireland and western Scotland. Today we might smirk at the skinheads, suedeheads, Slade, and Mott the Hoople, not to mention that early 'boy band' that was the Bay City Rollers, but their chanted anthems, tartan trimmings and strident beat captivated the youth of their day. So while in England, the 'bovver boy' culture usually started and ended with football club 'firms' and, in many cases, match day hooliganism, one local manifestation of that culture in Northern Ireland was in the so-called

'Tartan Gangs' that proliferated in urban areas in the 1970s, often associated with the burgeoning Loyalist paramilitary organisations, and most evident during riots. Over a short period, the new Blood and Thunder bands emerged in Belfast and other large centres with their ranks made up, in most cases, of these same angry Loyalist youths seeking ways to proclaim their identity, their loyalty and their pride against what they saw as an avalanche of international propaganda that favoured Nationalism. They brought with them all the raw energy of their interest in current popular music and applied it to their rendition of traditional Loyalist marching tunes.

Quincey Dougan of the Ulster Bands Forum, which acts as a media platform for most of the competitive marching bands, says the origins of Blood and Thunder was a 'political phenomenon and its genesis is through politics without a doubt'. During the period of great instability at the start of the Troubles, young Loyalist men wanted to express themselves in a way that would say, 'this is what I am and this is what I believe', he explains. 'Sometimes it's coming from the top of the head [consciously]; sometimes it comes subconsciously. There was the parading issue at the time and parading has always been a focal point in the [Loyalist] community. Even if you're a middle-class Unionist and you don't get involved, you still know about it; parading is still a part of you. So there was this parading thing and there was the Orange Order, the Black Preceptory, the Apprentice Boys and this range of bands. So the young men decided they had to get out there and they couldn't join the Orange; it's too much hassle to join the Orange because you have to get proposed and seconded at a meeting and in a lot of areas to this day, you'll not get into the Orange if you're not a regular church attendee. So from a youth perspective, this is what they found and people were searching for another way, and what better way to show people what is felt than to get on the road in a band?'

This resulted in a huge influx into the existing marching bands of the time – the pipe, accordion and traditional flute bands that had been around for generations in many cases. 'As more and more of the youth came into the bands, the elements of their own modern culture started manifesting more and more,' says Quincey. 'So there was an assimilation with more youthful culture and music and more aggression started coming into play because of the youth – you know the more physical thing that naturally comes into play because it is coming from male youth. And with that massive influx into the bands and the changes it meant, they began to say, "Right, we're going to start another band here, so what's the cheapest way to do it?" The answer, of course, was flute, because it is the cheapest instrument going. You know if pipes had been £10 a set, it would have been very different and we'd have pipe bands all over the place now. But the flute was a cheap instrument and that is how it happened. That is the origin of the Blood and Thunder, and I don't think that is disputable.'

Music played by the out-and-out Blood and Thunder bands has not changed much since the 1970s. It is loud, 'in your face' and stridently unapologetic. Familiar Orange traditional music is wrapped in a raw, basic rhythm, delivered in an aggressive and relentless torrent of percussion. Sometimes, consequently, the melodies of the flute are almost buried in a wall of thumping sound. These traditional Blood and Thunder bands parade in an aggressive fashion, filling the available road in a solid phalanx of drums (which make up the majority of the bands) as they march along and pound out their tunes. In its thunderous persistence, the music is fiercely assertive and to those of another political persuasion, fiercely provocative.

Of course, the Blood and Thunder bands draw on the fife-and-drum traditions associated with the Orange and other loyal institutions in Ulster. The thunderous bass drums, which provide the 'pulse' of the Blood and Thunder bands, also have deep roots in that musical culture. The bass drummers, who usually are also the focal personalities of the bands – familiar even to ardent followers of other bands from far away – fulfil the role of the traditional Lambeg drummer as they maintain the 'Loyalist heartbeat' of Ulster. To ensure that heartbeat never falters, many bands include a substitute bass drummer in the ranks when on parade, ready to take over quickly when needed, hoisting the big drum from one chest harness to the other between tunes and rarely missing a beat. Some bands, including the Castlederg

Young Loyalists, have marched with two and even three bass drums to emphasise the central role they perform. Their hugely energetic and muscular contributions are capable of stirring the blood of even the most sceptical outsiders and they follow in the tradition of the relentless pounding of the goatskin drumheads of the Lambeg drum, which is widely reputed to end only when the cane drumsticks have fragmented to stumps and the knuckles of the drummer are raw and bleeding – hence a popular explanation of the Blood and Thunder in the description of this musical genre.

Yet while the term Blood and Thunder is now associated in Northern Ireland (and urban Scotland) with the musical tradition of the bands, it has much deeper etymological roots as a form of 'minced oath'. In his nineteenth-century satirical poem, 'Don Juan', Lord Byron writes: 'Oh blood and thunder! And oh blood and wounds! These are but vulgar oaths …'[4] But the phrase features even earlier in the 1751 novel by Tobias Smollett, *The Adventures of Peregrine Pickle*: 'Smiting the table with his fist, he started up, and, with the most violent emphasis of rage and indignation, exclaimed, "Damn my heart and liver! 'Tis a land lie, d'ye see; and I will maintain it to be a lie, from the sprit-sail yard to the mizzen-top-sail halyards Blood and Thunder!"'[5] By the late Victorian era, however, the phrase had become the generic name for literary romances of historical melodrama. Reviewing Charlotte Brontë's *Jane Eyre*, G.K. Chesterton wrote: 'While it is a human document written in blood, it is also one of the best blood-and-thunder detective stories in the world.'[6] By the twentieth century, the term had been spoonerised into 'Thud and Blunder' to describe one aspect of the same branch of literature dealing with highway robberies. A century later, the term outside Ireland is perhaps most readily associated with a song by American heavy metal rock group, Mostodon, which includes the line 'Split your lungs with blood and thunder …' The song, which is actually called 'Blood and Thunder', is a firm favourite of US troops who have it fed into the radio headsets of their combat helmets during offensive engagements in war zones such as Iraq and Afghanistan. Significantly, it is the thunderous drumming that virtually drowns out the background melody which most appeals to these young men, the same attributes that stir the soul of modern Ulster Loyalist youth as it follows the marching bands.

Despite the rapid proliferation of Blood and Thunder bands in the past thirty years as a vibrant expression of modern Ulster Loyalist culture, they have received scant attention from general commentators, except as an unwelcome aspect of Orange parades. Indeed, there is a prevailing and entrenched view that the bands are merely the nasty side of the Orange Order and that they are inexorably linked and under the control of the Lodges. This is despite repeated disassociation of the Orange Order from the bands and the few academic studies of the bands which make the disassociation clear. Indeed, an article written by Queen's University of Belfast's Professor Desmond Bell in 1985 remains the most accurate and dispassionate account of this dominant Ulster Loyalist youth culture, then in its early stages of evolution.[7] The article deals with a marching band from the Fountain district of Derry city and its central importance for the Loyalist working-class youth. His independent survey of local schools in the city established that at least one in six Loyalist teenagers were involved in bands, many of them in what were recognised as 'Kick the Pope' bands and that they participated actively in band parades and other activities. He described the bands as 'independent self-governing outfits run by the young people themselves along roughly democratic lines' and how they acted as an alternative to the 'staid' Orange Lodge and the dangers of paramilitary involvement. 'Today it is the marching bands with their expressive display of Protestant identity and difference via a potent mixture of martial music, Loyalist symbol and Protestant self-image, that have become the most important mobilising agency for Protestant youth,' Desmond Bell wrote a quarter of a century ago, an importance which they retain to this day.

Not many have been paying attention to Bell's work, apart from a few other academic researchers who recognised the bands as a potent and popular force for Loyalist youth. Professor Bell followed up his article with a book in 1990 which dealt with the issue of links between the bands and the Loyalist paramilitary groups at that time.[8] However, his argument that the insignia and affectations of the bands were 'little more than acts of bravado' and unconnected with actual violence, was disputed by the most comprehensive academic study on the issue of parading, *Material Conflicts: Parades and Visual Displays in Northern Ireland* by Neil Jarman of the University of Ulster in 1997 which held that the relationship is 'more complex' than simply 'youthful defiance', citing cases of convictions of Loyalist paramilitaries who were involved in two particular bands.[9] He stated that while some bands were funded by paramilitary organisations and some carried flags showing their allegiance to the UVF and UDA, essentially the bands offered 'a means through which the harder, more militant, edge of Loyalism finds expression among the more traditional imagery of Orangeism'. While many involved in the band movement today concede that covert and overt links with paramilitary groups were important to some bands in the past, the overwhelming majority of bands have moved on from there after the Good Friday Agreement and the start of power-sharing devolved administration in Northern Ireland.

Adherents also brush aside criticism from those who would suggest that the Blood and Thunder bands do not play music of any merit. Quincey Dougan says, 'I've heard that said many times, even from some of the higher echelons of the brass band or melody flute bands, and it comes from outsiders who haven't a clue as well. But marching bands aren't just about music, you know. Blood and Thunder is not just about music. Blood and Thunder is about style and again it is this expression of youth on the street; it's an expression of identity and it's a way to get this out of you. The music is secondary as such and it comes along with the discipline and the marching, but by the same token it is music.'

Yet even though they are often dismissed as merely provocative renditions of traditional and popular airs, the Blood and Thunder performances of flute bands in Northern Ireland do encompass a huge range of musical ability, organisation and political (and religious) outlook, not to mention public behaviour. And while Blood and Thunder bands attract a natural antipathy from the Nationalist side of the community, often their most ardent critics come from the ranks of 'respectable' Unionism who have been happy to hide behind the antics of the bands when it has suited them. 'Unionism has used the bands to its own purposes,' says Quincey Dougan. 'That has always been the way with Unionism. The Blood and Thunder bands provided the foot soldiers when they were needed, but they didn't want to know them when it didn't suit. The media has a lot to answer for too. Over the years, the nature of the problem in this country has meant that the parades were a focus for the media and the world and the politicians and everyone else. So with the parades as a focus, it meant that any time anything did happen it became a big issue. All the media coverage, and public perception, came from the tip of the pyramid rather than the bottom of the pyramid. Really, trouble over parades has been the exception rather than the rule.'

The convenient disdain of conservative Unionists seriously

underplays the role of the Blood and Thunder bands in their communities. For instance, in her eulogistic representation of the Orange Order and its demand to walk down the Garvaghy Road in Portadown against opposition from local residents, Ruth Dudley-Edwards describes her early foray into Northern Ireland Protestant culture for a parade in Aughnacloy, County Tyrone: 'Of perhaps 90 Lodges and bands, only three or four were even faintly intimidating. The exceptions were what are known as the "Kick the Pope" bands of young men from places like Portadown, with earrings, shaven heads, vulgar and militaristic uniforms and a triumphalist swagger; in Scotland they would be on the terraces of Glasgow Rangers football club.'[10] It should go without saying that, even though they live in Portadown and other places in Northern Ireland, many of those young Loyalists are regularly on the terraces at Ibrox Park in Glasgow, for Old Firm (Rangers versus Celtic) games in particular, and Rangers football tops and jackets vie with Northern Ireland soccer team gear as the most favoured casual apparel of Loyalist youth.

It is also worth noting that in her book, *The Faithful Tribe*, Dudley-Edwards includes a footnote explanation saying that Orangemen describe these bands as Blood and Thunder bands, while 'Catholics (because they dislike them) and Loyalist youths (because they love them) call them "Kick the Pope".' In a later episode at the Drumcree/Garvaghy Road interface in Portadown, she describes the young members of the Craigavon True Blues who 'played the hymns like a call to battle' and while their 'macho, aggressive aura is off-putting' she still acknowledged that they are 'wonderful to walk along with'.[11]

Michael Ignatieff, a former history professor at Harvard, Oxford and Cambridge, who is now the leader of Canada's Liberal Party, takes a sympathetic and understanding view of these bands in his book *Blood and Belonging*. He describes his efforts to engage in conversation with a group of young men from the Rathcoole district of suburban Belfast and finding them generally uncommunicative and politically naïve. Yet when they don the uniform of the Whiteabbey Protestant Boys Marching Band, he notes, a change comes over them, allowing them to express through their music and marching what they have obvious difficulty expressing in words: 'The band is more than their club; the music is their speech. They may not be able to tell you, in so many words, what Britishness or Protestantism means, but when the big, pimply boy starts hitting the big bass drum, and Sheeran starts them marching to the beat of his snare [drum], and Marty, Paul, Deeky and Mudd take up the tune on the flute, they give a thundering account of who they are.'[12]

Michael Ignatieff notes that each of these young amateur musicians knows at least a 'hundred tunes on the small black ebony flutes they pull from their back pockets and a dozen rhythms on the short snare drums'. He also admires their dedication to the band as they practise all year long at their local youth club. During the marching season, there's hardly a night when they are not out parading and playing on the streets of Rathcoole and nearby districts. He follows them through the rain to the local Orange Hall, the route guarded by British troops, as traffic halts and onlookers applaud them. 'The drum brooks no argument,' he observes, so it is no wonder Nationalist neighbours describe this as the music of 'intimidation'. 'But it has its own fierce beauty, and the boys will tell you there is nothing to equal the feeling you get when you're marching in the downtown and the sound is echoing off the high-walled canyons of the city.'

In their aggressive assertion of Ulster Loyalist pride, it is significant that the Blood and Thunder bands emerged at a time when the very walls of Loyalism were tumbling down. Since partition and the foundation of Northern Ireland, the culture of Unionism and Loyalism had defined the state.[13] Loyalist culture comprised the essence of the identity of Northern Ireland. It was indistinguishable from the values, norms, ethos, world view and sense of place in history of the Unionist establishment that ruled from Stormont with little or no interference from the 'mother parliament' in Westminster. Loyalism essentially defined itself as being different from Irishness, by emphasising its cultural and historical differences, and by excluding the huge indigenous minority of Northern Irish Catholics from its purview. In this, it was aided and abetted by a southern political establishment and culture that emphasised its separateness from all the shared experiences with Britain stretching back through the centuries. While Dublin played down the huge cultural influences and its shared history with Britain, it also created an exclusive national identity that shunned the culture of its own shrinking Protestant minority. So as the south wrapped the green flag around itself, the north enveloped itself in orange and Sabbatarian respectability. Historical events such as the Glorious Revolution of 1690, which guaranteed the Protestant Ascendancy in Ireland, were marked with huge public celebrations of William of Orange's victory, while on St Patrick's Day or any other day that might be regarded as distinctly Irish, it was business as usual in Northern Ireland.

In the official calendar of the state, the 12 July marking the Battle of the Boyne was coupled with the tragedy of the Somme marked on 1 July to define a people who had paid with their very blood for the right to be recognised as different from others on the island they shared. The very manifestation of that separateness was the Stormont Parliament in all its grandeur and it was articulated time and again by reference to the 'people of Ulster'. Yet the 'people of Ulster' were not those who inhabited the nine counties of that ancient province of Ireland, nor even all the people inhabiting Northern Ireland, but the Unionist people alone before the world.

When Stormont was prorogued by Westminster in March 1972, Her Majesty's Government in London effectively wrenched away the abiding certainties of the Loyalist people of Northern Ireland. Cast into a political darkness where 'power-sharing' became a fundamental condition of any redemption or salvation, Loyalists searched for a way to express their Unionist identity in the 'new beginning' that Northern Ireland Secretary of State William Whitelaw presented as the only recourse to restoration of power at Stormont. So as the loyal institutions of Lodge and Preceptory that had guided the affairs of Northern Ireland were sent marching off into the sunset of their golden era, the Ulster Workers Council (UWC) emerged in their place. The UWC strike was called to wreck the new Sunningdale power-sharing administration. It heralded a new and assertive dawn of militant, working-class Loyalism, which manifested itself in a radically different collective identity to the sober ranks in bowler hats and dark suits. For as it teetered on a precipice, Loyalism had to develop an edge to withstand the steady erosion of its position by those it had relied on to guarantee its ascendancy. As the old order crumbled, the political thrust was in the new groupings defined by different levels of militancy in organisations that ranged from the Democratic Unionist Party (DUP) and the Vanguard Unionist Movement, to the Ulster Defence Association and Young Citizen Volunteers.

With the shift from deference to defiance, working-class Loyalist culture also changed radically. Emerging as they did from this new Northern Ireland cultural firmament, the Blood and Thunder bands acted both as a forceful reminder of Loyalism's place in the political structures, but also as a vitally important vent for the anger and frustration of young male Loyalists. The initial appeal was particularly to the young working-class Loyalists of Belfast and other large urban centres who searched for a place and identity in a more secular world robbed of the religious certainties that had sustained their parents – certainties that had also kept them in their place in the social rankings.

Yet young male Loyalists grow up and become their fathers over time and many of them spent their formative years watching or playing in Blood and Thunder bands. Moreover, over time the appeal of the bands spread. Many middle-class and middle-aged Protestants today still acknowledge the huge excitement they felt when first they encountered a Blood and Thunder band. For in a world of general uncertainty for Ulster Loyalism, here was a vibrant, vocal – if at times volatile – expression that they were 'proud to be Prod'. The aggression and swagger were also the 'forbidden fruit' on which respectable Unionism dined in its secret moments. They were the cultural standard that rallied the imagination of young Loyalists in towns, villages and rural communities, even as their parents might have expressed uneasiness or horror at their antics. For that reason, the abiding institutions kept them close rather than apart. From the start, many Blood and Thunder bands were formally linked to Orange Lodges, even if the Grand Orange Lodge worthies might pooh-pooh some of their excesses, particularly in those early days. In the new Northern Ireland that emerged under the watchful eye of Westminster, the Blood and Thunder bands were the least unacceptable means of harnessing young Loyalists who would otherwise have been disaffected to the point of open revolt, and directing their anger against the real and perceived onslaught on Loyalist culture and tradition.

While the wide proliferation of these bands was the main indication of the ascendancy of Loyalist radicalism over traditional institutions, there have been a few diversions along the way. Following the ceasefires that ended the conflict in the mid-1990s, the Blood and Thunder bands were drawn back en masse into the Orange fold. This occurred notably because of the protracted stand-off at Drumcree which reasserted the Orange Order as the focus of Loyalist defiance and attracted to its ranks many of those who were disenchanted with the promised possibilities of peace. In the shadows of the Drumcree church spire, where 'old antipathies were revived, old hatred recharged', it seemed at one point as if the Orange Order would prove itself as an immovable bulwark against which the political process of 'appeasement' would founder; yet even it could not resist the tide of history.[14] The Orange Order now has fewer than 36,000 members in Ireland compared to the record 93,447 members on the rolls at the start of the Troubles in 1968. Orange leaders attribute the decline to the growing secularism among Protestant youth in Northern Ireland and the requirement in many areas of employment to disclose membership of the Orange and other societies.[15] What had once been a useful network to secure employment is now seen as a handicap. For that and other reasons, the loyal institutions have had to find new ways to entice members and ensure survival.

Since the start of the twenty-first century, a further metamorphosis has occurred within Loyalism as the Orange Order follows the Apprentice Boys of Derry into a phase of cultural regeneration to stake a claim to a more secular identity. In this, it has been proclaiming and projecting its role as an expression of Ulster Loyalist identity and a clear manifestation of the Ulster-Scots presence in Ireland. In recent years, the Twelfth celebrations are packaged, if not always staged, as a festival of events centred on the traditional commemoration of the Battle of the Boyne. Gestures have been made for a more inclusive programme of events, but with very slow progress in winning over the traditional antipathy of Nationalists. For many on the Nationalist side of the community, however, the central role of the Blood and Thunder bands is cited as a clear indication that Orangeism has not discarded its triumphalist trappings. Leading commentator, author and columnist Brian Feeney sums up a generally held Nationalist view in describing Loyalist parades in places like Rasharkin as merely an opportunity to 'swagger and stomp' behind 'UDA or UVF members who use bands as cover for drilling exercises' in public events 'supporting a repulsive organisation that is virulently anti-Catholic'.[16]

Projecting Loyalist culture has been the aim of the traditional Orange, Black and Apprentice Boys institutions whose relationships with the Blood and Thunder bands over recent decades has been close, yet guarded. Before the 1970s, pipe and accordion bands considerably outnumbered the flute bands. Invariably, the bands that marched in Orange, or other official, parades were integral parts of the Lodges and were tightly controlled and directed by the loyal orders. That changed markedly during the 1970s when the Blood and Thunder bands emerged and proliferated, especially in urban areas of Northern Ireland and also in western Scotland, with its strong cultural links with the Orange traditions. What is not clear to many outsiders is that although some of these bands still fall under the aegis of local Orange Lodges by right of succession from former bands, and while they use the Orange Halls and other facilities for practice and rehearsal, the bands have established themselves as independent bodies and the crossover of membership is minimal. Now very few band members wear the sashes or shoulder ribbons indicating membership when parading with the loyal institutions.

In staying apart, the bands have developed styles of costume, regalia and performance that distinguish them from the more conservative demeanour of solemn Lodge members. Indeed, the evolution of the Blood and Thunder bands has been matched by a constant revision of the style of dress, and in recent years by increased emphasis on their musical repertoire and virtuosity. Whereas the early Blood and Thunder bands favoured a common style of paramilitary attire (Doc Marten boots with shortened 'parallel' trousers and 'bomber' jackets set off with tartan trimming), the styles of uniform today certainly tend towards full Victorian-style regimental military bands. That probably reflects the evolution of a musical culture that has now progressed through two or even three successive generations of Loyalist youth and blended, if not merged, with other strands of mainstream Ulster Loyalist culture.

The 'Kick the Pope' bands still have an added edge, however. Even when they veer over into the melody flute genre – with first and second flute to allow more ambitious musical scores and an added range of woodwind instruments such as the piccolo – the heavy percussion of bass and side-drumming maintains the Blood and Thunder aspect of the music. Because of it, they are hugely popular among their hordes of young local followers and draw large popular support for their parades and concerts. These programmes pivotally centre on their own local parades when they invite other bands to come to their city neighbourhood, town or village. Collections at local parades also provide the single biggest source of income for most bands and allows them to purchase instruments, buy new uniforms and cover other costs of parading into the next season.

While some critics might dismiss the bands of today as 'younger, brasher, more colourful and less sophisticated than those of the previous generation,' the phenomenon of modern Blood and Thunder bands runs the gamut from strident gangs who play a few provocative Loyalist tunes between bouts of drinking, to others – and the overwhelming majority – who take huge interest and pride in their culture and reflect that in constant and conscientious exploration of their musical tradition.[17] These latter bands use the full range of modern sophisticated communication techniques to maintain a cultural network and improve their performances and contacts with others who share their passion for this distinctive brand of Irish traditional music.

Yet since their emergence as a major cultural manifestation of Loyalist youth in the 1970s, the Blood and Thunder bands have also been the strutting in-your-face reminder of the Protestant supremacy won at the Battle of the Boyne and maintained down through the generations since. If nothing else, the flute bands with their 'wall of sound' rendition of martial airs – many of which would never pass muster for political correctness or acknowledgement of neighbourly difference – are the raw underbelly of a culture that has always felt itself under threat of being overwhelmed by the indigenous Gaelic tradition that surrounds it, a tradition that is promoted forcefully as the *only* legitimate culture of Ireland by the Irish Republic and internationally. In their choice of music, and in particular in their season of band parades, these 'Kick the Pope' bands are the defiant roar of Loyalism, repeatedly making their presence known in shows of bravado.

Even the order of marching marks out the Blood and Thunder bands from other traditional marching bands. In the case of pipe, accordion and brass/silver bands, the percussion is the secondary or background element. In order of procession, the pipes or accordions come first and then the drums, with the 'beaters' for the bass drum muted and the side-drums played softly as background accompaniment. With the Blood and Thunder flute bands, the drums have pride of place in a solid phalanx of percussion following immediately after the colour party carrying the flags and sometimes the drum majors who perform juggling tricks with ornate band-sticks and even acrobatics. The bass drum is given the central starring role at the heart of the marching band and the drummer wields his 'beaters' in a flurry of muscular performance, often wheeling around and weaving from side to side as he pounds. The flutes which give the band its descriptive name, take up the rearguard. So there is seldom any mistaking what has precedence in terms of melody and beat. In this regard, the flute bands obviously draw on the tradition of the eighteenth-century fife and drum corps that led armies into battle in Europe and North America. While the fifes provided the melody and rhythm to march the soldiers in step into battle, the drums played the role of intimidating the enemy.

Yet while there is nostalgic affection among Loyalists for the Lambeg drum in particular, which is seen as 'celebratory and enjoyable', this intimidatory role cannot be divorced from the ritual of performance that forms the wider perception of marching bands. In his book on the Ulster Protestant musical tradition, *With Fife and Drum*, Irish traditional musician and Protestant clergyman Gary Hastings describes the disassociation of the two as 'innocent, naïve and ignorant of the true spectrum of associations attached to the music and its ritual performance'.[18] There is, Hastings points out, 'another perception within that same community that tends to emphasise and identify with the triumphalist, threatening, tribal face of the whole thing. This is symbolised by shaved heads, dark glasses, paramilitary uniforms, violence, and alcohol abuse. It cannot be denied that this side of the music in one form or another has always been an element of the whole tradition.' The complex, multi-layered traditions of Loyalist music, he admits, evokes frequent images of 'drum-beating, banner-waving and territory marking' as well as 'drummers with blood streaming from their wrists, drunken mobs gathered round bonfires or frenetic, aggressive flute bands'. Yet he rightly points out that this annual ritual is not necessarily an act of provocation: 'Sometimes the most aggressive displays are intended for "home consumption", and are not specifically directed at anyone else. They are a ritualistic, internal definition of identity, territory and tribe, a rehearsal of mythic personality. They are a confidence-building, chest-beating, rooster's crow, meant for the community's own ears ...'

Reverend Hastings adds that this side of the music

is most visible at the interface with the other side of the community. Indeed, members and former members of Blood and Thunder bands readily admit that the choice of tunes and the level of provocation in performance are still sometimes cranked up deliberately when the bands come to an interface with a Nationalist neighbourhood. Even in towns and localities that are not known to the young band members, they point out, the police or other security personnel will usually provide a clear indicator by their blanket presence of where this musical provocation should begin. With considerable success, the Parades Commission has been reducing the provocation by restricting and altering parade routes and adding stipulations that include the absence of music at specific junctures. To their credit, it must be said, many bands realise that their future welfare and sources of funding for wider activities in their Protestant communities rests on acceptance or at least tolerance by those outside the Unionist fold. These bands have tempered their excesses of the past. However, they all insist that the music they play and the way they play it is a legitimate expression of their Ulster Loyalist cultural identity.

Whatever the view of Blood and Thunder bands, and contrary to the widely held view that they and their music are merely another facet of the Troubles, they have grown exponentially in number and strength in the past decade of relative peace.

CHAPTER 2

A BAND OF BROTHERS

Thursday, 15 January 2009

Legendary Ulster Unionist leader Sir Edward Carson gazes down on the proceedings from a framed photograph and his glowering expression shows the resolve of succeeding generations of Loyalists to maintain what they hold. Yet the band practice room at the back of the stage in the Bridgetown No Surrender Orange Hall beside the town centre car park at McCay Court, Castlederg, is also regally presided over by a more benign portrait of a younger Queen Elizabeth II and her royal consort Prince Philip. Around them, and on other walls, are other visual representations of what is held most dear by members of the Castlederg Young Loyalists Flute Band. There are photos from a couple of different eras of the band's mustered ranks in full uniform; a framed photo of Drumlegagh LOL (Loyal Orange Lodge) 626 parading through Castlederg on 12 July 1928; an iconic representation of King William crossing the Boyne on his white charger with sword raised, pointing the way forward; various Loyalist insignia; images of old UVF columns in drill formations from the early twentieth century; photos of young men gathered on a railway platform, possibly heading off to fight for King and country in the Great War; and of course the furled flags clamped against the wall in their properly designated positions – the Northern Ireland flag with its crown-topped Red Hand; the Scottish Saltire; the band's own standard modelled on the old UVF flag of 1913; and the Union Jack with pride of place under the portrait of the monarch.

Nestling amidst them all is a framed picture dedicated to the memory of 'Norman and Michael'. The emblems on it are the Union flag, the Irish harp and a Red Hand surrounded by shamrocks, an indication that members of this band are comfortable with their identity combining British and Irish symbols. Yet the identity of the two young men to whom the crest is dedicated is very much a unique heritage of this group of young Loyalist musicians. Norman McKinley and Michael Darcy were founding members of the Castlederg Young Loyalists Flute Band, young local men who were killed by the IRA during the Troubles in a period of tit-for-tat bloodletting during the 1980s, the echoes of which still reverberate through the community. Both young men were also members of the Ulster Defence Regiment (UDR). They had donned the uniform of this British army regiment in the general call to arms of young Loyalists to guard their homeland against those who would overthrow it. In the borderlands of west Tyrone, as in other frontier areas of Northern Ireland, their deaths were viewed in subsequent years by family, friends and neighbours – and accepted by most commentators – as part of a campaign of terror to drive border Protestants from their homes by murder and intimidation. In the panoply of martyrs to the cause of Unionism, Norman and Michael are numbered among thirty-two UDR men and women killed in west Tyrone between 1971 and 1991. In the annals of the Castlederg Young Loyalists Flute Band, they are among four serving band members who were killed by Republicans during the conflict.

Other young men now occupy the practice room in Castlederg town centre. Many of them are of the age when they too would have donned the uniform as part-time UDR soldiers back in those early years of their band's existence. But the UDR has long since been disbanded. Having been rolled into the amalgamated Royal Irish Regiment (RIR) home battalions, its part-time ranks have now been demobilised. Yet its legacy lives on and today the UDR has been accorded the same iconic status in the nostalgia of this Loyalist frontier community as the 'B' Special Constabulary which preceded it as the home guard. The 'B' Specials, disbanded in 1971, had been formed as a part-time local police militia (along with the full-time 'A' Specials and the reserve 'C' Specials) at the time of partition, its members coming from the surviving ranks of the original Ulster Volunteer Force. That fractured succession and the memories of these forces are melded into a deep communal pride that those who served in the ranks of the UVF, the Specials, the UDR and the RIR answered the call to protect their community and guard their God-given homeland from those who would destroy it and them.

So when the young men of the Castlederg Young Loyalists Flute Band gather for practice or performance, in uniform or in their casual street clothes – which include Northern Ireland soccer tops and jackets, several Glasgow Rangers shirts and a couple of zipped jackets with the band's insignia – they carry their history with them. They may not have answered a call to arms, but they are clearly proud to wear the uniform of this band of brothers. Even on a bitterly cold winter night, they are infused with enthusiasm for the year ahead when their band will carry the colours and march to the sound of their own flutes and drums, proclaiming the loyalty and allegiance of their community.

Bandmaster Trevor Donnell sits at the head of a table around which four other drummers stand. All five have their drumsticks raised in readiness. Trevor gives the lead, brattling a staccato beat onto the formica table-top. The others join in in unison and the sound raised by the drumming is relentless and precise; then the seven flute players ranged around the room, standing or leaning against walls, come in together and the Castlederg Young Loyalists Flute Band is up and running with its first tune of the year. Immediately the band hall is enveloped in the thunderous sound of a familiar yet unidentified tune and, to my relatively untuned ear, the synchronisation and rendition is note perfect. In the background, meanwhile, the relentless 'pulse' of the bass drummer's large sticks on the table top is the beat to which my toe taps. Table tops are used for practice sessions, as the actual drums are too loud to play indoors. The tune segues into another familiar air with a slightly different beat and the pace is continued at that relentless rhythm to the end.

A brief silence … but the lull is momentary with no commentary on how they have performed. Bandmaster Trevor, who has lapsed into a reflective silence, simply says, 'Eighteenth of December' and he starts a table-top drumbeat once more with the rest of the band immediately falling in behind. At the end of that tune, Trevor looks over in my direction. 'What do you think?' he asks, obviously more out of a sense of politeness to acknowledge my presence than any passing notion that I might have something worthwhile to contribute.

'Sounds to me like you boys need no practice,' I say, smiling.

'Would you like to join in?' he asks, his drumsticks still poised over the table top.

'I'd probably need my own table,' I reply and a few of the young bandsmen laugh.

The bandmaster then explains, for those who might not know, that I am there because I am writing a book to 'make us all famous'. His explanation makes me feel only slightly less self-conscious as an intruder on the band from outside its traditional constituency.

But no more of that frivolity; band practice for the Castlederg Young Loyalists is a serious business and they are back into it immediately. I turn my attention from the concentrated expressions of the drummers and fluters back to the surroundings of the practice room. On a noticeboard which occupies most of the stage-side wall, there is a large collection of candid photos of band members and supporters enjoying themselves at recent social functions, indicating that they take part in the band activities as much for the social aspects as the music and marching, and they clearly enjoy each other's company. To the right of these on the noticeboard are a number of pennants awarded for competition successes, including the Blood and Thunder prize for best bass drum at the DUP South Down Band Parade in 2008. There are also a few 'official' band notices, including signed undertakings that flutes – which are the property of the band – will be properly looked after and, if lost, will require the payment of £200 within a fortnight.

I notice a cutting from a local newspaper about the Dedication Parade that formalised the setting up of the Castlederg Young Loyalists Flute Band in 1977:

Torrential rain which preceded a dedication service and band parade in Castlederg on Saturday afternoon did not dampen the enthusiasm of hundreds of supporters as the streets echoed to the shrill of the fluters, who had come along to add their approval to the formation of the Castlederg Young Loyalists Flute Band.

The dedication service, which was held at Bridgetown, was conducted by Rev. J. H. Lyons. Mr John Dunlop MP addressed the large gathering before the service and congratulated the new band on their splendid turn-out, and in his remarks said that 'in his opinion, the Nobel Peace Prize should have gone to the security forces, instead of the Peace People [Mairead Corrigan and Betty Williams]'.

Mr Derek Hussey, who was chairman, expressed thanks to Kilclean Pipe Band for being the only local band to turn out for the parade, and also to the parents of the band members who had been responsible for a smart turn-out of the boys. He thanked everyone who had contributed to band funds.

The band, which has upward of sixty members from Newtownstewart, Sion Mills, Ballymagorry and a majority of local youth, started practising only four months ago.

At the end of the parade, the Castlederg band formed at the side of the bridge and applauded the other bands who had taken part in the parade, and a special ovation was given to the Kilclean band.

Altogether fifteen bands took part. They were Birney Memorial and Fintona Silver Jubilee accordion bands; Sergeant Lindsay Mooney Memorial, Londonderry; William King Memorial, Londonderry; Ballymena Young Defenders; Foyle Defenders, Newbuildings; Pride of William, Donemana; Derrylonan Boyne Defenders, Cookstown; Star of the Roe, Limavady; Blair Memorial, Omagh; Omagh Protestant Boys; Enniskillen Young Conquerors [all flute bands]; Lack and Kilclean Pipe bands.[19]

So a total of ten Blood and Thunder flute bands marched through the streets of Castlederg that day in 1977. How the young members of the new band must have thrilled to the reverberations of the drumbeats off the familiar buildings of their own town. The golden era of Blood and Thunder flute bands had begun in the rural west in the very year that British policy on Northern Ireland, under Labour's Secretary of State Roy Mason, shifted decisively to 'Ulsterisation' and gave the primary security role to the Royal Ulster Constabulary and its police reservists, as well as to the UDR, rather than the British army regiments seconded to duty outside 'the mainland' on Operation Banner.

Close to the entrance to the practice room, a pair of young women – 'cuddies' in local parlance – sit as close as possible to the relatively inadequate heat generated from a bottle-gas heater. At one point they rise from their seats in the interval between tunes, gather their jackets about them and go down the short flight of stairs and outside into the car park, perhaps for a smoke. Their role as members of the colour party for the band will become apparent later. For now, their contribution is confined to foot-tapping as they memorise the beat of the tunes.

Occasionally the brief lull in the rapid succession of tunes, each one moving effortlessly into another, is punctuated by a rapid verbal exchange between Trevor and his more accomplished fluters. At one stage one of the fluters goes to a table and copies over from his binder to a notebook the note sequence of a tune. There are brief consultations, delivered in the rapid musical west Tyrone accent of the 'Derg and gradually it becomes clear that the bandmaster and band are compiling and practising a programme of tunes for a forthcoming performance. They are businesslike and efficient, and it is quite clear that all of the participants are encouraged to co-operate in getting the best out of the collective performance. Apart from bandmaster Trevor, there does not appear to be a hierarchy of members and all contributions are well received.

Robbie McKinley arrives as expected for this first practice of 2009. In the thirty-two-year history of the Castlederg Young Loyalists Flute Band, he has missed very few nights or days. He used to be the band's bass drummer and later he points to a photo in another newspaper cutting on the wall. There he is, immediately recognisable but younger, with the big drum strapped to his shoulders, pounding out the beat. In the photo he has large bushy sideburns curling down his face, which is stretched in a broad grin as the boys in the band of that era surround him on the parade ... clearly happy times that Robbie McKinley is unwilling to let go of easily. He offers to tell me about his memories of the early days of the band and we go down a few steps into the expanse of the Bridgetown Orange Hall. From the practice room, the Blood and Thunder sound still envelops us as the band practice continues, the music and even less comprehensible verbal exchanges between the participants coming through the light partition wall. Robbie casts his mind back to 1977: 'We had an accordion band here back at that time and that fell though and we decided we'd try a flute band because that was all the go at that time,' he explains. 'The accordion band had been a Lodge band, so we were taken on by the Lodge, too – Bridgetown No Surrender LOL 379.'

Robbie says that while the band was, and still is, affiliated to the Orange Lodge and uses its facilities, it has its own independent structures and, while there is some crossover in membership between the Lodge and the band, some of the drummers, fluters and colour party – as well as the helpers – come from localities outside the Lodge's remit. Among the founding members of the Castlederg Young Loyalists Flute Band, back in 1977, were Robbie and his brother Norman, as well as Derek Hussey, then a young teacher at Castlederg High School. The teacher's involvement was crucial to its successful establishment, because he had grown up in a working-class family in the Tyrone county town of Omagh. He had gone off to train as a teacher at Stranmillis College in Belfast, taught in the city for a while and then returned to west Tyrone to settle in Castlederg. His Omagh contacts were crucial to the successful launch of the new band in Castlederg, as was his teaching presence in the local high school from which the band still recruits members.

'Back then, there was a flute band in Omagh, the Protestant Boys,' Robbie McKinley recalls, 'so we got in touch with them and they came down and got us started.

It was a fluter and a drummer came down to us and they worked with small groups, teaching us the basic tunes we needed, and it went on from there.'

The visiting flute instructor from the Omagh Protestant Boys Band was Kenny Porter. He showed the eager young bandsmen from Castlederg the basic scales and then taught them a few familiar Blood and Thunder tunes to get them started – 'The Sash', 'Derry's Walls' and others. From then on, it was a matter of picking up the music from wherever they could get it. Again, teacher Derek Hussey proved an important resource and he had the notes for new tunes printed up on large cardboard displays at the school. On practice night these would be posted on the wall where the big noticeboard now hangs and the fluters would be lined up in chairs in front of these to learn the notes and rehearse them over and over again, while Robbie on the big bass and the side drummers took up the beat on the periphery. But the seeds of fluting struck fertile ground and soon the band's repertoire grew as tunes were learned from other bands, from recordings and other sources, and then passed on to the other band members and other bands. Even as beginners, the Castlederg Young Loyalists Flute Band was not without its initial successes. 'We won a few trophies back then,' says Robbie. 'We held our own all right.'

As the bass drummer, Robbie points out that he had a 'very important part in the band. The bass drum is the pulse of the band and all timing goes by the drum.' But even though he and five others – including his brother Norman – had come from the accordion band, they had little advantage over the new recruits lined up in front of the flute notes on the wall of the practice room: 'We had played with the accordion band, as I said, but this was a different style altogether with the flutes. It was like starting all over again.'

In those early days, the Castlederg Young Loyalists could muster dozens of fresh young musicians eager to be part of the band and learn the music. It was more than a marching band, of course, it was a cultural movement that had begun in Belfast and was now spreading to the far reaches of Tyrone where Castlederg was a pivotal centre on the western frontier. Like a busy hive of bees, the band drew in young enthusiasts, who later swarmed to establish new colonies of this popular cultural phenomenon elsewhere in Tyrone.

'We got quite a big number from the start,' says Robbie. 'There might have been forty or fifty fluters at one time, and they would have come from all over – from Omagh and Newtownstewart and Donemana and from Artigarvan.'

Over time other bands were formed in the area, such as the Red Hand Defenders Flute Band in Newtownstewart and Robbie thinks there was a flute band in Artigarvan also competing for recruits among the youngsters at Castlederg High School. That proliferation was a crucial part of the establishment, a process of stamping the Loyalist identity on every outpost of Northern Ireland, a resounding, pulsating assertion and affirmation that the Loyalist heartbeat was every bit as strong in the far reaches of Tyrone as ever it had been.

In the early days, the learning curve was steep and the dedication required of band members matched it. There were twice-weekly practices on Tuesday and Thursday, and then Friday and Saturday were spent parading at home and away. Robbie recalls that the young Castlederg band went as far as Randalstown a few times and often to Moygashel, down beyond Dungannon, but the parades were mostly local: 'I have good memories of back then, especially the friendships we struck up and the camaraderie. I have some great friendships through the band.' He nods towards the wall at the back of the stage where the practice continues. 'It's a smaller number now but the music is a lot better than we played back then.'

Robbie also recalls that from the very start there was a close co-operation between all bands in the district of west Tyrone and beyond as the band moved on from local parades to venture further afield: 'We'd get on with most of the bands and they would support one another.' From encouraging and helping to train new bands, to exchanging notes for tunes and even instruments, the network of the Blood and Thunder bands had been carried along with the zeal of conversion from pipes and accordions to flutes and drums. The passion of those early days still inspires Robbie McKinley to turn up on this bitterly cold January night for the first practice of the year and it brings him back week in and week out for practices, performances and parades. So why does he do it?

'Because it's our culture; it's what we are,' he says matter-of-factly.

Robbie remembers that, even before the accordion band of his youth, there had been a pipe band in the town and his father, who was also a member of Bridgetown No Surrender LOL 379, says that there was another flute band in Castlederg in his boyhood. The transitions have obviously marked periods when the bands simply fell apart because of lack of engagement, a dearth of enthusiastic leadership and a consequent drop-off in new blood.

The Castlederg Young Loyalists' bandmaster occasionally sent out letters to source new members and sometimes put an advertisement in the local newspapers. But from the very start, the local Castlederg High School provided the most fertile recruiting ground for the fluters, drummers and other participants for the new band. With little else to engage young males apart from organised sports, the band provided a controlled and energised environment to explore and give voice to their cultural identity. There was always strong community support for the band and its activities: 'Down the years it has kept young boys together and it's kept them off the streets,' Robbie points out. 'This was a great meeting place.'

If the memory of all those meetings brings joy, there is more than enough sorrow in the partings, particularly those that were unexpected and violent. Robbie's brother, Norman McKinley, of Breezemount Park, Castlederg, was one of two Castlederg Protestants killed in a 200lb IRA landmine explosion in the nearby townland of Second Corgary on 14 July 1984. He was 32, single, a private in the Ulster Defence Regiment. He was Robbie's brother and, with him, a founder member of the Castlederg Young Loyalists Flute Band and a member of its flute corps.

'It was a Saturday morning and we were all in the house, and Norman went out on patrol that morning,' Robbie McKinley recalls. 'He also played guitar and he had a wee group and I remember him telling our mother to have the hot water for him for a bath when he would get back because he was playing somewhere that night. Then shortly after that we got the word. I remember it was a reverend and a member of the UDR who came to tell us.'

Private McKinley died immediately in the blast which ripped through his military Landrover when it was detonated from a vantage point just across the border at 11 a.m. on that summer Saturday morning. Two other members of his eight-member UDR patrol were seriously wounded in the attack. The IRA ambush party opened fire in the immediate aftermath of the explosion and pinned down the patrol survivors. By the time a helicopter rescue party reached the scene, Corporal Heather Kerrigan, a twenty-year-old single woman from Kilclean Road in Castlederg was beyond saving. She died in the helicopter on the way to hospital. On at least one occasion in Belfast, Heather had carried a flag in the colour party of the Castlederg Young Loyalists Flute Band. Her brother, also in the patrol, was seriously wounded but, luckily, he survived.

'I knew that wee girl very well too,' says Robbie McKinley. 'You know, I still feel it the same as I did back then and it will be twenty-five years on 14 July next.'

The murders on the slopes of Meenbog Hill had a huge impact. In a few short months of that fateful year, five violent deaths had devastated the Protestant community in Castlederg. Norman and Heather had been best man and bridesmaid at the marriage of Heather's sister Elma to Tom Loughlin, another UDR member. He had been killed just a few months before them in March 1984. Another guest at the wedding was Robert Gregory 'Greg' Elliott. He was the first of the local UDR quartet to die in an almost relentless onslaught that Elma Loughlin, Tom Loughlin's widow and Heather Kerrigan's sister, said seemed to be a campaign by the IRA 'to get all our loved ones, particularly around Castlederg'.[20]

Greg Elliott, an electrician, was also single and a part-time member of the UDR. He was gunned down on 2 January 1984, as he got into his van to go to work at the house he shared with his sixty-nine-year-old widowed mother on Lislaird Road, west of Castlederg near the border – not far from where Norman McKinley and Heather Kerrigan were later killed. It is believed that two gunmen were involved in the death of Greg Elliott. One shot him at close range through the windscreen with a handgun and the other fired a hail of bullets from a rifle through the driver's door of his vehicle. It is reported that at least fourteen shots were fired.

Greg's mother rushed outside when she heard the shots and found her son's body slumped over the steering wheel. Meanwhile the IRA men made off on foot to their car and then drove across the border two miles from the house.

Because Greg was an active volunteer in his church, the Presbyterian Moderator attended his funeral and he reflected on the response of Loyalists to the huge electoral support for Sinn Féin in the recent local elections: 'To the Protestant people and indeed to the world at large, 100,000 votes for a party which will not renounce violence means 100,000 votes in support of violence,' the Moderator remarked. 'Any other explanation is facile.'[21]

However, there was another troubling aspect to the murder of Private Elliott and that was the role of an RUC Special Branch informer within the Republican ranks, Declan 'Beano' Casey. As quartermaster for the IRA in Strabane, Casey cited this as one of the murders in which he was involved with the knowledge of his police handlers. When that revelation appeared in the *Daily Mirror* in June 1993, it caused outrage in, among other places, the House of Lords, where former Northern Ireland Secretary Lord Roy Mason said: 'I raise the issue of Declan "Beano" Casey, alleged to be a double agent and the startling revelations in this week's *Daily Mirror* of him being the quartermaster for the Provisional IRA and working for the security forces. Now, what is the truth of the matter? If the Secretary of State says that we are upholding the law in Northern Ireland, does his law include this type and style of operation? Paying informers and having secreted agents within the terrorists' ranks is one thing, but this is an entirely different matter. I think that the air must be cleared and the Government must tell us the truth. Have we used and employed a mass killer? There is no need for an investigation, the RUC and the security forces must know.'

'Beano' Casey was also implicated in the death of Tom Loughlin, a UDR part-timer, who worked for the Department of the Environment's Water Service. A father of four, he was heading off to work on 2 March 1984 in his DoE van, while his young wife Elma, with their three-month-old daughter, was waving goodbye from their doorway in Drumnabey Park, Spamount, to the north of Castlederg and within a very short distance of the border. A booby-trap device under the van exploded and, oblivious of the danger, Elma rushed to the wreckage where she comforted her husband until help arrived. He was rushed to hospital but died three hours later.[22]

Robbie McKinley points out: 'It doesn't get any better with the years because nobody has ever been charged with it, so there is no closure in that way. We did speak to the Historical Inquiries Team [a special investigation unit set up to look into dormant murder files], and they said they would get around to looking into it. But they are still working on all the cases before that, so it could be some time, if ever, before they get to it.'

Hardly had the mourners dispersed from that funeral, than they were back at Castlederg First Presbyterian Church for the burial of Trevor George Elliott, an RUC Reserve Constable who had been killed by an IRA bomb as he and a colleague, Constable William Neville Gray, drove along the road from Crossmaglen to Camlough. Constable Elliott was 29, married and the father of two daughters, and while he was living in Tandragee, County Armagh, had continued to be a member of the Castlederg congregation.

While each of the deaths that year had a huge impact on the Protestant community in Castlederg, the death of Heather Kerrigan brought a wave of revulsion and condemnation. In the aftermath of her death, the Tyrone Brigade of the IRA said members of the security forces should leave and then contact the IRA: 'Provided we are satisfied that such a person has not committed grievous war crimes against our people, and is not engaged in a ruse, we shall remove that person's name from our target list.'[23] To the Loyalist community of Castlederg, it was like spitting on the graves of their dearly departed loved ones.

But the tragedy did not end there. Four years later, on the night of Saturday 4 June, 1988, Michael Darcy was pulling into the driveway of his home at Dergview on Castlederg's Killeter Road where he lived with his widowed, seventy-six-year-old mother, Kathleen. She later described what happened: 'It was near half twelve or a quarter to one when he came in and I was in bed when I heard the car coming in. And there was the wee dog and I says to the wee dog, 'There's Mikey back', and it jumped down off the bed and away out and then I heard the shots, six shots. I ran out and I couldn't get the car open. The car was locked, the engine was still running, the music was still playing, and I couldn't get into the car. I just stood there and screamed. He was shot six times in the back. I remember screaming and screaming but no one came. Not one person came out of their homes. I couldn't get help for ages.'[24]

Michael Darcy was a lance corporal in the UDR, in which he had served for ten years. He was a member of Bridgetown No Surrender Orange Lodge and another founder member of the Castlederg Young Loyalists Flute Band. His fellow band members carried the coffin from his home and at Castlederg Cemetery they handed it over to a UDR colour party. His UDR commanding officer said, 'We think that the actual targeting of Lance Corporal Darcy was done probably from within the community in which he lives. He was a very professional and competent soldier. He was a fine young man who was popular with his peers and well respected by his superiors.' His local church minister added, 'This murder was extremely cruel. Whoever carried it out must have known that Michael was the only son of a widow. We have had similar killings before and people are almost living in an atmosphere of expectancy.'[25]

Robbie McKinley says that Michael Darcy was a huge presence in the Castlederg Young Loyalists Flute Band. He was deeply involved in teaching the younger members and he always took some of them in his car to and from the parades. His death had a devastating and lasting impact on the band. 'It was like losing another member of my family because the band is very close knit and is like a family,' says Robbie. 'The longer we're together, the stronger the bond gets.'

In 1998, Michael Darcy's mother told Press Association reporter Melissa Kite that she had voted against the Good Friday Agreement. 'I did it for Michael,' she said. 'They talk about prisoner releases but not one person was ever caught for all those boys in Castlederg Cemetery.'[26]

In the top right corner of Castlederg Cemetery lie the mortal remains of four of those killed while wearing the uniform of the Ulster Defence Regiment. The surrounds and headstones are of uniform black marble and each headstone bears the emblem of the UDR – a crown-topped Irish harp – and each has the epitaph 'killed by terrorists' with the date of death.

Elsewhere in the graveyard, the grave of Michael Darcy, shared now with his mother Kathleen (who died in 1999), has the legend: 'He lived and died for Ulster'. For Michael Darcy, like other residents of the locality, Castlederg was a place of 'us and them'. A lengthy article by BBC correspondent Fergal Keane, published in *The Times* of London on 20 May 2000, relates how the young soldier and bandsman had warned his mother that if anything should ever happen to him, she must not allow 'them' to see her crying. Yet they both were conscious that in the convoluted world of Northern Ireland and its tribal identities, it wasn't as cut and dry as that. For as Fergal Keane then revealed, Michael Darcy was the son of a Roman Catholic from the Republic of Ireland called Mick Darcy and he had been baptised and reared as a Catholic in London until the tragic death of his father when he was six. Kathleen Darcy then brought the boy with the cockney accent home to her Loyalist community in the deeply divided town of Castlederg and raised him as a Protestant. By the time Michael was told of his Catholic beginnings, he had already staked his colours firmly to the mast. 'He wanted it [kept] quiet because he knew what they were around this place,' his mother told Fergal Keane. So he helped to form the band of which he became such a pivotal member and he even joined the local Bridgetown No Surrender LOL attesting in doing so that he was 'born a Protestant'. There was never any question of where his loyalties lay and up until his return from that parade in Omagh to the fatal ambush awaiting him on his doorstep, Michael Darcy was as loyal as any in Castlederg. Even beyond the grave, the double identity life he chose to live has not tarnished his memory. When Fergal Keane disclosed the secret to Derek Hussey after Kathleen Darcy's death, the Ulster Unionist politician said that his friend's death – part of an ongoing sequence in the local Loyalist community – propelled him into politics: 'The killing has to stop,' he said. 'There can't be any more Michael Darcys.'[27]

When Ian Sproule's cortège passed through Castlederg town centre in April 1991, it was the twenty-third funeral of an IRA victim to make its way to the local cemetery on the Drumquin Road. Ian 'Cracker' Sproule, twenty-three, was shot as he was parking his car outside his house at Lisleen Road, Killen. At his funeral in Castlederg First Presbyterian Church, the local minister said he personally had buried nine of the twenty-three victims of the IRA and that 'no one has been charged' for any of the murders.

Ian 'Cracker' Sproule was also a member of the Castlederg Young Loyalists Flute Band and, at the time of his death, the IRA justified the murder by showing a document to a journalist which suggested that the young man was a Loyalist paramilitary activist. It was from a Garda Special Branch file and it identified Sproule as a suspect wanted for questioning about the planting of incendiary explosive devices in business premises in the Donegal towns of Ballybofey, Castlefinn and Letterkenny four years earlier. The document had a stamp saying 'UVF' beside Sproule's name.[28] In the political furore that followed the disclosure of the document, it was pointed out that the firebomb attacks had been claimed by the Ulster Freedom Fighters (UFF), a cover name for the Ulster Defence Association (UDA), and not the UVF. Then, a month after Ian Sproule's funeral, a UDA/UFF gang smashed down the front door of Donegal Sinn Féin Councillor Eddie Fullerton in Buncrana and shot dead the fifty-six-year-old father of six at 2 a.m. on 25 May 1991. A UFF statement claimed that Fullerton had passed on Garda information about Ian Sproule to his IRA killers.[29]

The horror of violent death is infused in the consciousness of the community to which the members of the Castlederg Young Loyalists Flute Band belong. The band's official Roll of Honour on its website includes its four former members in a list of twenty-three dead. The roll begins with Winston Donnell, the first UDR soldier to be killed in the Troubles, shortly after the regiment was founded. Winston was the uncle of current bandmaster Trevor Donnell and his 1971 death was quickly followed by two others mentioned on the Roll – UDR sergeant Kenneth Smyth and Daniel McCormick, who had recently resigned from the UDR and is the only Catholic on the band's Roll of Honour.

The final entry on the Roll of Honour was also a band member. Former Loyalist prisoner Charles 'Christopher' Folliard was a thirty-year-old gardener from Douglas Bridge – one of nineteen children – and his brother had been injured by an IRA bomb while serving in the UDR. Christopher was shot dead by dissident Republicans as he said goodnight to his sixteen-year-old Catholic girlfriend in Oakland Park, Strabane, in the staunchly Republican Ballycolman area of the town. Two masked men walked up to his car and pushed his teenage girlfriend out of the way, before opening fire on Folliard who was preparing to drive off. In a clinical execution, one of the gunmen then walked to the front of the car and shot him three more times with a police issue Heckler and Koch rifle, causing wounds to the head, chest and legs. Folliard was pronounced dead on arrival at Altnagelvin Hospital in Derry.[30]

In one of the more bizarre twists of the Troubles, the gun used to kill him had been reported as having fallen from a police Landrover as it rushed to an emergency in Strabane town. While the Continuity IRA claimed it had recovered the rifle and had it in its arsenal, the cold-blooded assassination of Folliard was believed to be the work of the INLA which had maintained a strong dissident Republican presence in Strabane. Whoever was actually responsible, Sinn Féin MP Pat Doherty described them as 'enemies of the peace process, enemies of Republicanism'.

Folliard had served half of a jail sentence of fourteen years for conspiring to kill a Catholic workmate at a quarry in Newtownstewart. In fact, having been involved in the murder plot, Folliard then called The Samaritans help-line and gave details of the bomb planted under a lorry. His warning meant the device was found before it could be triggered. On being sent to prison, he chose not to go to the Loyalist wing of the Maze Prison but to serve his sentence as an ordinary prisoner in Maghaberry Jail. His family said he had severed all paramilitary links and his Presbyterian minister pointed out at his funeral, 'This part of his life was something which he deeply regretted.'

In talking to Robbie McKinley about his earliest memories of the band, I am conscious of a detail I read about his brother's death long after the local revulsion had been covered by so much more blood. It was in a report about the disbandment of the Royal Irish Regiment (RIR) and the reaction of retired UDR Sergeant Leslie Finlay who spoke of how this disbandment dishonoured his fallen comrades in the Castlederg area of west Tyrone, including his own nephew William Pollock. In particular, he recalled the three deaths of Tom Loughlin, Heather Kerrigan and Norman McKinley: 'I was in the store in Omagh when Norman's kit was brought in. His leather boots, they were like two porcupines. The bones of his feet were sticking out through them.'[31]

Robbie McKinley is no longer an active member of the Castlederg Young Loyalists band – although he has a central role in the CYL Old Boys – yet he still marches to the beat of his own drum and he points out that the good times far outweigh the bad days for the Castlederg Young Loyalists Flute Band: 'There were some bad times and some good times down the years. It was hard times when the membership would drop off, but we're getting strong again now. We have to keep it going because this is who we are and those that have gone would certainly want that.'

CHAPTER 3

AIR ON A BLUETOOTH

Thursday, 22 January 2009

The annual general meeting at the Bridgetown No Surrender Orange Hall is down to the crucial vote for bandmaster and little knots of paper ballots are assembled on the 'drumming table'. Band members lapse into conversations as they are counted. Johnny, who is standing right in front of the gas heater, complains there is no heat from it. Perhaps for my benefit, Trevor Donnell points out that the other positions are already filled and there are three contenders for bandmaster. He doesn't seem anxious and the result is overwhelmingly for him to stay on.

'OK, so I'll take it on again for this year but it will be my last,' Trevor says. 'I was going to quit in the anniversary year but I'm still here …' He pauses. 'I was going to take on somebody as assistant bandmaster this year to share the work. I've spoken to him already about this and that person is Davy Lowry, if that's all right with the rest of you.'

Nods and some shifting and shuffling signal the silence of

assent as young Davy smiles; then it's back to the rehearsal. The Castlederg Young Loyalists Flute Band does not stand on ceremony, even for an AGM. I learn afterwards that the Treasurer is informed by phone that he has been elected in absentia for another year.

Indeed, mobile phones and other new technology have revolutionised the Blood and Thunder scene. As with any gathering of young people, phones are in constant use. They are used to record and transmit tunes, recruit substitutes and, travelling to and from parade venues, they are an audio SatNav system to co-ordinate arrival. They are also used for taking photos and video clips of parades and practices, transmitted to absent band members and posted on Internet social networking sites.

Band old-timers marvel at the new technology, acknowledging that it has raised standards and discipline. In the early days of the band, rehearsals were formal classroom-style events. Today, members are supplied with flute notes and the band CD and DVD recordings, which show precisely the performance and tempo of popular tunes. The Castlederg Young Loyalists have three recordings to date – an early cassette tape called 'Loyal Tunes of Glory', a first CD called 'Marching Along the Border', and the bumper CD/DVD package to mark the thirtieth anniversary in 2007, called '30 Years of Marching'. Currently, the band is putting together a charity CD and together these recordings will comprise more than fifty tunes, many of them medley arrangements. Meanwhile, the Internet has been flooded with Bebo and more formal websites hosting band news and history, YouTube video extracts, comment boards and more. The University of Ulster research project, CAIN (Conflict Archive on the Internet), has noted that Loyalists in general have embraced new technologies because of their deep distrust of the mass media.[32] They share a general Unionist view that mass media has misrepresented their culture and consistently favoured Nationalism. CAIN observes: 'Loyalist band websites and the associated guestbooks, discussion forums and even online radio stations, make up the most intensely active corner of Loyalist and Unionist web space. Band members have lots to discuss and organise during the marching season and many are clearly enthusiastic about the new information and communication technologies. The Net provides a new means for distributing recordings of their music. The use of text-messaging abbreviations in band guest books and online forums illustrates the continuities and crossovers between mobile-phone use and Internet use. The intensity and frequency of discussion on several of the guest books suggests that these websites have become an important focus for a significant proportion of band members.'

The University of Ulster research also notes that the political content of Blood and Thunder band websites varies widely in scale and tone, and many bands assiduously avoid any overt political content on their websites, which are devoted to the music and the competitions. However, it notes that one band posted candid photos of an illegal paramilitary 'firing party' at its 2002 parade. Such links are seldom acknowledged, much less boasted about now.

Websites present a more acceptable face for bands and access has been tightened to prevent sabotage. Yet the ephemeral nature of Internet activity and the turnover in bands means that there are hundreds of discontinued and inactive sites dedicated to bands that may have ceased to exist. CAIN notes: 'By March 2005 almost a quarter of the sites listed … were defunct.' A Google search on the Internet turns up almost half a million results for the term Blood and Thunder. Thousands of these are for video/sound clips of Blood and Thunder performances on YouTube; hundreds more are for websites dedicated to Blood and Thunder bands. Many are merely cloned Bebo sites with adolescent content and, occasionally, inappropriate comments. One could expect little else given the historical legacy and sectarian climate of Northern Ireland and the bravado of young adolescents who make up the bulk of the Blood and Thunder participants. However, it should be pointed out that the level of abuse is markedly higher on Bebo sites for Republican flute bands.

The Castlederg Young Loyalists Flute Band has a Bebo website dedicated to it – notably without sectarian or political content – and it includes links to the Bebo sites of band members for invited friends only. Nobody seems to know who set up that Bebo site, although its very existence prompted this prominent advisory on the band's dedicated website: 'Welcome to the only Official Web Site of Castlederg Young Loyalists Flute Band, 30 Years Marching Along the Border – Quality not Quantity – 1977–2007'.[33]

The official website acts as a source of information on all that the band's current members and all those who have gone before them hold most dear. There are promotional videos and advertisements for CDs and DVDs; photo galleries and badges and emblems; a variety of historical accounts and commentaries on landmark events; links to other websites; and musical resources such as flute notes and lyrics for popular Loyalist songs. There are also fun pages, games (one called 'Shoot the Provos'!) as well as computer 'wallpaper' for Glasgow Rangers Football Club. There are sections on charity events such as the Castlederg to Portrush cycle for Children in Need, bonfire night and an extensive account of the thirtieth anniversary dinner. Finally, there are interactive sections including a guestbook, a section for old messages which had been posted on the website and a section called 'What People Are Saying' about the band.

The history/commentary sections provide a window into the thinking of those who organise and support the Castlederg Young Loyalists Flute Band. They are unapologetically Loyalist, with brief historical accounts of the Battle of the Boyne, the 36th (Ulster) Division at the Battle of the Somme, the role of the 'B' Specials along the border for the first fifty years of Northern Ireland's existence and the Ulster Defence Regiment which succeeded them as the part-time militia. There is a UDR Roll of Honour for the local company, as well as an account of the Troubles in Castlederg and a section entitled 'Bloody Sunday, Bloody Waste' decrying the huge cost of the enquiry into the 1972 shooting of thirteen Catholic civilians by British paratroopers.

What is on the official website is largely down to Nigel, an adult volunteer who has devoted much of the past decade to learning about web technology and building the site for the band. He has done so largely by trial and error, and he and Trevor Donnell agree what should be posted there. The site has had its moments. At one point a notice on the site declared: 'The band regret that due to people abusing the guestbook we had no alternative but to remove it until this problem is resolved. We hope to have a new improved guestbook soon. Signed Trevor Donnell, Bandmaster.'

Nigel explains: 'We started taking a lot of abuse. There would be comments aimed at different band members and rows about what was going on in the town. People were getting at each other through the guestbook and stuff like that. It actually got to the extent that you might have some people putting on comments about such and such a one having a wain [child] and so and so is the father. People would be coming to us saying there's a comment on the guestbook about me ... get it off! So we changed the guestbook completely so that we would have a tracer on it and a warning at the start of it that anyone leaving a comment could be traced ... but hands up, we don't have the ability to trace them. We don't have the equipment, like. Sure the PSNI couldn't even get that information unless it's a sex offence, so the chances of us getting it would be very remote. But because of that [warning], now we get a very small amount of comments, which is a major disappointment because many of the comments were very, very good.'

Nigel has worked on the official website as a labour of love and his efforts resulted in two Golden Web Awards in 2003 and 2004. He points out proudly that this is an achievement that stands out in the world of marching bands.

'It started off just as a hobby, you know, but it grew from there,' admits Nigel, who is Trevor Donnell's brother-in-law, with other close family links (three brothers-in-law and two sisters have been active in the band at various stages) that gave him a ready and detailed insight into the band's history and outlook. 'It started off about 2002 as one page and basically that was the front page. After that, I got interested in building a website and I experimented with several free web providers ... and I just couldn't get the thing to work out. You see, I had no qualifications or experience in computers or anything else and finally one night the whole thing just came together. Admittedly it was just a front page and there was nothing else on it. It was this big black page with an orange banner on the side of it that you could put the names of the other pages on and, of course, there was the name of the band across the top of it. This occurred about maybe half twelve, maybe a quarter to one at night, so I had to ring Trevor to tell him, "We've got a website; we've got nothing on it but we've got one." So the next night we scanned the band badge; that's because we had no band badge digitally, so we scanned one into the computer. We even had no photo of the badge, so it was from the actual badge onto the scanner. We filled out the blank areas and made it a little brighter and I put a frame around it. I put it on the website and it's on there yet. The only other thing we had on it at the start was a notice about when the band had practice and that everyone was welcome to join. And we had a counter at the bottom of the page and that's basically how it all started … And then once I got into it, I started to think, "Now what else could I do?" and I wanted to put photographs on it but nobody knew how to do that at the start but we learned how to do that as we went along.

'The band's badge is based on the badge of the 36th Ulster Division and this area of Tyrone and Donegal had a large contingent – the 88th Rifles – and they made up the bulk of the 36th Division that went to the Somme. And because of that, there was always a very tight connection between the band and the memories of those from the area who were lost at the Somme. So one of the first pages was the one about the 36th Ulster.'

From the outset, Nigel's idea was to build a website that

did more than just proclaim the band's presence. He wanted it to express the pride of band members in their Ulster Loyalist culture at a time when their side of the Northern Irish community felt it was being eclipsed by Nationalism and dismissed as nothing more than tribal bigotry.

'I really wanted to have the history of what it was like growing up a Protestant in this area and the Troubles around it, because this area was badly hit, very badly hit. Several times, I mean, we were reduced to a town of rubble and I wanted to get that across. I also wanted to dedicate it to those we grew up with and went to school with, who died as a part of the Troubles. You know, many times in modern politics those people are forgotten.' Yet the website was not intended to be triumphalist, nor to glorify militarism. He fears that this has been a deliberate intention of other Loyalist websites and it tarnishes the memory of those Protestants who died during the Troubles. 'You know, you see websites and they have guns on them and that ... We didn't want something that was distasteful to their memory. We wanted a dignified website in their memory,' says Nigel, who agreed the tone and ethos of the website in discussions with Trevor Donnell and his predecessor Derek Hussey.

'So it went on from there and I spent hours on it, sitting down at maybe nine o'clock most nights. You see, I live with two wains and they went to bed maybe about nine o'clock and I would then sit down and start to do something on the website and you were still at it at maybe four o'clock in the morning. Of course I had no training, so I just experimented and tried to see how to get what I wanted and even that changed as I went along. You know, I'd be talking to Trevor and maybe going around different band sites and you'd come across one and there would be music playing on it and you'd wonder, "How the hell do you get music playing?" And so then you would read different things and you would try different things and eventually you would get it. Every time you got something, it was great. You would get a real buzz.'

Trawling through different websites to see what could be achieved was about all the outside help he got. As an amateur, Nigel's creation was built by doing rather than by reading or being told. After a few failed attempts to solicit help, he decided that this was the only way to go. 'I did e-mail a couple of them [websites] but I never got any response that was any good or most of them didn't respond at all. One guy did respond and he gave me a whole clatter of information but honestly you would need a degree to understand it. So I just went back to trial and error until we finally got it built the way we wanted it.'

Even with the Golden Web Awards for 2003 and 2004, he was tweaking the design and the content. The livery colours changed and the site grew. Photographs posted willy-nilly were organised into albums to ease navigation and sections were added. 'There was another page added to it in the middle of the Bloody Sunday Inquiry, because it was something the limelight was on at the time. You know, whatever happened that day in 1972 is not going to change from whatever viewpoint you look at it. I find it scandalous that barristers were getting two grand [£2,000] a day as it sat in Belfast for maybe a year and a half. There was never going to be a case where the British army would come out and say, "We killed innocent people" and there was never going to be a case where Republicans would say, "Listen, we were doing more than just walking up the street" … To me it was just a total waste of money because it was never going to clarify anything.' Nigel insists, however, that the Bloody Sunday section is more than his personal view. 'There would have been comments about it [in the website guestbook] at the time it went up. I should have saved all those old messages but what we didn't realise at that time was that we had the website for free and we were only allowed a certain amount on each page. Now the website is paid for and it's unlimited, but at that time it was just a free website. You know, we posted every message sent in because we wanted people to be able to go in there and see what was being said, but when we went in to look we only had about a tenth of the messages. That was because the page couldn't take them all and the rest were just gone, which was sad, because there were some good ones. I remember one of the earliest messages was from a man from here who had gone away to Australia and he talked about how the website brought back so many memories and he had a tear in his eye, you know. People like that remember those who have died and they appreciate all the hard work that has been done to keep their memory alive. That message was one of the nicest ones we got and it makes it all worthwhile.'

Messages falling off the precipice was not the only problem in those early days. It was only after a long, frustrating time that Nigel learned the site had to be formally registered with search engines. 'But eventually we got there through word of mouth being passed about. We got it right and it was great,' he says, acknowledging the contribution of the local Castlederg High School. He laughs, 'And then, at one stage you know, the site was banned up at the school because the kids were spending too much time on it …'

In the busy coffee shop at the Old Courthouse in Markethill, County Armagh, Quincey Dougan hands me a leaflet to read while he goes off to order tea. It is headed 'Loyalist Marching Bands: Misunderstood and Misrepresented?' and it points out that the bands represent a culture that has evolved over centuries to become the 'largest musical youth movement in the United Kingdom and Ireland' providing a disciplined social outlet for more than 20,000 active members. Over the course of the next couple of hours and several brews of tea, Quincey expounds on this in a gush of unbridled enthusiasm to put the record straight and he has set his sights on the World Wide Web to spread this message further. Quincey is the webmaster of the Ulster Bands Forum website and a pioneer of web activity in the movement for the Kilcluney

Volunteers Flute Band. The wider forum, he points out, provides for a huge and growing network of those interested in the culture and organisation of Blood and Thunder bands.

'Over the last few years, we have been trying to get a bit more guidance and direction for bands and the Internet has been the primary means of that,' says Quincey, who describes the Bebo websites as 'pure rubbish' that perpetuate the image of bands as irresponsible, adolescent and often sectarian. The Ulster Bands Forum provides a platform for the views of people actively involved in marching bands and its aim is to promote Ulster Protestant cultural traditions. He reckons active contributors represent between 300 and 400 bands and tight security allows members to express their views openly and have them analysed and challenged by others. All participants must give a full name, address and other information so that they can be vouched for by *bona fide* members and endorsed by the committee.

'People are joining as individuals,' Quincey explains. 'They're not joining as bands and there is continuous clearing of dead wood. If people don't come back [online] in a month, then I just wipe them. The membership is around a thousand people. It's quite easy to get a thousand people on an Internet forum but our site is different because something like sixty-three per cent are people who log on every day or several times a week. It's a very active and living forum. If you go to it at any time, there will be something new.

'The basic idea of it is to discuss happenings in the band

world. That's broken down [into separate sections] because there's a lot of marching bands in England; there's a lot of bands in Scotland and there's about twenty-four in the Republic and then there's a few in Australia and a few in Canada and they all come into it as well. But that obviously would be the most active section. Over and above that then, there are sections for funding, public relations, promotions, education – that obviously is all-important. The most active part will be Upcoming Events – you know, who is organising what, and reports and pictures and videos of those events. Those have been the most popular topics and they will be even more so in the coming months. But then there's a forum for community chat and community discussions – to cut the nonsense a bit. News and politics will be discussed regularly but I have to say that the forum is exclusively orientated to bands and what is relevant to our movement. Now there's also a lot of crossover on a lot of occasions; some issues are very emotional and they will get activity but it still tends to be very much about bands.'

While my request for admission to the Ulster Band Forum has been politely declined because I am not a band member, Quincey takes out his Blackberry and logs on to the website. Flicking through the various categories, he illustrates what is exercising the thoughts of people in the band world. In the traffic for the last hour of postings, this ranged through Wrestlemania, a Shankill Road Defenders album on eBay and even a discussion about an academic paper on 'bands and territory'. Quincey names the PhD student author and remarks, 'I didn't like her essay at all, incidentally.' He continues flicking through other topics – the Sons of Ulster parade; a nightclub event; tickets for a Northern Ireland football match; and a discussion on wads, springs and pads for flutes. 'Whenever it gets into the evening time, you would have more discussions related to what's going on maybe, but that is an indication.'

Quincey argues that the Ulster Bands Forum, which has existed since 2003, must remain closed to casual lurkers and posters: 'This forum is for the people who are involved in the culture and who are supportive of the culture. It's very deliberate because that was felt to be the best way to make changes. It was the best way to maintain focus and its mission, as the website states clearly, is to "promote unity, encourage understanding". If it was opened up to just anyone, it would not be following that mission. There are people who just want to keep all that other kind of stuff going and that has been a huge contributing factor in holding a lot of things back. But when the anger's up and the blood's up, you know you don't tend to be thinking about that. You don't pre-plan, you react and it's often not rational. What is happening at the moment is that the movement is becoming less and less reactionary. The Internet has allowed a degree of networking and information exchange between bands that just was not possible before. Besides the help it has given in organising events and raising the standards of musical performance, the website has allowed the bands to explore the essence of what they are doing and to formulate discussions that might allow them to change deeply ingrained and widely disseminated public perceptions that are wrong in their view. So the bands are like every other movement in the world that has decided to use the Internet. There's debates taking place between people who are not just in different counties but in different countries, so that opens everything up for new perspectives, new ideas, new viewpoints.'

He brings to the mission his experience as a pioneer of new communications technology in the Blood and Thunder community. 'The first band to set up a website was Kilcluney Volunteers. I did that in 1998. It's [the band website] offline now because I started to concentrate on something else and didn't get back to it, but there would be archives of it on the Internet. Back then there literally was no Loyalist website ... well there was one site devoted to the LVF [illegal paramilitary Loyalist Volunteer Force] or something, but there were no other Loyalist cultural websites at all. I started a very simple website, then over the years it took off. With a tendency to go for that Bebo stuff which is for children, you'll get a lot of extreme stuff because they just don't understand. Then the individual band websites never seemed to keep going because the networking takes prominence now. The general pooling of information and trying to learn from other people and wanting to be in touch with other bands seems to have taken preference, and more and more bands don't feel that maintaining an individual web presence is really of major benefit to them. There are a few, but there are very, very few that are constantly updated. But then a lot of bands would actually record their practice and put it on YouTube and the number of bands with proper recording equipment would surprise you. At Kilcluney Volunteers we're recording our next CD with our own recording equipment and a lot of bands record practice CDs for the benefit of members. If you go on to YouTube you'll get thousands and thousands of clips of bands. A lot of them are poor quality because they're just done with mobile phones, but it'll get better over time.'

Access to the Internet has been a huge boost to Blood and Thunder bands and the preferred means of communication within and outside their own community for Ulster Loyalists who strongly distrust the mass media. Added to the hundreds of thousands of video clips of bands already posted, a new channel called 'Bandxparades' was added to YouTube in 2009. In one season, it compiled almost 500 video clips of reasonably good quality.[34] For outsiders, this allows a fascinating window into the world of Blood and Thunder bands with all the fervour, colour and showcasing of the regular band parades that few outside the movement ever see. Meanwhile, the Ulster Bands Forum website continues to be the internal communications channel for those within the Loyalist marching band world who are committed to dialogue aimed at creating a more positive image of their activities and their culture.

CHAPTER 4

FOR GOD AND ULSTER

Thursday, 29 January 2009

Bandmaster Trevor Donnell interrupts the rehearsal for the Castlederg Young Loyalists Flute Band's first public performance of 2009, in just over a week's time, to query the title of a tune. He has been given an alternative name for it and, when he points this out, several band members join in to disagree with the alternative suggestion. 'That's the Lord Is My Shepherd,' insists Kenny Sproule, who is organising the stock of the band's CDs for merchandising. 'That's the way it is sung in church too.' Several others agree and Trevor accepts their explanation. He has been wondering if the band wants more hymns on the programme for the forthcoming Somme commemoration night. The band members, however, seem happy enough with the tunes already chosen which also include '18th of December', 'Farnross', 'The Outlaw Josey Wales', 'Albert Reid', 'Killaloe', 'Billy McFazdean' and the 'Green Fields of France' or 'Willie McBride'. While some band members wear their Christianity openly, they are content that the band itself is no more than a secular expression of their identity and culture. Given the huge disparity of Ulster Unionist affiliations and the varying degrees of their practice of faith, it could do little else.

Neil Johnston found Jesus and was saved on the side of the road between his home in Irvinestown and Enniskillen, County Fermanagh. He had just been in a critical accident and was suffering from serious head injuries, spine damage, a punctured lung and his right arm was hanging by a few remaining threads of nerves. Yet Neil firmly believes that divine fortune ensured that vital help was at hand and, as he began the slow and painful path to recovery, his faith in the Lord and his passionate desire to rejoin the ranks of a Blood and Thunder flute band kept his spirits up and his hopes alive. In 2006, a year after the accident, however, Neil was told that he would probably never walk again because of the damage caused to his spine. He proved the medical experts wrong and in late 2008, just a couple of months after enlisting in the Castlederg Young Loyalists Flute Band, he completed a charity cycle of seventy miles from Castlederg to Portrush, County Antrim, in aid of Children in Need.

'A total of thirteen cyclists did the run from Castlederg to Portrush,' bandmaster Trevor Donnell explains. 'We left Castlederg at 8 a.m. and arrived in Portrush an hour ahead of our [planned] time at 3.30 p.m., soaked to the skin. It was well worth it and we got a very good reception the whole road down from the other road users, which helps you on the way. The youngest to do it was just nine years of age, but I have to mention one guy who joined our band recently and had been told a few years ago that he would never walk again following a road traffic accident. He cycled the whole thing. It did our hearts good to see him cycling into Portrush. Anyway we raised a grand total of £2,717 for Children in Need, so it was well worthwhile.'

'About ten or so undertook to do it and there were three of us who completed it from start to finish,' says Neil. He explains: 'Since the accident I have to keep going. It's four years ago just there on 25 January – back in 2005. I was on my way to band practice that night with the old band I used to be with, Defenders of the Rock, in Lisbellaw. The last thing I remember was going out of Irvinestown that night. I have no memory of it [the crash] whatsoever. I hit into another car but they were all right, luckily enough.'

His matter-of-fact recounting of the surgeries he underwent seems like a litany of relatively simple procedures. Yet all of these operations were on the spine and the consequences were considerable each time the young north Fermanagh man was brought back to the operating theatre up in Belfast. 'After the fifth operation then, that's when I started to get better … When I was getting into bed, I used to have to wheel the wheelchair over and then catch one leg and lift it in and then catch the other and lift it in too. What I started to notice then, coming into Christmas, was that the legs started coming up to my hands and I thought, hey what's going on here? It was the greatest Christmas present ever ... they thought maybe I could walk again and they started to give more attention to the spinal injuries with physiotherapy. I was in Musgrave [Park Hospital, Belfast] and it really helped me, you know. The physio was really hard but it helped. I had the physio twice a day when I was in there and then I would come home at the weekends.'

After Neil Johnston's slow and painful road to a relatively full recovery all he 'really wanted to do then, when I was walking again, was to get back with the band. You know, I used to dream about that all the time. At the start of it all then, of course, I was on crutches, but I used to follow Lisbellaw around, and then I was on one crutch and all. Then on 11th night, it was my first night with no sticks or crutches or anything and I walked around with the band, but I wouldn't have been able to march or anything. So it came around September time and the parade in Tamnaghmore; that was my first parade back again in 2007. I was a bit shaky at the start, but when I got into it I was able to do it all right. So I was back then to the end of the season.'

Having surmounted the painful challenge of walking once more, to the point of being able to march and play in a band parade, he set a new ambition to explore further the music and marching tradition he loved. His ambition was fuelled by his new-found religious fervour as a born-again Christian.

'And then for 2008, I was with Lisbellaw still, but there were a lot of things going on,' he explains. 'You know the band didn't want to learn new tunes and I wanted to do new tunes and all, but they didn't want to learn the tunes. So I was on my own, more or less … So I said, look I have had enough, and I left them then. But my brother, he's still in the Lisbellaw band, so he is.'

Neil Johnston was a young, experienced and remarkably enthusiastic fluter in search of a Blood and Thunder band and he immediately looked to the Castlederg Young Loyalists Flute Band. In terms of travelling to and from practice, there was little difference in the twenty miles between Irvinestown and Castlederg and the sixteen miles to Lisbellaw through Enniskillen. However, convenience was not the deciding factor, he quickly points out, noting 'I've always admired this band'.

Neil has been an active member of a marching flute band since an early age, having been recruited to his first through a family connection when he was still in the Primary Five class at school, which puts him at about nine years of age.

'There was no band in Irvinestown, but my uncle … he would have started the band, it was called the Milligans down about Lack, the USC Memorial Band [Ulster Special Constabulary]. My father got me into it, and that was my first band and my older brother was in it as well, so he was. My father would have been big into flute bands too. He was never in a band but he could play a flute. And he got me into the bands and I was only in P5. I used to play in the parades near home, but then at the weekends they'd go away to parades and I'd be left behind. But I just loved the parades, so I did. A band is more than parades and music though; it's a social club and it's all your friends.

'I was in the Lack band until 2002. But it was in County Fermanagh and there's something funny about flute bands and County Fermanagh. You see, there's not as great an interest among the young ones and that's what happened with the flute band at Lack; they ran out of members. In all County Fermanagh there's only four Blood and Thunder flute bands, whereas in places like Armagh and Down, you'd have one every two miles maybe. You're spoiled for choice there like, but when the Lack band disappeared, there was no flute band to join in that whole part of Fermanagh.

'After that then, I joined Lisbellaw Defenders of the Rock because a lot of my school friends were in it. I went to school in Enniskillen High and, with a lot of my friends, there used to be a lot of banter about which band was best and all. So I joined the Lisbellaw band in 2003 and I was in it until 2008, so what's that, five years? I suppose I was two years out because I couldn't march, but I was still counting myself as a member and all. And then I joined Castlederg last October. I always admired this band and I remember years ago when they had two bass drummers and when I was wee and all, I used to wait for the band with the two bass drummers to come along. That would have been after Robbie [McKinley] was on the bass, but my mother remembers Robbie and she says he was a great bass drummer.'

Again, the decision to move to the Castlederg Young Loyalists was facilitated by the network of contact and movement between the Blood and Thunder marching bands. 'There's a boy, Gary Braden – he hasn't been at practice because he's been working – but he was in the Lack band with me and I was over chatting to him, you see, and at this time I still wasn't back driving. But he had joined Castlederg and I said to him, "When I get back driving, I'll come down to practice." He passed on the word and then they offered to come up and collect me, but I didn't want to put them out, so I waited 'til I got everything right, you know, the car and all, and I got here about two weeks before the charity cycle. There wasn't much time to train with the others, but I was out on the bicycle all the time anyway.'

Although he is still embarking on his first year of parading with the Castlederg Young Loyalists Flute Band, Neil has already gone the distance, even though he had to take a break, just as in the long cycle to Portrush. 'There was about 500 yards of it I didn't do,' he admits. 'You see, at the top of the Coleraine Hill I was struggling a bit. Trevor [Donnell] was behind us and I was the last cyclist; the two other boys were on racing bikes and they were away on and I was coming up the hill real slow. At the top of the hill I stopped and I was gasping for air and Trevor got out and put my bike into the van, and then about 500 yards on were the other boys on the racing bikes. So I got out then and cycled on to Portrush, and all the others had to get out as well and we all cycled into Portrush. It was really great, everybody cheering and clapping and all.'

Neil points out that during the closed season part of the year, the charity cycle was a good bonding exercise for a new band member. 'I really got to know everybody, so it was great.' Being mobile again with his own car and his role in the Castlederg Young Loyalists band has turned Neil's life around, bringing him back from his invalidity to a full and active life. He has quickly established himself as a more than willing member of the band, volunteering to go out of his way to facilitate it by collecting other bandsmen for a lift to parades, and even going to big parades the band can not attend to sell the band CDs and DVDs. His enthusiasm for the band is matched by a strong work ethic and he points out that he is now working part-time in the Marks and Spencer store in Enniskillen. Nor has his enthusiasm for his car been dampened by his traumatic experience. 'I love driving, so I do, even though I had the accident, because I don't remember anything about it.'

Neil says other members of his family share his enthusiasm for Blood and Thunder bands. His older brother was in the Lack band and acted as its bandmaster for the final three years of its existence. He has also paraded with the Lisbellaw Defenders of the Rock on occasion and was a member of that band. While he doesn't take an active part any more because 'he's thirty-three now and he's married and all with a family', he is still interested and often goes to parades to watch Neil and their younger brother who, while he would have been 'big into bands', while growing up, only joined when he turned sixteen in 2007. 'He went to all the parades and all, but he was never interested in joining. Now he's marching and all with Lisbellaw, so that's good,' says Neil, who adds that the brothers also share an interest in football and other sports. Just like a normal family of young men, 'there'd be a lot of banter and all ...'

He candidly points out that he is a born-again Christian who attends Kilskeery Free Presbyterian Church, a small hamlet of south County Tyrone, outside Irvinestown. The congregation is not far from the spot where he had his roadside epiphany while he lay seriously injured with his very life hanging, like his all but severed arm, by a thread.

'While I was recovering, I knew that God was telling me that I would walk again if I put my trust in Him,' says Neil. 'I was thinking, you see, what would have happened if I had died that night at the side of the road with all the people that were there helping me and all. I was thinking, what reasons have I to live? What purpose do I have in life? And then it just gave me a new lease of life kind of thing. It has really helped and now everything is starting to fall into place with God. You see, when I was in hospital and real bad, a minister came in and he asked me if I was saved and I told him I was, even though I wasn't at the time. That got me thinking, you see and it was because of that I became a Christian.'

However, Christian fervour for Neil is not expressed through unwelcome proselytising, but in his calm, friendly demeanour. Even within the band, he smiles understandingly when some of the banter among the group of young men and women occasionally slips into bawdy remarks, or when comments or remarks are accompanied by expletives. The band is his social club now and he accepts the norms of membership and must incorporate that with his Christian principles. On the very rare occasions when the band might have to do something on a Sunday, Neil is known not to be available. But he does not allow his status as a born-again Christian to completely preclude the normal social life of a young man. 'I would go into pubs but I don't drink any more,' he observes. 'I don't know what it's going to be like with this band, but I know they don't drink before they parade and so I don't think it should be too bad, you know.' He is perfectly aware of the reputation of Blood and Thunder bands on that score: 'Some bands would drink a lot and act the eejit and I was having some problems with that in Lisbellaw. But this is a great band and I always admired them.'

The involvement of a born-again Christian in Blood and Thunder music probably is not that unusual given their huge numbers in the Protestant population of Northern Ireland and the broad spectrum of bands now involved in that musical genre. According to a recent study, one in eight adults in Northern Ireland is an evangelical, born-again Christian, and they hold more conservative views and are more committed to their churches than others who identify themselves as Protestants. The findings of Claire Mitchell of Queen's University Belfast and James Tilley of Oxford University, based on data in the 2004 Northern Ireland Life and Times Survey, show that Ulster Protestants should never be regarded as a homogenous group holding similar views on politics and society in Northern Ireland.[35] However, previous research by one of the co-authors of this study, Claire Mitchell, concludes that while religious practice varies greatly among Northern Ireland Protestants, religious ideas and symbols continue to be important in the imagination of Protestant identity: 'Concepts of Protestant freedom, honesty, religious siege and anti-Catholicism still permeate the language and values of many Protestants, even amongst those who do not go to church or see themselves as religious. Whilst not specifically referring to theology or doctrine, Protestant ideology continues to help people make sense of social relationships in Northern Ireland. Protestant ideology retains strong explanatory power, particularly when it overlaps with other cultural, political and economic issues.'[36]

Given the strong evangelical tradition and disparate congregational nature of Northern Ireland Protestantism, as well as the tradition of strong religious identity in the cultural affairs of Unionism, band parades provide a ready market for proselytising. Yet such activities are low-key and generally amount to little more than distribution of leaflets and other reading matter. So in the course of a mere handful of parades, a visitor might come away with advice on free Bible Camps for children during the long summer school holidays; a fundamentalist magazine dealing with issues ranging from humanism, creationism and the 1859 Protestant revival in Ulster; a Way of Life Calendar for 2010 with prominent and familiar quotes from Scripture on every page; and a remarkably lurid leaflet on the Battle of Aughrim in 1691 with a religious warning built into the failed tactics of the Jacobite forces under the Marquis de St Ruth which led to another, and this time conclusive, Protestant victory for the Williamites.

This growing collection of ephemeral literature distributed at band parades is in sharp contrast to the secular nature of the Protestantism on display at events that are not held under the auspices of the three traditional institutions of Loyalism – the Orange, Black and Apprentice Boys. For apart from the very occasional hymns played by some bands – and notably by the more traditional accordion bands which participate – the musical fare tends to range over modern march tunes, show tunes and countless variations on traditional airs that would not be out of place at any cultural gathering in Ireland or Scotland. It is possibly this overtly secular aspect of the marching bands and, in particular, the Blood and Thunder movement, that has ensured its continuing popularity. If one fervent belief is expounded at band parades, then it is the faithful adherence to the Northern Ireland football team and, to a much lesser degree, the football clubs of Glasgow Rangers and Liverpool.

Religious practice and observance have subsided in Northern Ireland in line with the fall-off elsewhere, although on a somewhat delayed timescale. Because of that, the most obvious markers in the divided community have become secular. Today, Catholic/Nationalist and Protestant/Unionist youths are distinguished most readily by their street clothing – Protestants/Unionists wear Northern Ireland soccer tops, and occasionally those of Rangers and Liverpool, while Catholics/Nationalists wear GAA jerseys and sometimes Glasgow Celtic and Eircom Republic of Ireland tops in larger urban centres.

Quincey Dougan of the Ulster Bands Forum believes that the overwhelming majority of bands are now apolitical, as they have no direct political mission, and he contrasts that with the GAA which has had a clear political objective of promoting Irish Nationalism since its foundation in the 1880s. So while he agrees that bands play the same social role in the Ulster Loyalist community as the GAA clubs do on the Nationalist side, he argues that the bands do not have the same hidden agenda. 'A lot of people from a Nationalist/Republican viewpoint would totally disagree with this, but from my point of view, I think we have less political trappings. We bring things with us into bands because that's who we are, but there are no implants and there's no overarching constitution or objectives. There is no central objective that we're going to maintain Northern Ireland as part of the United Kingdom at all costs. We don't have that element and whilst there is broad acceptance that this is our belief and our values, we don't have the trappings that I think the GAA has.'

He does not dispute the fact that some bands were formed on the fringes of the burgeoning Loyalist paramilitary groups of the 1970s, but the overwhelming majority of bands that have survived have evolved far from that. Indeed, there has been a concerted effort to rid band parades of the once common spectacle of young men in paramilitary garb wearing dark glasses. Given the close scrutiny of Loyalist band parades, there is virtually no opportunity of staging the paramilitary spectacles which were common during the darkest days of the Troubles.

'There are obvious exceptions and there will always be exceptions, but you'd be hard put to find even one GAA club that doesn't carry the name of someone who could be regarded by my community as being a terrorist during some era,' Quincey charges. 'My band's a band, just a band; the politics that's talked about is one member talking to another. The band doesn't talk about it. The band doesn't decide that they're going to go out and leaflet somewhere. The local GAA football club in my area of County Armagh is O'Donovan Rossa. It stuck me immediately that [Jeremiah] O'Donovan Rossa was one of the first men who ever threw a bomb in England. But we have been told that we have to ignore that because it was a certain while ago. But then when it gets into other later periods and modern times, then there is this whataboutery and whatifs and so on. Our people believe the GAA has more contradictions in it than the bands ever had and it seems to get away with them.'

In the pantheon of Loyalist marching bands, generic names are favoured, with endless variations on Protestant Boys, Defenders, Pride, True Blues and Volunteers attached to local place names. Where an individual's name is used, it is invariably King William, although in one notable case, that is reversed in the name of William King, a very early innocent Protestant victim of the Troubles who was kicked to death in Derry city in 1969.

CHAPTER 5

IN THE FOOTSTEPS
OF HEROES

Saturday, 7 February 2009

'This will bring a lump to the throat, a tear to the eye and have the hairs standing on the back of your neck,' promises host and one of the singer/performers Derek Hussey, as loyal Castlederg gathers on a bitterly cold February evening for a special performance. The show, entitled 'In the Footsteps of Heroes – From the Somme to D Day,' starts at 9 p.m. in the Castle Inn and is billed as an 'event to recall in music and words the heroic sacrifice of those who went to war for King and country'. The occasion, staged with energy, pace and colourful presentation by the amateur members of an Omagh-based Under the White Ensign Cultural Association, also brings a glint to the eye, a swagger to the step and quite a few raucous cheers as well.

The loudest cheers of the night are for a typically defiant 'Winston Churchill' and finally for an excerpt from 'The Sash' in a medley of Loyalist tunes played as an encore finale by the Omagh Protestant Boys Melody Flute Band. The visiting band has been renamed the Omagh Drum Corps for the night and, in keeping with the fairly elaborate production, its members march briskly to the stage at the start of the evening dressed in bright red full regimental uniforms. All other participants are wearing authentic armed services uniforms and in a few cases suitable civilian dress. Without asking, one knows that the uniforms have been preserved in loving memory of those heroes who answered the call to arms and those who supported them ardently on the home front. With that spirit of unquestioning tribute so prevalent, the huge cast delivers a feast of song and verse that often manages to evoke the grim reality of the 'War to end all Wars', the plucky 'gallows humour' of the trenches and the defiant spirit of the Blitz. So even in the close confines of the small band stage at the back of the Davy Crockett Lounge, a three-hour programme of music, song, poetry recitals and readings from letters sent home from the front, is presented in an absorbing performance that ends almost too quickly in a rousing chorus of 'Keep the Home Fires Burning'. By then, all the extended cast of performers is crowded onto the stage and the audience is singing along at the persistent urging of Councillor Hussey.

The evening begins, however, in a fittingly sombre mood with the call to war elicited in a reading by Diane Beckett of John Scott's classic poem 'The Drum':

I hate that drum's discordant sound,
Parading round, and round, and round:
To thoughtless youth it pleasure yields
And lures from cities and from fields,
To sell their liberty for charms
Of tawdry lace and glitt'ring arms;
And when Ambition's voice commands,
To fight and fall in foreign lands.

Then as the Omagh Drum Corps settles onto the stage, a reading by Andrew Burnside of a letter home from the front written by a young Tyrone soldier in the 36th Ulster Division captures the mood at the Somme on the night before battle when the horror was yet to unfold and the concern was merely for lack of home comforts. Yet we know that young Irishmen were answering the call in droves to the sound of old favourites, 'Killaloe' and 'It's a Long Way to Tipperary', now played by the Omagh Drum Corps. These are followed by music hall favourites 'Take Me Home to Dear Old Blighty' and 'Hello, Hello! Who's Your Lady Friend' before the lengthy narration by Kenny Porter to haunting background flute music recounts in detail the sequence of actions at the Battle of the Somme on that fateful day, 1 July 1916, when so many lives were lost. The venerable silence in the packed hall testifies to the resonance of the story that is so well known to the Loyalists of Ulster.

Northern Ireland Loyalist culture is pervaded with

an absolute conviction that Northern Ireland's Unionists have done more, suffered more and sacrificed more for their British identity than any other people. The ritual of public performance and recognition that inspires, motivates and compels the marching season right through to Remembrance Sunday ceremonies in mid-November is an acknowledgement and public celebration of their past loyalty and sacrifice; the culture of politics is there constantly in the daily reminders of the flags and emblems. The martial airs and the military-style uniforms of many Blood and Thunder flute bands is a modern statement that this militant commitment to their British identity continues today and has been won in the blood of their fathers, uncles, brothers, sisters, sons and daughters. It asks constantly and repeatedly, how could you even begin to doubt that we are more entitled than anybody else? For although Ulster Loyalism is deeply rooted in the Ascendancy established in the Glorious Revolution of the seventeenth century, the shibboleths of modern Loyalist identity are drawn from and constantly associated with the Great War, and particularly with the fateful Battle of the Somme in 1916. The image of young men paying the ultimate sacrifice for their beliefs and their identity is deeply and lovingly ingrained in modern youth through participation and support of the marching bands. That is particularly apparent in the choice of band emblems. The iconography is everywhere, silhouetted figures in British battle-dress against a battle-scarred hill. It is the scene on the bannerette, flag standard and drums of the Castlederg Young Loyalists Flute Band. Other Blood and Thunder bands display similar images of soldiers from the 36th Ulster Division going over the top at the Battle of the Somme and urging others to follow in their wake. While there is also the open acknowledgement in the music itself that the sacrifice of the Somme was a terrible waste of young lives and ill-conceived from the outset, that does not in the least diminish the allure of the historical legacy which is constantly and repeatedly remembered from that fateful battle and all the others in which loyal Ulster did its bit and more.

It is a remarkable feature of modern Blood and Thunder bands that their iconography largely focuses on elements from the Ulster Volunteer Force whose members made up the Ulster Division of the British Expeditionary Force that took up its positions on the Western Front in 1914. At parade after parade, it is the image of those young men from ordinary Protestant homes throughout Ulster that adorn the flags and banners and big bass drums. While King William of Orange features here and there in the names of bands, it is the image of the sons of working-class Belfast and of towns, villages and farms throughout the nine counties of Ulster who joined up in force and paid the ultimate sacrifice that inspires the modern Loyalist youth. The image of a reigning monarch on a white charger may inspire the more traditional institutions of Ulster Protestantism such as the Orange Order, but it is the legacy and image of young men from homes just like theirs that inspires and motivates the young men and boys who flock to join the Blood and Thunder bands and eschew the more staid and formal organisations. Those young men gave their all and felt they were ultimately betrayed by the ruling class of England when the majority of the island was granted independence in 1921.

In this adherence to the image of the glorious defeat of the Somme over the victory of the Boyne, strangely, this youthful strain of Loyalism mirrors the blood sacrifice tradition of Irish Nationalism. Like the commemorations of Easter 1916, Bloody Sunday and the hunger strikers, the emphasis on the Somme is a celebration of bravery beyond endurance in the face of insurmountable odds rather than opportunist victory. For all the plucky courage and do-or-die daring shown by young men from Protestant Ulster during that horrific battle, the gains were momentary and the lines quickly reverted to where they had been before the loyal Sons of Ulster went over the top. So in a real and evocative sense, the celebration of the Somme echoes the assertion articulated in Republican ideology by the words of Terence MacSwiney, the jailed Lord Mayor of Cork who died on hunger strike in October 1920: 'It is not those who can inflict the most but those who can endure the most who will finally conquer.'

The 36th (Ulster) was made up of members of the Ulster Volunteer Force, which had been formed under the command of Lieutenant-General Sir George Richardson, veteran of the

Afghan wars, to oppose Home Rule for Ireland.[37] Mobilised in the Home Rule crisis of 1911, the UVF had engaged in open drilling and public shows of defiance against the imperial parliament, including gun-running, with shipments of arms landed from two ships, the *Fanny* and *Clyde Valley*, at Larne on 24 April 1914 (with subsequent arms shipments landed at Bangor and Donaghadee) and dispersed to strategic dumps in Orange Halls throughout Ulster. Significantly, the illegal guns, which would have been used to resist the application of self-government for the Irish kingdom by His Majesty's Government, had been procured in Germany almost on the eve of war.[38] Yet a few months later, in September 1914, with the formation of the 36th Division as part of the new army to fight Germany, Lord Kitchener got a highly disciplined, moderately well trained and enthusiastic force of thirteen additional battalions for the three existing Irish regiments drawing recruits from Ulster and County Louth: the Royal Irish Fusiliers based in Armagh and drawn from that county as well as neighbouring Monaghan and Cavan; the Royal Irish Rifles based in Ballymena and recruiting in Antrim, Down and Louth; and the Royal Inniskilling Fusiliers based in Omagh and recruiting in Tyrone, Fermanagh, Donegal and Derry. Those who only months before had defied the will of the Empire, went forth into battle to preserve it under the divisional insignia of the Red Hand of Ulster which, significantly, is also the emblem of County Tyrone. The Division served with distinction and suffered heavy losses on the Western Front for the duration of the First World War.

Yet one day stands out in the collective folk memory of Unionists – the first day of the Battle of the Somme, recalled in vivid detail in the performance on this night in Castlederg. On that day, the Sons of Ulster had been given the unenviable task of taking a German position known as the Schwaben Redoubt between the village of Ancre and Thiepval Wood.[39] Before they emerged from their trenches, however, attacks by other divisions of British imperial forces further along the line had been repulsed. The advancing Tommies had been easily picked off from the better German vantage points as they made their way in proper military order through No Man's Land. The fighting men from places in England, Scotland, Wales, Australia, Canada, South Africa and other imperial forces – not to mention the French and French-Africans who fought alongside them and who also advanced against the German lines on 1 July – were mown down because they were expendable cannon fodder in the military machine.

However, while the other offensive actions by divisions of the British army's X Corps followed proper military proce-dure, the Ulster Division threw away the rules of military protocol and gave it their all for God and Ulster. Consequently, the 36th was one of the few divisions to make significant gains on that first day of the Somme. According to military historian Martin Middlebrook: 'The leading battalions (of the 36th (Ulster) Division) had been ordered out from the wood just before 7.30 a.m. and laid down near the German trenches ... At zero hour the British barrage lifted. Bugles blew the "Advance". Up sprang the Ulstermen and, without forming up in the waves adopted by other divisions, they rushed the German front line ... By a combination of sensible tactics and Ulster dash, the prize that eluded so many, the capture of a long section of the German front line, had been accomplished.'[40]

While the Ulster Division was the only division of X Corps to achieve its objectives on the opening day of the battle, the capture of the Schwaben Redoubt came at a heavy price. In two days of fighting, the division suffered the loss of 5,500 officers and men, killed, wounded or missing. When news of the slaughter reached home, a pall of mourning for the 2,069 lives lost descended on the homes of Ulster. It could be argued that it has remained to this day in the sense of righteous folk memory of a terrible price paid for loyalty and a justification of the assertion of Ulster Protestantism and its values in the political and social life of Northern Ireland. Set against the total losses of over one million from that offensive, the deaths of the young soldiers from the Ulster Division might seem paltry. Yet hardly a Protestant home in Ulster was left untouched by the carnage and the cenotaph and other war memorials which have pride of place in almost every town and village are constant testimony to the terrible legacy of that time.

Yet strength is also drawn from the acknowledgement of the bravery of those who went over the top in the hour of need. In his report from the front line of that fateful day, celebrated *Daily Chronicle* and *Daily Telegraph* war correspondent Philip Gibbs wrote of the men of Ulster in the 36th Division: 'Their attack was one of the finest displays of human courage in the world.'[41] Nine Victoria Crosses – the highest honour awarded to members of the British forces – were allocated that day to those who had taken part in the big push. Three of the Victoria Crosses were awarded to men of the 36th (Ulster) Division and two of these were posthumous awards.[42]

Yet that demonstration of bravery and prowess in capturing the Schwaben Redoubt was in vain because other objectives had not been reached along the front and reinforcements dispatched into the continuing carnage of No Man's Land never reached them. Isolated and surrounded by the German army of the Western Front, the men of Ulster were forced to retreat right back to where they had begun on the morning of 1 July 1916. On 2 July, what remained of the tattered and traumatised Ulster Division was withdrawn from the battlefield, in the words of one modern commentator, 'to re-group and march directly into the political mythology of Ulster Unionism'.[43]

While Protestant Ulster commemorates that loss, it remains perplexed that there is no similar public acknowledgement of the part played by other Irishmen in the Great War. Just a few months after the Ulster losses at the Somme, the 16th Division, formed into regiments such as the Dublin Fusiliers and Connaught Rangers in large part from former members of the Irish Volunteer Force set up to counter resistance to Home Rule, was ordered down to the Somme from its Western Front positions further north at Loos in Belgium. On 3 September 1916, it was sent into battle to capture the villages of Guillemont and Ginchy. History records that these Irishmen fought with the same reckless courage that had distinguished the 36th (Ulster) Division on 1 July, but after ten days of attack and counter-offensive, the 16th had lost half its strength of 11,000 men through death and injury. Two of those who fell, a private in the Connaughts and a young officer in the Prince of Wales Leinsters joined their three Ulster Division heroes in receiving the Victoria Cross.

However, unlike their Unionist comrades who returned home demanding recognition for their loyalty, the Nationalists who went off to fight the good fight for King and country in the hopes of securing Home Rule in return, had already lost the day to erstwhile colleagues who had stayed home and rebelled in Dublin just weeks before the carnage of the Somme began.

By the time the Somme offensive lapsed back into the waiting game of trench warfare in the weeks leading up to Christmas 1916, it had already been firmly implanted into the psyche of loyal Ulster as one of its finest hours. Almost

100 years later, on a night in Castlederg, it still has the power to set hearts beating and bring a tear to the eye in the vivid description of the battle read out in the lengthy narrative listed in the programme for the evening with a picture of soldiers cheering and holding their helmets aloft as they march off happily en masse into battle.

But enough of the tears for now as Councillor Derek Hussey takes to the stage to lead the Castlederg audience in a rousing chorus of 'Pack Up Your Troubles in Your Old Kit Bag' before Lynn Gibson and Kirsty Rutledge deliver recitals of 'In Flanders Field' and 'The Response' and the Omagh Drum Corps rally the spirits once more with 'The Girl I Left Behind Me' and 'Goodbye Dolly Gray'. Yet if anything is calculated to raise the mood of the Castlederg gathering, then it is the arrival of the 'Sensational Nicola Moody' backed by 'the Moodettes' dressed in their Women's Army Corps (WAC) uniforms to entertain the troops. As the Moodettes (Diane Beckett, Stacey Connor and Leanne Jeffrey) provide backing vocals, the sensational Nicola launches into upbeat numbers with 'Yankee Doodle Boy', 'Over There', 'Deep in the Heart of Texas', 'She'll be Comin' Round the Mountain' and 'Pistol Packin' Mama'. In the Davy Crockett Lounge, even the boys at the bar are now paying full attention.

But back to Jimmy, the young Tyrone squaddie. He is still at the Front and writing home to his mother on 14 September 1918, but by now he is bitterly disillusioned by the death and injury he has witnessed and perplexed at what it has all been for. His disillusionment is shared in the performance of Eric Bogle's great anti-war song, the 'Green Fields of France', sung by Neil Moody, before the Omagh Drum Corps heralds the intermission with a tribute to the young local soldiers who had gone to war with the Royal Inniskilling Fusiliers playing 'Fare Ye Well Enniskillen'.

The intermission belongs to the Castlederg Young Loyalists Flute Band. Marching briskly into the vacant dance floor space between the stage-front tables and the bar to the rear, the two-member colour party stakes a claim for the largest local element of the evening's entertainment with the band's first public performance of 2009. They deliver a selection of appropriate tunes, although many are repeats of airs that have gone before – 'Tipperary', 'Green Fields of France' and 'Killaloe'. Yet the sight and sound of the familiar faces and playing style of the local band, noticeably lifts a large segment of the attendance that may not have been paying the closest attention to much of what had been happening during the first half of the programme. Local fans sitting furthest from the bar strut their way up to order fresh rounds of drinks and they do so in marching time with the music. There are roars of approval from the crowd at the back when a change of side-drums raises the tempo and the decibels in the hall.

Yet as the local Blood and Thunder band marches off the floor and the final part of the programme commences

114

to the wail of Second World War air-raid sirens, the loudest cheer of the night so far is reserved for the avuncular rotund figure who had once dismissed the unyielding 'integrity of the quarrel' amidst the 'dreary steeples of Fermanagh and Tyrone'. In the guise of Alan Gregg – and with his stentorian tones tinged with a more markedly Northern Irish accent – Winston Leonard Spencer Churchill epitomises the 'Not an Inch' mindset professed by Loyalists amidst those same dreary steeples to this day: 'We shall fight in the fields and in the streets, we shall fight in the hills, we shall never surrender.' That firm promise from the wartime Prime Minister of Britain rouses the large crowd now congregated around the bar with several exuberant echoes of 'No Surrender' and a chorus of accompanying cheers. After the 'Peace in our time' appeasement of Neville Chamberlain which had preceded it, along with the performance of the Luftwaffe march 'Aces High' by the Omagh Drums Corps, Churchill's No Surrender attitude is more than enough to rouse the audience for the second half of the night's entertainment and the downhill course to Victory Day. For now, the 'Sensational Nicola Moody' leads her Moodettes back on to the stage to 'Bless Them All' as they 'Hang Out the Washing on the Siegfried Line' and thrill some male members of the audience with 'Kiss Me Goodnight Sergeant Major'.

Yet truly, this second half of the night's performance only serves to illustrate that the war against Nazi Germany is a distant runner behind the vivid folk memories of the Somme and the trenches of the Great War. For while there clearly is something inspiring and uplifting drawn from memories of the heroism and sacrifice in the mud and mayhem of the Ardennes, the story of the Second World War in Northern Ireland is shrouded in recollections of deprivation, want and being shown up generally for a less than exemplary performance.[44]

Perhaps under normal circumstances the most vivid and abiding image would be of a once-divided community rallying and uniting in the face of unimagined horror and adversity as the Blitz descended on Northern Ireland. Yet there has been little appetite since for the image of fleeing crowds evacuating Belfast and other centres, even if they went off according to contemporary descriptions 'talking to one another' and 'sleeping in the same sheugh, below the same tree or in the same barn' and 'saying the government is no good'.[45] So while that spirit of the Blitz is meat and potatoes to rebellious Londoners, it actually goes against the grain of Loyalist Ulster Unionism. Indeed, there is little of home-grown origin in which to take pride, given that the enlistment from south of the border actually surpassed that of the loyal north and given the treacherous machinations of the imperial government that sought to trade Irish unity and all that entailed in exchange for agreement by the neutral Éire government to enter the war on the Allied side.

Having been spared conscription by the insistence of Westminster, Northern Ireland's one claim to 'doing its bit' beyond the call of duty during the Second World War was devoting more acreage than before the war to tillage farming during the early years – even if the increased land use was accompanied by lower crop yields – and shipping more fresh milk across the Irish Sea during the worst times of the Battle of Britain. However, the Second World War in Northern Ireland also brings to mind a host of uncomfortable home truths: the Unionist Party's trenchant opposition to food rationing; the provincial government's hopeless provisions for defence against Luftwaffe raids, apart from its elaborate plans for protecting the statue of Lord Edward Carson at Stormont; Sir Basil Brooke's pointed decision to site the office to drive enlistment at the Unionist Party headquarters and thereby alienate Nationalists who might answer the call; under-performance in war industries; and strikes in the shipyards. Above all, however, there is the abhorrent memory of wealthy loyal citizens ensconced under the blazing lights of a plush hotel across the border in County Donegal attired in evening wear and dripping with jewels and silver fox fur stoles.[46]

Little wonder therefore that the most celebrated folk memory of the Second World War is not drawn from indigenous effort but from the 'invasion' of Northern Ireland by those former colonial rebels – the Americans.[47] Particularly in the months leading up to the D-Day landings in Normandy, the six counties had been turned into a vividly colourful armed camp. Castlederg residents, too, were swept

117

up in the change, with airmen and GIs based throughout Counties Tyrone and Fermanagh and US Navy personnel heavily concentrated on Derry's docks from which the defence of the North Atlantic lifeline route was co-ordinated. Camel cigarettes, sheer stockings and chewing gum brought jitterbugging excitement and illicit fun to dour Ulster, where shortly before the death toll from air raids on central Belfast was only curtailed by the absence of people kept at home by the strict Sabbatarian laws that closed practically everything that might have drawn people out of their homes and into the cities and towns.

So apart from nostalgic classics such as 'We'll Meet Again' performed by Shirley Hussey, the second part of the evening's entertainment is dominated by the Omagh Drums Corps playing celebrated theme tunes from the movies – 'The Great Escape', 'Colonel Bogey' and 'The Longest Day' – and, of course, by the sensational Nicola and her Moodettes with their colourful renditions of equally evocative songs such as 'This is the Army Mr Jones' and 'Rum 'n' Coca Cola'.

It makes for a rollicking wind-up to the second half of the night and the crowd is fully primed for the final 'Exhortation' in which Alan Gregg invokes the familiar refrain of Remembrance Sunday ceremonies: 'They shall not grow old, as we that are left grow old; Age shall not weary them, nor the years condemn. At the going down of the sun, and in the morning, we will remember them.' Two minutes of silence follow before the final advice: 'When you go home tell them of us and say – For your tomorrow we gave our today.'

Then it is the turn of all the performers to crowd onto the stage and, with Councillor Hussey urging on the audience, launch into a couple of verses of 'Keep the Home Fires Burning' to bring the night to a formal conclusion. There is also a promise from the local councillor that he would do his best to have the whole night repeated in Castlederg some time before Remembrance Sunday itself. But the boys at the back want more now and the Omagh Protestant Boys oblige with their rendition of a Loyalist medley, which includes the familiar refrains of 'The Sash My Father Wore'. A couple of men near the entrance are sauntering about in a makeshift dance as some family groups with children take their leave. The crowd is still milling about the bar and though the night's entertainment has gone on for more than three hours, every face in the Davy Crockett Lounge wears a broad grin of satisfaction. If the night's performance has dwelt on war and sacrifice, the remembrance of the bloodshed and needless death has plainly been a soothing balm to the spirit of Castlederg Loyalism.

Outside, the bitterly cold night is crisp with hoar frost and Neil Johnston is returning from the Orange Hall ahead of some other band members. With this first performance of 2009 behind them, the Castlederg Young Loyalists bandsmen are up and out of the trenches and ready for the fray.

CHAPTER 6

JANUARY, FEBRUARY, MARCH, MARCH, MARCH

Tuesday, 17 March 2009

It is 9 p.m. on St Patrick's Day and they are dancing in the streets of Killylea, County Armagh, to the tune of a jaunty Irish jig. Crowds of young men and a few young women mill around the pub at the top of the village and at the foot of its main street, while family groups are scattered along the way. They are all delighting in the performance of the hundreds of musicians who have shown up for the party atmosphere on a clear but chilly spring evening when the cool air is warmed by the brisk pace and the wafting aromas from a stall dispensing burgers to the assembled horde. Young musicians in colourful, retro-military uniforms grasp their burger buns with both hands and set off up the road. Some hold the snacks as if they were flutes and they munch to the beat of the other bands as they walk along. Frequently they pause with friends and acquaintances, greeting them like long-lost family. After the long winter break, the Blood and Thunder party has begun again for Ulster's marching band fraternity.

A police checkpoint has been set up just at the start of the Killylea bypass on the main A28 road connecting the Ballygawley roundabout through Aughnacloy with the Nationalist cities of Armagh and Newry. The checkpoint is shrouded in ominous gloom because of the heightened security that follows the slaying during the previous week of two young British army 'sappers' at the Massereene Military Barracks in Antrim, the simultaneous wounding of two pizza delivery messengers and the murder of a veteran police constable in Craigavon, County Armagh. To avoid further security risks, the police use only glow-stick lights to signal traffic to stop at a road barrier that directs the through traffic on a diversion around Killylea bog.

Long lines of cars are already backed neatly onto the hard shoulder and facing out to where others are hurriedly reversing into place. The decanted occupants set off on foot towards the village. Without car lights or street lights, the road is almost pitch black. Yet through the deep gloom, shadows hover everywhere. Even in silhouette, it is clear that most are dressed in uniforms; some could even be police. From the sides, shapes loom up heading towards the sparse lights of the village. Some carry side-drums, the harnesses jangling a beat along the way. Others lug folded banners and flags. Around the front of a van with its parking lights turned on, a small cluster of bandsmen surrounds a large-framed young man struggling to put on his tunic. One of his companions tries to help: 'Houl on there, I'm hardly fit to get her on,' the big fellow grunts in exasperation as the others laugh. Like athletes laid up over the long closed season, some clearly will struggle to get back in shape for the marching season ahead.

Nearer the village, bands are assembling beside a row of portable toilets. They seem to know instinctively what to do as they form into orderly lines under the direction of their bandmasters. Final adjustments are made and, with well-practised timing, they move off on command to the single beat of a drum in the wake of the band in front whose music is starting to fade into the distance.

The Portadown True Blues are next, their ranks filling the road with a large colour party, more than a dozen side-drums and a couple of dozen fluters. After the initial few paces, the leading drumbeat suddenly changes into a roll and the music strikes up. And as the band saunters off on its circuitous course around and through the village, the bass drummer raises the thunder with his first frantic flurries on the drumheads and he begins a zigzag dance from side to side through the swaggering ranks of his band.

Occupants of the parked cars along this stretch – mostly elderly couples, but also a few younger parents with small children – have their engines running for heat against the evening chill. In relative comfort they enjoy the start of each band's performance as the parade sets off in a strikingly ordered rotation of bands. Meanwhile, the arriving bands assemble back on the edge of the gloom, then move into position and set off on a signal from a marshal, moving along the parade route that begins at the Darton Gate Lodge and goes along Kennedies Road towards Armagh city, then swings up along the curving Main Street past the handsome St Mark's Church of Ireland church at the crown of the village, before spilling down to the dispersal point opposite Esker Park.

Around this point, a few stalls have been set up selling colourful wares – Union Jacks, Northern Ireland flags and other mementoes. There is a notable absence of shamrocks or other familiar symbols of St Patrick's Day. Meanwhile, a stall with a large banner for the parade's host band, the Cormeen Rising Sons of William Flute Band, is doing a brisk trade in burgers and soft drinks in aid of the Buddy Bear Trust in Dungannon, the only dedicated educational facility in Ireland for children with cerebral palsy.

Out on the street, a parade marshal in a red winter jacket with the initials 'CSW' for Cormeen Sons of William inscribed on the back, holds a small walkie-talkie radio while he directs the successive bands into place for their finale. Further back, the bands mark time as they wait their turn before the final gallery (the main body of spectators) and the judges for this first competitive parade of 2009.[48] As they follow along in sequence, the variety of composition, style and performance becomes strikingly apparent. There are the accordion bands, comprising mostly young female members, playing jaunty tunes and familiar hymns in a style that is oddly reminiscent of rural Northern Ireland before the Troubles and television images of more aggressive parades. The Enagh Accordion Band from nearby Tynan village, where Counties Tyrone, Armagh and Monaghan converge, receives a burst of polite applause as it finishes and disperses into clusters of family and friends. The Killylea Silver Band, also playing to a home audience, completes its marching set with 'Killaloe', and falls out to a burst of applause. But the night belongs to Blood and Thunder as wave after wave of heavy percussion moves down through the streets, marking time at intervals as the bands make their way to the final post. From Fermanagh, Tyrone, Derry and Down they have come to join their County Armagh counterparts in a huge celebration of St Patrick's Day.

From Fermanagh have come Magheraveely Pride of the Village Flute, South Fermanagh Loyalists and Lisbellaw's Defenders of the Rock. Joining the Cormeen Rising Sons of William from County Armagh are Pride of the Frontier from Drumhillery and Drumderg Flute, then Portadown True Blues, Upper Bann Fusiliers, Craigavon Protestant Boys and Kilcluney Volunteers from Markethill, as well as the Bessbrook True Blues. County Down is represented by the Loyal Sons of Benagh and South Down Defenders from the Newry area, Mourne Defenders and Rising Sons of the Valley, both from Kilkeel, Skeogh Flute from Dromore and Pride of the

Hill from Rathfriland. From County Tyrone have come the Moygashel Sons of Ulster, Derryloran Boyne Defenders from Cookstown, Omagh True Blues and Omagh Protestant Boys, Newtownstewart's Red Hand Defenders, the Tamlaghtmore Tigers from Ardboe and, of course, the Castlederg Young Loyalists. From County Derry meanwhile, is the Tobermore Loyal Flute Band. The bands pass through in almost a blur of musical entertainment and geographic confusion.

My re-education in the geography of Loyalist marching bands has commenced during this exposure to the public celebration of a culture that is virtually ignored by mainstream media when it is not the source of trouble. For here, on 17 March, in a small Northern Irish village, a parade of forty-two bands playing Irish tunes, in what is recognised by all those taking part as a St Patrick's Day parade, goes unremarked and unnoticed by people outside. Indeed, a similar St Patrick's Day parade hosted by the Ulster Protestant Boys Flute Band in Coleraine includes another couple of dozen marching bands. Neither parade receives even a mention in the mainstream media amidst all the coverage of events whose catalogue of parades – all of which must be notified to the Northern Ireland Parades Commission – totals some seventy venues.[49] The largest parade is reported to be in Belfast with an undetermined number of bands and participants. On the Nationalist side, the event hosted in the County Derry town of Maghera by the Glen Ancient Order of Hibernians Division 367 and the St Patrick's Accordion Band, has twenty bands.

In Derry city the parade has two bands, in Strabane there are three bands, Omagh has two and in Newry there are six bands taking part. These and others receive extensive coverage. Yet two of the biggest events in terms of participating bands go virtually unheeded, as does another event in Portadown organised by the Edenderry Ulster-Scots Club with twenty Lambeg drummers.

It is little wonder that there is widespread resentment among Northern Ireland Loyalists at what they see as the dismissal of their unique culture. Quincey Dougan of the Ulster Bands Forum points out that with forty-two marching bands, Killylea is 'the biggest St Patrick's Day parade in Northern Ireland'. In terms of its discipline and structure, he regards it as the best celebration in Ireland of the patron saint's day and he compares it with the parades he has seen in television coverage. 'The Dublin parade, to be quite honest, is abysmal. It only has seven marching bands. You see, we come from a perspective built into us now over the centuries of Protestant parades and we see some of the effort on the other side as comical. The Belfast St Patrick's Day Parade is laughable. They call it a parade and they are going down the line of some of these American events, but the American parade has scale and it sort of benefits from having a lack of its own culture. That means there's a lot of time and effort put into it, whereas everything over here seems very haphazard and very thrown together.'

Quincey sees the unheralded success of the Killylea event

as a long-overdue expression of Ulster Loyalist celebration of an annual festival from which they have been excluded, or indeed from which they have excluded themselves in the past. The village just down the road from Patrick's Primal See in Armagh city will become a prime focus of attention, he believes. 'In a few years the [Killylea] parade will be on during the day rather than at night because what I'm finding in regard to St Patrick's Day amongst Unionists, or Ulster-Scots if you want to use that term, is that people are absolutely itching to get out and do something. Now Cormeen [Killylea] is the main event for those who know of it. When they started [the annual parade] there was nothing else and this is their fifth year. The first year they were chastised by different ones who did not see any reason for Protestants to celebrate St Patrick, but they have gradually made it a great night. Meanwhile, the Ulster Protestant Boys in Coleraine had about twenty bands for their parade on 17 March. They would not have a major profile, but they are also trying hard and they've been at it a few years as well.'

Quincey Dougan agrees that parading on St Patrick's Day does not have to be divided on sectarian lines. He points to an initiative undertaken by his own band, the Kilcluney Volunteers. 'I was anxious to do something different with the band a few years ago and I came across this marching bands festival in Limerick on St Patrick's weekend. I said to our boys that we should go. Aye we'd go anywhere you know. We got a grant for it, which was a help; whenever you're getting the hotel and all free, it's easier convincing the boys. So we went down and paraded through Limerick. We carried the Union Jack and all our band's flags and we did not make any compromise, no changes whatsoever; every tune we play up here, we played down there. And we walked through Limerick and we ended up at Limerick's Church of Ireland cathedral, which was weird for us in a way. But the reception we got ... there literally wasn't one adverse reaction in any shape or form about that parade.'

Public tolerance of Blood and Thunder in Limerick contrasts with his experience closer to home, where the virtually unknown St Patrick's Day parade in Killylea is the prelude to thousands of further parades during a season that goes on into October, before indoor events resume. And while some commentators portray the issue as one of give and take, the fact remains that the tradition of parades is overwhelmingly rooted in one side of the community and the other has resented and opposed it at every turn. In the middle sits a ten-year-old agency that must negotiate the tightrope of public opinion while balancing tradition and public order in the process.

Michael Boyle, Director of Policy in the Parades Commission, has a bird's eye view of his native Belfast from an office on the twelfth floor of the Windsor Tower, the tallest building in Northern Ireland. It is probably a good vantage point from which to view the issue of parades which have so often erupted into conflict on the streets down below. Yet he also brings to this role the perspective gained from more than a decade as a police officer with An Garda Síochána in Dublin, two masters degrees and a doctorate on issues of conflict resolution, as well as his experience as an accredited monitor of elections for the United Nations in trouble-spots around the globe. It probably requires all of these perspectives to retain the necessary critical distance from a perennial issue that draws such sharply divergent responses from nearly every other individual in Northern Ireland. Yet while his opinions are often couched in striking analogies, they are direct nonetheless, a personal demonstration perhaps of how the adjudicating body perched high in the tower has managed to chart a course to relative peace from the nest of confrontation and crisis in which it was hatched.

The Parades Commission was set up in 1997 by the Westminster government as a result of a recommendation drawn up by Sir Peter North with the assistance of the special commission he headed. This commission, the Independent Review of Parades and Marches in Northern Ireland, also involved two respected clergymen from both major traditions then facing each other across the divide between Drumcree Church of Ireland and the overwhelmingly Nationalist Garvaghy Road in Portadown. It also had the backing of the police officers who were previously charged with determining, as well as regulating on the ground, the parades and marches throughout Northern Ireland. Indeed, it was because of the sudden about-turn by the police on the issue of the

Drumcree parade in 1996 that the Independent Review was set up. In that year, Chief Constable Sir Hugh Annesley first banned the parade and then sanctioned it at the last moment as the possibility of a violent backlash loomed. His actions infuriated both sides in turn and convinced political leaders that an independent body was needed on the issue.

However, Michael Boyle sets out immediately to dispel the notion that the Parades Commission he serves has a direct role in permitting or banning parades. That, he explains, is not within the brief of the commission nor any other statutory body. 'People often ask us why we gave permission for a particular parade, but we don't give permission and those parading are not even required to seek permission,' he explains. 'There is a human right of assembly and that includes the right to have a parade. It is a right that comes from civic society; so when people ask me who gave permission for a particular parade, I say, "You did, because you are a member of our civic society." The problem, of course, is that people never like other people exercising their rights when it comes into conflict with their own rights.'

Because of the particular circumstances of Northern Ireland, where people share a history but with sharply divergent interpretations of the past and how and what to celebrate or remember of it, the human right to assemble and parade must be regulated. In other societies – in England, Scotland, Wales and the rest of Ireland – the respective police authorities undertake the governance of parades. In Northern

Ireland, of course, that led to a partisan approach to the issue, what Michael Boyle describes as deciding the question of where 'the pet gorilla sleeps'. Given the gorilla's propensity to violent assertion, the answer was 'anywhere he wants'. So the Orange administration and the Royal Ulster Constabulary allowed the Orange and other Loyalist institutions to parade wherever and whenever they wanted, thus creating an open book on the traditionality of parade routes on behalf of the favoured and dominant side of the community. But politics and geography have changed since then and many of the traditional parades – including those that cause the most conflict – are in areas that have been transformed in terms of their demographic profile. The new era requires new rules and procedures, yet most people still see things in sectarian terms.

Because the right to parade may infringe on other rights, there is an official requirement to file a Notification of Intention with the police at least twenty-eight days before the planned date. The only exemptions to this are for funerals and Salvation Army processions. The police pass on a copy of this Notification of Intention to the Parades Commission. Meanwhile, all parade-related protest meetings must also be notified to police at least fourteen days in advance and a copy of this is also forwarded to the commission, which then looks carefully at those events that it considers to be 'sensitive'. The grounds of sensitivity are clearly defined on a determination of whether the parade is likely to have a negative effect on community relations, lead to public disorder, or damage the life of the community. To determine this, the Parades Commission gathers information from local interested parties – organisations, political representatives, police and its own authorised officers – and it considers the feedback and other information to determine if there is a chance of local agreement. If agreement is achieved, the commission does not intervene further. If not, the commission then has to consider the need to impose conditions or restrictions on either the parade or the planned protest. In doing this, the commission must decide whether there is a necessity to interfere with the right to parade and, if it decides that there is, then any restrictions imposed must be proportionate. Such restrictions must then be issued five working days before the parade date. Furthermore, all determinations of the Parades Commission are published in full with detailed attachments outlining the guidelines on behaviour for those participating in parades (see Appendix 1).

The fall-out from any decision of the Parades Commission to impose restrictions is entirely predictable. Nationalist objectors to parades demand outright bans which are outside the scope of the Parade Commission powers; for instance, the Drumcree parade is restricted to a modified route that does not permit the proposed return route along Garvaghy Road, but it is not banned. And because the Orange Order believes that giving an explanation is akin to asking permission, it refuses to even deal with the agency established by Her Majesty's Government to handle the issue. The marching bands, including those in the Blood and Thunder genre, have adopted a more practical approach to ensure their parades take place, and they now engage constantly with the Parades Commission. However, that does not alter the fact that the Loyalist side of the community generally regards the Parades Commission as an unnecessary infringement on their recreational pastime and a sop to those who complain loudest and longest about it. They draw attention to the relatively trouble-free staging of thousands of parades as proof that there really is no problem to solve. When there is a flare-up, it is not caused by active band members, they point out.

'That's not to say that bands are always totally blameless,' says Quincey Dougan, 'but I'm not even sure if there was trouble at any band events last year. Maybe there was in the aftermath or whatever, but not during the parades.'

When it is suggested that perhaps the very existence of the Parades Commission as a monitoring agency with the power to impose restrictions, has prevented trouble in recent years, the bands' association spokesman reiterates the view that the agency is not needed. 'At the moment, there would definitely be two trains of thought on what the Parades Commission has achieved. The almost unanimous one on our side would be that they have created more issues and more concerns than they have solved. Things change; everything changes and natural evolution was, and is, happening on parade routes and within bands. But the inconsistencies within the Parades Commission's approach tend to create more confrontation and it must be pointed out that these [Blood and Thunder bands] are youth cultures and youth cultures don't react well whenever they are confronted.'

The bands also believe that the Parades Commission too often bows to unwarranted opposition from tiny factions and blames the loyal orders and some bands for not 'engaging' with what they consider unrepresentative trouble-makers who foment community opposition for political reasons. After ten years of determinations by the Parades Commission, Quincey Dougan says that a recognisable pattern has emerged. 'All that you will get in any part of the country – whether it is Castlederg, Downpatrick or anywhere else – is that this or that parade is going to cause trouble. They say you won't talk to the residents, you won't do this or do that; we have concerns about this, that or the other. So the bands have met with the commission, addressed all of the concerns, proved beyond a doubt that they are not going out to create bother, conflict or trouble, tried to facilitate in every way they can, and yet it has always come down to the fact that a threat of violence on the other side has still contained that parade ... and that is always something that you will get repeated continually. It's a result of almost farcical human rights ... the ascendancy of individual rights. Human rights are obviously important but it seems to be disproportionate how that emphasis on individual rights over society is coming across now in the media and even on the ground.'

While the objections are taken by the Parades Commission at face value, moreover, the culture of the marching bands is disparaged and even dismissed as no more than sectarian posturing and provocation, he points out. Yet he contends that many from the Catholic Nationalist side of the community admit they secretly enjoy the bands. 'I used to work with a boy from Keady and he would have been a very staunch Sinn Féin supporter and he told me – because we would have talked about these things – that, whenever he was a child, he loved to get out to hear the bands whenever they were playing in the street. And by the same token, he said his daughters were always after him to go out and hear the bands and yet he would bring them in and close the doors. One of the arguments laid down in past years is that this is a deliberately provocative and sectarian movement; that it is only here to cause trouble and keep the conflict going. The fact is that we have had calm for over a decade now and the bands are thriving; they're growing again.'

In countering the argument that the Parades Commission is necessary to draw the line down the middle and guard against civil turmoil, Quincey Dougan returns repeatedly to the issue of provocation. He is particularly incensed by the allegation that the Blood and Thunder bands are merely there to foment trouble by playing their music.

'Of primary importance at the minute is something

that hasn't been addressed properly; that is this idea that a band is provocative. That's a very important one to address … particularly that the music we play is provocative. It's something that even very, very recently has been thrown up. Let's get this straight, music is not provocative. People may take offence to it, but music cannot be offensive and music cannot be provocative as far as we are concerned. Yet that is constantly put forward. There was an example raised over the Rasharkin parade last year, where one particular band played 'Here Lies a Soldier' when parading past a Nationalist protest. The comments made and reported on were that this was an offensive tune to Nationalists and the lyrics of it are offensive to them. These are typical things that are said, so I'm just using it as an example. Now there was nobody singing [in Rasharkin], so it's a piece of music that they chose to take offence to. But that's the theme of the John Wayne film, *The Quiet Man*. It is exactly the same piece of music and in the movie they call it 'The Isle of Inishfree'. But nobody takes offence when they're watching *The Quiet Man*.

'So there's this lack of honesty within that element of Nationalism that always protests against parades. You know there is offence taken even against an individual walking down the street, but this pretence that it is offensive music or an offensive style of music is an absolute farce and there is a total lack of honesty in it. That is something that we are trying to delve into at the minute. You see, I remember being at a conference in Dundalk a few years ago and, like a lot of bandsmen, you'll find that when you go to my car there'll be a tin-whistle or a fife in it. Anyway, we were staying over in Dundalk that evening and there was a broad cross-section of people there. I had the tin-whistle in the car and I brought it in and I'm footering about and there was a young fellow there and he said he was in the Lurgan Martyrs Republican Flute Band. So, besides the fact that he couldn't play that well [Quincey laughs], we were playing tunes, and the weirdest thing to me was the fact that one of the tunes he would have found offensive when we played it – "The Sash" – he actually played. It was "The Sash", albeit a bastardised version of it with the notes slightly changed. He played "The Sash" because it's an Irish tune called "My Irish Molly". There are even closer ones, too. Our bands play "Crossmaglen" and to Republicans it's "The Fighting Men of Crossmaglen".

'By the same token, there has been stuff that has been borrowed the other way. I went along to the Easter Parade in Armagh, the Republican one. I went in to it once a few years ago and there were three bands there from Scotland. And I was sitting in Market Street waiting for this parade to come along and the next thing I hear was 'Pack Up Your Troubles' and then 'It's a Long Way to Tipperary'. Then they were walking through and they were playing what we know as 'Absent Friends', and that's a country and western tune. It's a strange crossover. Our tune 'Sandy Row' – that's 'The Wearing of the Green'! So it becomes a farce when people say they are offended by a tune. How can you be offended by a piece of music? Music can't offend. If I take that same piece of music and put it on two CDs, played by my side and your side ... and if you listen to your side first and then you listen to my side, can you seriously say you are going to be offended by one of the pieces of music and not by the other? Music is not intrinsically offensive, but it is one of the sticks the Republican protesters have used to beat us over the years with the backing of the Parades Commission.'

Quincey Dougan reflects the prevailing belief in the leadership of the Blood and Thunder bands that they are conveniently misunderstood, underestimated and dismissed for political reasons. 'Over the past number of years, for instance, the musical standards in the bands have been raised and raised and the standard of marching bands at the minute is very, very high. Maybe to the untrained ear standing outside all they hear is this noise, but even they should admit that it is not easy to get twelve or more musicians to play the same tune, and to get them to walk up and down the road while they're playing it; well, that has to be an accomplishment anywhere in the world. Yet there's this preoccupation or idea within Nationalism that these bands gather up on 12 July morning, they part that evening, and that's it. It's nonsense. You know, we practise several days a week every week of the year to do what we do ... and then there's all the expense as well in keeping a band going. Castlederg's probably doing about sixty parades a year and we're [Kilcluney] doing eighty every year and that doesn't count all the other wee events, like indoor events in the winter which has become a bit of a growing phenomenon over recent years. There are different trains of thought on that, but to be honest I think it is more dictated by finance than any big underlying reason. But this winter has been phenomenal. I mean there was one weekend when there were twenty-five different indoor events for marching bands to go to. It was getting ridiculous at one stage, you know, there was far too much going on.

'You know this argument about bands, that our core reason for being is to create conflict and to somehow maintain a Protestant ascendancy or something. It's nonsense and even some people in academic circles are talking about the "territoriality" thing – where you're basically pissing up agin' a local pole like a dog. There are minor elements of that, as there are in any culture. But what blows it out of the water is the fact that our band plays in eighty parades a year and of those eighty parades, ninety per cent of them are in areas where there are no people of other traditions. You know, Markethill is ninety-one per cent Protestant and I'm from Markethill and I'm in a band from Markethill. There are other bands here and when you're playing in Markethill, you're not trying to annoy anybody. Why would you? If I was just trying to annoy people, would I be practising two nights a week to do it?'

From his perch in Windsor House, Michael Boyle of the Parades Commission readily accepts that the overwhelming majority of marching bands are fully compliant with their stipulations for behaviour and that huge efforts are devoted now to raising the standards of music and the decorum of the marching bands. There has also been huge progress as well in discouraging the 'blue-bag' aspect; the coteries of hangers-on with drink carry-outs who formerly trailed in the wake of their bands. However, he also points out that the source and nature of complaints about Blood and Thunder band parades are changing. 'Increasingly the protests are less related to the alleged sectarian or political context of the parade, but to the disruption of lives – the economic damage to business, restriction of traffic movement, disruption of children sleeping – and increasingly they come from within the very community that is supposed to be staging the parade.'

Controversy still surrounds the very existence of the Parades Commission, of course, but on a much more muted level than heretofore. Another 'strategic review', specially commissioned by the Westminster parliament under former Liberal Democrat leader Paddy Ashdown, is examining the future of the parades body which those on the Unionist side have pledged to bring down. Lord Ashdown's group has had to postpone its report on several deadlines. Unionists claim that this is because of Sinn Féin's resistance to relaxing control of parades, but it is not easy to arrive at a consensus on an issue that is so divisive within Northern Ireland. While Nationalists believe the Parades Commission does not go far enough in curbing the loyal orders and the Blood and Thunder bands, the Orange Order and the

Unionist parties see the very existence of the agency as an unnecessary encumbrance on Loyalist cultural traditions. For in Northern Ireland, the American expression that 'everybody loves a parade' does not hold true. While nobody loves a parade more than the Ulster Loyalist, Nationalists insist they dread the annual marching season. So while the number of parades staged annually in Northern Ireland has now levelled out at just under 4,000, the balance of these remains overwhelmingly weighed in favour of the Loyalist side of the community. However, while many Nationalists believe that this imbalance is merely continuing a tradition of humiliating and insulting their neighbours in shows of supremacy, there is no doubt that recreational parading is the main cultural activity of Loyalists. So of the 3,849 parades that came before the Parades Commission between 1 April 2007 and 31 March 2008, 2,691 (seventy per cent of the total) were organised by groups in the Unionist tradition, including the loyal orders.[50] Of the remainder, only 203 or five per cent of the total, were organised by Nationalist groups and invariably these were much more localised and smaller. The remainder were classified as 'other' parades and included charity, civic, rural and sporting events, as well as church processions.

Analysis by the Parades Commission has established that forty-eight per cent of the parades staged by Unionists were organised by the Orange Order, seventeen per cent by the Royal Black Preceptory and ten per cent by the Apprentice

Boys. Another seven per cent were classified as 'other' Unionist parades and eighteen per cent were organised by Loyalist bands. The vast majority of the parades organised by the various Loyalist institutions featured bands. Of all these 4,000 or so parades, only 250 notified cases (or six per cent of the total) were deemed to be contentious and, of these, fifty-two related to the weekly notifications submitted by the Portadown District Orange Lodge that it wished to parade down the town's Garvaghy Road from Drumcree church. Parades not deemed contentious are not considered by the Parades Commission and those that are reviewed simply have conditions imposed in terms of an alteration of route, which applies in eighty per cent of cases, timing or numbers taking part, and whether music can be played at certain places along the route. In other cases, the Parades Commission might impose conditions on the type of music, mode of dress and behaviour of those parading.

In the absence of any agreed alternative to be sanctioned by Westminster, the Parades Commission will continue to exist in one form or another. Michael Boyle points to the case of the Maryfield Secretariat set up under the Anglo-Irish Agreement of 1985. The Unionists pledged to bring it down and, sure enough, it no longer exists, but the British-Irish Secretariat established under the Good Friday Agreement carries on its work. 'If the commission was gone,' says Michael Boyle, 'we would have something else to do the job. It would really be an exercise in face-saving and no more.

In other jurisdictions, the determination on parades remains with the police. Here the police don't want to touch it.' The Northern Ireland Police Federation Chairman, Terry Spence, has said his members would oppose any move to replace the body, saying, 'Whatever the outcome of the deliberations on the future of the Parades Commission, this federation will be difficult to persuade that the present process which is free of political manipulation needs to be replaced.'[51]

Meanwhile, Paul Goggins, Minister of State at the Northern Ireland Office, has publicly stated that the body 'has done an extremely good job in difficult circumstances. However, we know that there are people and organisations in Northern Ireland who do not share that view. If it is possible for all the parties and all sections of the community to arrive at a consensus on an alternative system, we will obviously be prepared to consider it, because in the longer term we need a sustainable approach to parading. We cannot lurch from parade to parade and season to season, unsure about the future. We have to have a sustainable approach to parading, so that peaceful parading can be guaranteed.'[52]

Meanwhile, back in Killylea on St Patrick's Day, the crowd's attention is caught by a small band in tight formation marching briskly to a tune called 'Go Man Go' and following up with 'Lannigan's Ball', the new medley of Irish airs it is unveiling on an appropriate occasion. The Castlederg Young Loyalists Flute Band draws bursts of spontaneous applause from many of the young bandsmen now lining the route as spectators. Family groups, with young school-going children are heading home and the night is ending. But the 2009 marching season is barely at its dawn and already it is whetting the huge appetite for much more to come.

CHAPTER 7

GO MAN GO

Monday, 30 March 2009

The strains of a well-known rebel song reverberate around the walls of Killeter Church Hall: 'I wish I was in a land of cotton/Old times they are not forgotten/Look away, look away, look away, Dixie Land.' Samantha's powerful voice rises and falls to the plaintive lyrics. Soon the young fluters from Castlederg join in as she shifts into the equally familiar strains of the 'Battle Hymn of the Republic': 'Glory, Glory, Alleluia, His truth is marching on.' Despite minor adjustments by fiddler and musical arranger Matt McGranaghan, the sequence of American Civil War songs is just one of several high points during a relaxed rehearsal in a rural Church of Ireland parish hall that explores and challenges the versatility of four young Blood and Thunder bandsmen.

The collaboration with the energetic and quick-tongued musician from Castlefinn in County Donegal is under the aegis of Border Arts, a Castlederg-based community arts organisation headed by Gordon Speer. Leading by example, Gordon plays keyboards for the session, while his son, Christopher, plays guitar, with much ribbing from McGranaghan. The younger pair are members of Kintra, the traditional Irish and Scottish music and dance group which received a standing ovation for its show at a recent St Patrick's Day celebration at Stormont. There is an easy atmosphere in the Killeter parish hall and the young musicians, who include Castlederg Young Loyalists fluters Davy, Johnny, Ryan and Neil, are happy to explore musical collaboration along with their bandmaster Trevor Donnell, who plays the side-drum on several of the numbers while the ornate wooden bass drum of the band rests unused on a small easel at the fringe of the circle.

The Castlederg Young Loyalists bandsmen are clearly excited about the Border Arts project and they plan to use these songs, with other material, on a new CD. But with competing commitments on all sides, it is not easy to bring it all together: even the venue for tonight's rehearsal is a last-minute choice because the Killeter Heritage Centre is being used for dancing classes. And with the parade season now underway, finding time to finish the charity project will pose another major challenge for an organisation that limps along in dire need of funding.

The schedule of an active Blood and Thunder band is motivated by two major considerations – money and esteem. Bands that travel to many venues attract a lot of the host bands back to their annual parades. Bands that perform and look well on their home turf – and that entails having a big annual parade – contribute hugely to local pride and attract recruits. The result of both is a large attendance at the band's annual parade, which is its main source of revenue. The cycle sustains the band, even when their energy is sapped by late nights on the road and early morning parades at home during the high part of the summer season. For the Castlederg Young Loyalists the parade season entails a lot of travel and cost. Quincey Dougan of the Ulster Bands Forum says many bands are now curtailing their travel because of the financial strain, and concentrating efforts on the parades closest to home. His band, Kilcluney Volunteers, has racked up bills of £10,000 for bus travel in one season. For a small band like the Castlederg Young Loyalists, that is not an option and travel to and from parades is invariably in a small convoy of cars for which the members receive no expenses and rely on contributions for petrol from their passengers. With school-going and unemployed band members, this is not always feasible.

Thursday, 2 April 2009

To the strains of the music coming out of the open doors of the Bridgetown Orange Hall, the colour party marches up and down Castlederg's main car park on a fine spring evening. Kenny Sproule is to the fore of a tightly packed cluster of three flag-bearers. They go through their paces, carefully avoiding parked vehicles, their standards held aloft. Inside meanwhile, bandmaster Trevor is warning the fluters to take care of their instruments or risk the £200 fine. 'You have to oil the flute regularly to make sure it doesn't crack,' he advises. When someone remarks that the brass part doesn't really need to be oiled, Trevor suggests they take no chances and oil the entire instrument. 'Oh, and make sure you dry the outside with a towel when you're finished using it as well,' he says, to several knowing nods.

The band is practising for its first Tyrone outing of the season – the Omagh True Blues parade. There are several new faces in the hall. Robbie McKinley explains that they were with the band last year – one of them is from Newtownstewart, the other is living in Omagh, so they haven't made it along to practices before now. Trevor reminds them they will have a lot of rehearsing of the new material to do before Monday 13 April, when the band will be in Larne for the huge Easter Monday Apprentice Boys event hosted by the Scottish clubs.

'What about "Sandy Row"?' somebody suggests during the next lull. 'You always play that when you're going up and down the hill in Omagh.'

'Do I?' asks Trevor, obviously unaware that this is his usual choice for the Courthouse Hill, where marching Blood and Thunder bands revel in the echoes of the percussion bouncing off the five-storey homes of banks and solicitors' offices close to John Street, regarded as the Nationalist centre of Tyrone's county town. So 'Sandy Row' gets a twirl as the first members of the colour party come inside.

'Michaela, did yous do the fall out?' Trevor asks. 'I noticed the last day it wasn't right and we need to fix that.' Kenny, who has been carefully furling a flag at the entrance doors, comes up. 'Kenny, I want yous to fall out here ... and I don't mean fight with each other,' Trevor laughs. A very brief discussion about the drill follows and, moments later, the bandmaster is sounding a closing drumbeat on the table top as the colour party marks time. The order rings out with the final brattle and they get it nearly right. Kenny admits the fault: the exercise is repeated. This time, the final steps, a brisk right turn and they snap to attention in unison. This earns Kenny a brief cheer from fellow band members and the practice resumes.

Later, local Young Unionist activist Ryan Moses arrives to tell the band about a possible grant from Airtricity, which has invited grant applications from local groups. The company's Northern Ireland arm based in Omagh has added wind farms at Bessy Bell Mountain and Slieve Divinia to its existing operations at Tappaghan and Bin Mountain. Airtricity also has proposals for Tievenameenta, Slieve Kirk, Glenconway, Bellmore and an extension of the Tappaghan site – all within short distances of Castlederg. Ryan Moses explains that community funds totalling £6,000 have been earmarked for Unionist groups in the area and a couple of small applications are already in. Trevor Donnell immediately suggests they apply to buy twenty-five new Guards-style caps which cost between £60 and £70 each. There's some discussion on the need for new uniform trousers. The Young Unionist representative says the cap idea fits better because, in theory at least, different band members can use them. It would be harder to make a case for trousers, he says. So caps it is and Ryan says he'll put in for further grant aid from the Ulster-Scots Agency which has responsibility for dispensing specially allocated EU peace funding. One proposal the band hopes to pursue is for a supervised disco for youngsters to help keep them out of 'divilment about the town'.

Finally, as band members disperse, Trevor points out that they need to meet here at 7 p.m. tomorrow so that they can parade early in Omagh and be back in time for some members to do the door at a charity fundraiser in the Castle Inn. 'There'll be a big crowd coming back from Omagh and some of them might be trying to get in for nothing to have a late night back here,' says Trevor. 'So we want to have plenty on the door to make sure we get everybody paid in.'

Friday, 3 April 2009

The Omagh bus depot car park is a hive of Blood and Thunder activity and the excitement is palpable in the raised voices punctuated by an occasional tattoo on a side-drum. Members of the Castlederg Young Loyalists Flute Band muster around their vehicles, strategically parked for a speedy exit. Across from them, a burger/chip van is doing steady trade and at a market stall an older couple examine the array of plastic flags – Union Jacks and Red Hands – and other trinkets. Among the novelty wares are bright pink cowboy hats with 'Slappers on Tour' printed across the front – Ulster honesty in all its glory.

Two parade stewards from the Omagh True Blues stand at the pedestrian ramp opposite the Garden of Remembrance for victims of the 1998 Omagh bombing. The parade will be underway by 8.45 p.m., they promise, only fifteen minutes behind schedule. They outline the route – a figure of eight along Drumragh Avenue, Dublin Road, left into Irishtown and back along Crevanagh Road to the Swinging Bars Roundabout and then straight back through Campsie, Market Street and on up to the courthouse, turning back down High Street and left into Bridge Street for the bus depot. It's about two miles, enough to put the forty bands through their paces in one of the first outings of the 2009 season.

One of the stewards advises that the best spot for spectators is the junction of Market Street and Dublin Road, precisely where the Real IRA bomb wreaked devastation a decade ago in the aftermath of the Good Friday Agreement with all its promise of mutual respect for cultural, political and historical difference. My suggestion that the most spectacular views might be up at the courthouse brings a cautionary retort, 'Well, you'd be at the very outer extremity up there, so you would. You would probably be better with the crowds down this end of the town.'

Around the corner, police officers keep the traffic flowing in the confusion of vehicles, many stuffed with young bandsmen. Along the footpaths, crowds gather. Outside a fast-food takeaway in Campsie, a group of East Europeans are probably wondering what is happening. Then off in the background, familiar drumming above the din, followed by flutes. I hurry back as the Castlederg Young Loyalists round the corner at the Omagh Community House and come towards Campsie Bridge, against the parade route, with a steward leading the way. Kenny Sproule's colour party steps smartly in close formation, but the drummers and fluters have to compress their ranks to negotiate a path between the parked cars and the two lanes of traffic that have created a bottleneck towards the junction. The tune never falters.

I assume the parade route has been adjusted and decide to use a nearby footbridge over the Drumragh river to catch up with the band heading back into the town centre. Where better to meet the loyal sons of Ulster than on the historic King James' Bridge, which the forces of the deposed Jacobite monarch crossed on their 1688 route to Derry's Walls? But there is no sign of the band. I return back through more car parks where bandsmen adjust uniforms, and skirt the crowds at the main junction, where collection buckets jingle as they fill, replenishing the coffers of the Omagh True Blues. At the finish point the Castlederg Young Loyalists are marking time. A relatively brisk fall-out and Trevor breathes an obvious sigh of relief. So how did it go? 'We just followed the steward and he took us up through Campsie and then back down again and we broke a drum along the way,' he reports.

'Now, though, we've got to get going for some of them have to be back in the Derg for a party.'

As the Derg contingent departs, other bands edge to the starting point opposite the Omagh College campus and go thundering off. Most band members are in their late teens or early twenties, but some seem as young as five or six, while a few are over thirty. Different in style but united in purpose, they pour along the route with just enough of a time-lag for spectators to pick up the rhythm of the next contingent as the one in front fades away. There are occasional cheers for recognised bandsmen, the loudest for members of Omagh's three large bands, the host True Blues, Blair Memorial and the Protestant Boys.

In Market Street the sound reverberates in the canyon of five-storey buildings. Bands starting on the parade route compete with others coming over Campsie Bridge on their return to the heart of the town. The effect is a cacophonous jumble of melodies and relentless percussion as each band tries to outplay the others. Yet this is where the crowd concentrates, drawn to the spectacle and thrilling to the sound.

On up the town, the bands thunder beyond Scarffe's Entry. The Pride of the Derg band belts out its raw and ready rendition of Loyalist tunes. Created by disaffected members of the Young Loyalists, the Pride favours no-frills Blood and Thunder. With eighteen flutes and a dozen drummers, the other Castlederg band dispenses with the Courthouse Hill and wheels right into Bridge Street on the heels of the band turning from the opposite direction. Other bands follow the assigned route up High Street where the spectators are reduced to a couple of smokers outside Daly's pub and several police officers at the mouth of John Street, regarded as the town's Nationalist heartland. A band goes thundering down the hill as another comes up. As they meet, the rival bass drummers give it all they can to outdo each other. At this point, a young man in a tracksuit carrying a large sports bag emblazoned with the letters GAA walks down the Courthouse Hill, as if ambling through a deserted town centre. His obvious refusal to acknowledge the presence of the bands is deliberate, a practice born and bred of mutual suspicion that has kept apart close neighbours – even in a town with a well-earned reputation of community harmony to set alongside its horrific recent history. That customary standoff is underlined when the local Blair Memorial Band swaggers up the hill belting out 'The Sash'. As the descending band comes alongside, the bandsmen take up the tune in unison. A few Blair bandsmen do improvised jig steps as they turn at John Street where flags still celebrate Tyrone's 2008 All-Ireland Gaelic football victories and inside the pubs, young revellers ignore what is happening around most of the town.

Thursday, 9 April 2009

Under normal circumstances in Northern Ireland, a parade involving forty bands with up to 1,000 young musicians coming in wave after wave through a town centre with colourful flags, uniforms and acrobatic drum majors, would be largely ignored, even in a town of some 25,000 inhabitants. The exceptions come when the parade leads to something other than the normal complaints of traffic disruption, lost business and noise. So the assumption that last Friday's events would not merit coverage in the following week's local newspapers serving both sides of the local population, was premature. The *Ulster Herald* reports that the Parades Commission is demanding an explanation for an 'illegal Omagh march':

Police have rushed to defend their handling of security at Friday night's illegal Loyalist band parade at John Street in Omagh. The True Blues parade took place in Omagh on Friday evening but, after it was over, three bands went to the Kevlin Road and marched up to John Street in the direction of the Courthouse. They played 'The Sash' outside pubs in area, which prompted immediate condemnation by local business people who said it could have led to a riotous clash with young revellers.

A spokesman for the police said the bands congregated as they usually did at Johnston Road car park and then went to the bus depot where the parade started. They travelled along Drumragh and up Market Street and High Street. At the courthouse, a police officer indicated that the bands were to turn and go back down the street again to the bus depot. The PSNI spokesman said that around 11 p.m. police received a call that the bands were marching along the Kevlin Road and John Street, which are forbidden areas for these parades.

'We have been told by those involved that the three bands were from Belfast and Portadown and that they mistakenly turned down at Scarffe's Entry and travelled to the Kevlin Road. One of the bands went home while the other two continued marching until John Street. They then turned right and went to the Courthouse and down the hill again.' The spokesman added, 'This has never happened before in Omagh and the matter has been referred to the Parades Commission.'

The incident was on the agenda at yesterday's meeting of the Parade's Commission ...

[Sinn Féin] Cllr Begley also said he would be contacting the Parades Commission to reiterate the strong opposition to such parades through John Street, which is a Nationalist area of Omagh town. The Councillor also rejected the PSNI's claims that the parade was policed in a professional and proportionate manner.

'If this had been the case both bands wouldn't have been facilitated in their coat-trailing exercise. We don't have objections to people parading but in the case of these particular marches, there is absolutely no consideration given for Nationalist people of this area,' concluded Cllr Begley.[53]

Saturday, 11 April 2009

Easter weekend and the West Ulster Bands Forum host a concert in Newtownstewart's 2000 Centre featuring seven bands – accordion, pipe and Blood and Thunder. The line-up includes Convoy Pipe from Donegal and Castlederg Young Loyalists.

Monday, 13 April 2009

The Castlederg Young Loyalists are in Larne, County Antrim, for the traditional Easter Monday parade of the Apprentice Boys of Derry hosted by the Scottish clubs.

Friday, 17 April 2009

The Loyal Sons of Benagh Flute Band celebrates its thirty-fifth anniversary with a parade of forty-nine bands in a 'very well marshalled and incident-free' event in Newry during which the host band unveils a new uniform of 'sharp blue and orange, topped off with white peaked caps'.[54]

Saturday, 18 April 2009

Randalstown Sons of Ulster parade draws twenty-six bands, while in north Belfast, Pride of the Shore Flute holds the final of the 2009 Battle of the Bands won by Gortagilly Coronation Flute from Moneymore 'who took to the floor immaculately turned out and proceeded through a strong and entertaining set that was very crowd pleasing ...'[55]

Friday, 24 April 2009

Lurgan, County Armagh, is the venue for the annual parade of the Star of the North Flute Band from Dollingstown, while the William Savage Memorial Band event is taking place in Killyleagh, County Down.[56]

Friday, 1 May 2009

Castlederg Young Loyalists are among a turn-out of thirty-two bands at the Red Hand Defenders Flute Band annual parade in Newtownstewart where the East Bank Protestant Boys Flute and Gortagilly Coronation Flute from Moneymore are among the 'stand-out bands of the night'. The hosts parade at the end with 'a band of over forty members and one of their best ever performances'. On the same night in Dromore, County Down, Skeogh Flute had thirty-nine bands parading to the 'distinctive town square'.[57]

Saturday, 2 May 2009

A turn-out of eighteen bands in Ahoghill, County Antrim, for local Sons of William Flute parade; in Belfast's Shankill Road area, the Sons of Ulster parade has fifty bands; while in Lurgan, County Armagh, the Craigavon Protestant Boys 'one of the oldest Blood and Thunder bands in the Province' has another fifty bands among whom 'the small bands of Cormeen Rising Sons of William, Lower Woodstock Ulster-Scots and Castlederg Young Loyalists were a testament to their commitment and dedication'.[58]

Friday, 8 May 2009

Castlederg Young Loyalists is among a cross-section of sixteen pipe, silver, accordion, melody flute and Blood and Thunder bands that parade through Enniskillen, County Fermanagh, for the local Star of Erne Pipe Band event where large crowds turn out. Meanwhile, in Lisburn, County Antrim, another forty-five bands parade for the Pride of Knockmore; in Limavady, County Derry, forty-eight bands are out for the Star of the Roe parade; and in Newtownhamilton, County Armagh, twenty-three bands including 'strong Blood and Thunder' bands from Keady parade with 'exemplary style and appearance' are out for the Carnagh Accordion Band event.[59] Not everyone shares that assessment, however. Sinn Féin councillor for the Fews district Jimmy McCreesh says the Newtownhamilton parade in South Armagh is 'excessive and provocative' and criticises the handling of the event after being contacted by several constituents who accuse the police of following an 'Orange Order agenda' by allowing the bands to indulge in an 'exercise of unadulterated triumphalism'. 'There can be no justification whatsoever for these bands invading a small town in such numbers,' says Councillor McCreesh. 'They virtually laid siege to the town, causing widespread disruption. These sectarian bands wreaked chaos for those living in Blayney Hill and the Armagh Road. In no way did they attempt to communicate or consult with local residents.' While respecting the rights of all traditions to express their culture, says Councillor McCreesh, the parade was a 'great affront' to local residents.[60]

Saturday, 9 May 2009

In north County Tyrone, ten bands parade for the local Sons of William through Donemana village 'with a relaxed atmosphere adding very much to the family-orientated proceedings'. Castlederg Young Loyalists and Pride of the Derg are said to have 'put on a good show'. In Larne, another parade features twenty-three bands.[61]

Thursday, 14 May 2009

In the Davy Crockett Lounge and fresh from being hauled over the coals by the Parades Commission in Belfast, bandmaster Trevor Donnell is frustrated by the lack of enthusiasm for the planned trip to Scotland to celebrate the 'Glasgow Twelfth'. At his side are drummer Andy and his partner, with their toddler son playing at her feet. She seems equally puzzled by the general reluctance to commit fully to a trip to Scotland with all expenses paid. 'I mean, it's all for nothing,' she remarks. 'Anybody else would be jumping at the chance.' Trevor agrees, 'Aye, but you'd want to throw in another £100 each to get some of these boys to say yes.'

Some say they are going, some aren't and some can't decide. Trevor warns that final confirmation has to be given by next week and he reminds them that everyone agreed to the Scotland trip when it was put to them back in January. 'There's ten members of the [Orange] Lodge going and we have a bus for thirty-six, the hotel booked and we signed a contract that means we pay a £2,000 fine if we don't show up. So tell me, what would you do if you were in my place … if you were the bandmaster?'

Various combinations and permutations are suggested; lacklustre computations suggest four, five, six and seven flutes. Trevor says that the band cannot turn up for the 'Glasgow Twelfth' with fewer than ten flutes. 'Maybe we should just tell another band to go in our place. Give them the bus and the hotel for free because they are already paid for. At least then we'd save ourselves from the £2,000 fine.'

That suggestion doesn't please those present, all of whom – with two exceptions – have now fully committed to going. Niall doesn't know if he can make it, but says he is more than ninety per cent sure he can. Davy the drummer says he can't get off work, but by the end of the session, he agrees to make one further plea to his boss. 'I've really been looking forward to this trip,' remarks Neil to cheer up the gathering, and several others nod in agreement.

'Will we be wearing our tunics in the parade if we go?' asks Niall. 'Just … last time it was a really hot day and it's a long parade.' Andy's partner suggests that each of the travelling band members could buy a matching short-sleeved shirt for a fiver so they could wear them if it's another hot day. 'We'd have to get the name on them though,' observes Trevor. 'Not your own names … the band's name.'

He is particularly sensitive about proper identification of the band on all livery and equipment. Yesterday he was summoned to Belfast for an inquiry by the Parades Commission arising out of the Craigavon Protestant Boys parade on 2 May in Lurgan. Trevor says the complaint probably came from local dissident Republicans who were protesting. Two bands were before the Parades Commission inquiry – Castlederg Young Loyalists and 'I think it was that band from Magheralin – they're a new band.' The complaint was that both had contravened the parade conditions by not having the band name on their bass drums and thus not properly identifying their band.

'I said I wasn't one bit happy about using that drum,' Trevor tells his young bandsmen, explaining later that the drum had been substituted because the regular bass was in the boot of Andy's car. He was off working on a job in England and, because he now lives in Cookstown, he had no opportunity to pass it over to someone else for the Lurgan parade. 'I told the Parades Commission Andy was to blame,' Trevor jokes, 'and our proper drum was in his boot somewhere in England.'

Yet he obviously takes seriously the alleged breach, pointing out that every time the band parades, they sign a commitment on certain rules including proper display of the band's name on the drums. 'So hands up ...' he says, adding, however, that it particularly rankles to be singled out for complaint by 'political allies of Colin Duffy', a Republican veteran from Lurgan.

'We're not as bad as the other band, I think, because we had our name on the bannerette,' Trevor adds. 'They showed me a great photo of Kenny with the bannerette, so it was us all right. At least we had the bannerette with our name on it. The other band had no bannerette, so we may not be too bad ...'

Friday, 15 May 2009

At Billyhill near Shercock in County Cavan, Protestant marching bands from Cavan and Monaghan parade in support of the local accordion band.[62]

Saturday, 16 May 2009

An East Belfast Protestant Boys parade on Newtownards Road is arranged to be more family friendly and appeal to tourists to the city. The starting time is brought forward to 6.30 p.m. and the parade ends at 10 p.m. with the host band in fancy dress and sweets distributed to the children along the packed route. On Belfast's Shankill Road, the Warkworth Purple Star Flute hosts an event at the Ulster Rangers Supporters Club.[63]

Friday, 22 May 2009

Every town in Northern Ireland has sectarian geography, usually discerned in the display of flags, murals and painted kerbstones and lamp-posts. Yet even without such hints, Cookstown is no exception to the geography of tribal division, even though the town appears at first to be one long street with a few minor offshoots. Going south to north, the sectarian fault line is where the street rises to Fairhill and then spills down into the 'old town'. That is where the police check traffic as the late spring evening descends on the Cookstown Sons of William annual parade.

After Fairhill, there is a noticeable buzz as people wait for almost fifty marching bands. On the fringes, a smiling Sinn Féin MEP, Bairbre de Brún, peeps out from posters between ornamental trees. Further along, Ulster Conservative and Unionist MEP Jim Nicholson – who has held the seat for twenty years – urges a 'Vote for Change'. A parked van has a picture of Democratic Unionist Party candidate Diane Dodds on the side and, moving through the crowds, a man hands out leaflets for incumbent Jim Allister, running as the Traditional Unionist Voice candidate for the seat that the DUP wants back. But little heed is paid to such trifles nearer the main junction where spectators are out in force, mostly in family groups with children waving little Union Jacks, twirling toy band-sticks or punching the air with inflatable giant hands in true blue colours. A few roadside stalls are doing brisk business and a mobile trader, sporting a Union Jack Stetson, pushes a shopping trolley filled to the brim with flags, yo-yos and sparkling fancies – all conveniently priced at £1. More pound coins are being dropped into the collection boxes carried by host band volunteers in bright reflective bibs.

At 8.45 p.m. the Omagh Protestant Boys Melody Flute Band, in their distinctive colonial pith helmets, are first over the brow of the hill from the Moneymore Road end of the town. After that, the marching bands spill along in rapid succession. Soon bands on the return leg are competing with those setting out and the main junction at Molesworth Street is enveloped in a torrent of sound. Blood and Thunder dominates, although into the midst of all the flutes and drums march two accordion bands; one from nearby Desertmartin and the much-vaunted Dunloy Accordion Band from County Antrim. Middle-aged women predominate in both accordion bands and Dunloy's fast-paced delivery earns applause before the fluters return.

A trio of short-statured women – a mother and daughters – elbow their way through the crowd. 'H'mon the Sons,' shouts the mother in a rasping Belfast accent, vocal encouragement for any number of Sons of Ulster, Sons of William and Sons of the Conquerors among the bands. 'H'mon the Shankill,' she adds helpfully as her daughters add yelps of delight. A stalled bandsman shouts, 'Hey you, stop making all that noise,' and laughs. The trio dart through the parade to the traffic island where the Sons of Ulster from Belfast's Shankill Road are on the return leg and take up position behind them. One daughter smiles proudly while smoking a cigarette with her arms folded, a stance used by comedians to typify the 'Milly' characters drawn from Belfast's once plentiful numbers of factory girls.

A bottleneck develops at the foot of the hill. Everything halts. The Sons of Ulster from Moygashel unhook drums as fluters break ranks and mingle. Several minutes later, their lone banner-bearer, an older man who has remained fully at attention, rests his ceremonial pole on the road and turns to inform those behind that the parade has stopped. A chorus of laughter as somebody says, 'So what else do we not know?' The mood is patient, light-hearted, but as the delay persists, even the young drum major stops twirling his band-stick and balances it on his nose to impress onlookers.

Further up the street at a parked car, young bandsmen who have completed the route drink furtively from concealed bottles. Outside the pubs, smokers who have been watching the parade, go back indoors. Yet most of the crowd waits patiently. Movement returns, bands reassemble hurriedly and set off again on a shortened route that just goes up and down the main drag. Then, out of the gloom, the familiar Battle of the Somme banner of the Castlederg Young Loyalists comes over the hill and here they are, marching along to 'Lannigan's Ball'. A few bursts of applause greet them and they march off into the distance before wheeling about and returning up the other side of the street. Then another brief pause and the band members relax and chat. Bandmaster Trevor explains that they had been assembled and waiting to go for a full hour. 'Then a young police officer came along and told us someone had died and the body was being taken back to a house along the route and there were a lot of cars so the bands couldn't get through.'

We chat about the parade. Trevor says the band in front is very good, referring to the Skeogh Flute Band from Dromore, County Down, which has just been playing 'The Star of the County Down', a hugely popular tune with many older spectators. The parade begins to move again and, in a concertina movement, the Derg boys are back marching jauntily with only one other band a good bit behind. The parade is winding up. Pub doors close as customers move inside. Cars pull out and the traffic police are still at Fairhill as host band Sons of William takes its triumphal tour of the town.

The Castlederg Young Loyalists pack away their instruments and set off across the Black Bog towards Omagh and then home. Tomorrow they are back this way and on to Ballymena for Ballykeel Loyal Sons of Ulster, an event with seventy-five bands deemed 'sensitive' by the Parades Commission. The first long weekend of the summer unfolds and the high season beckons for the Blood and Thunder bands.

Sunday, 24 May 2009

A Loyalist gang descends on the Heights area of Coleraine to remove Irish tricolour flags after Glasgow Rangers clinch the Scottish Premier League football title. Kevin McDaid, a middle-aged Catholic youth worker trying to prevent trouble, is killed. His widow Evelyn, a Protestant, is injured. Assistant Chief Constable Alistair Finlay says, 'There was a suggestion there was going to be an impromptu band parade. That was not going to happen, but the indication was that the community in the Heights believed there was to be some band parades and that there would be a number of exhibitions of triumphalism coming from the Loyalist community. In response to that there was the building of some barricades and the raising of some flags in that particular community.'[64] The policeman explains that police organised negotiations, a settlement was reached and the dead man was pivotal in this and handled the removal of barricades. About fifteen people then came from a nearby bar 'intent on removing flags' which were due to come down anyway. Bedlam ensued with hand-to-hand fighting and Kevin McDaid was killed. The *Newsletter* quotes the senior police officer dismissing reports of UDA paramilitary involvement: 'There is no evidence that this was anything other than a maverick group of yobs, who made their way down from a pub, intent on violence.' The paper quotes a community source saying phone calls were made to the bar taunting the Loyalists to come and remove the flags.

Thursday, 28 May 2009

A report in *The Irish Times* mistakenly credits the Orange Order for re-routing a band parade in Coleraine after the sectarian murder of Kevin McDaid. The decision to alter the route is taken by the band organisers in the Pride of the Bann Flute Band, which expects forty other bands and more than 20,000 marchers and supporters to attend its annual parade. The decision is made following a series of meetings with the Parades Commission, which also heard from Sinn Féin, the SDLP, police and others. Meanwhile, one of the dead man's sons is reported to have received a death threat from the UDA.[65]

Friday, 29 May 2009

The Pride of the Bann's parade passes off without incident as forty bands parade peacefully through Coleraine, defying fears that violence would erupt. During the parade, the remains of father-of-four Kevin McDaid are brought to his family home. The Pride of the Bann Flute Band initially planned to march near the scene of Mr McDaid's murder but organisers decide not to cross the town's Bann Bridge. Local supporters line the parade route, with around a dozen armed police officers at the bridge where a handful of the McDaid family's neighbours gather to protest close to where the bands pass. Later, Declan Kennedy, a nephew of the dead man, accuses the Loyalist band of disrespecting his memory by staging Friday's parade which can be heard from the wake house as it passes through the town. 'There's fear in this estate. Nobody wants more trouble but that's what the parade means – trouble. I know they're not crossing the river now but it should have been called off, it's disrespectful to his memory, everyone thinks so.'[66]

Monday, 1 June 2009

The *Newsletter* reports that an unofficial Bebo website dedicated to Pride of the Bann is carrying a number of distasteful and threatening messages in relation to the parade, including the UDA motto, 'Quis Separabit' (Who will separate us?). The band points out that this is not its site and joins calls for its removal from the Internet. Among the messages posted online are some referring to the re-routing of the parade away from the murder scene, with one contributor urging bands to play 'loud so they can hear you over the river' and another remarking, 'Heard parade passed peacefully last nyt well done to all involved don't let the taogs [*sic*] bring u to their level.' A third wrote, 'The McDaid family could hear you loud and clear as the coffin returned home. I think they (and the world) got your message. No Surrender! Hate is all we have left.'

Meanwhile, PSNI Chief Superintendent Alan McCrum praises the parade organisers: 'They deserve credit for the voluntary steps that they took in altering the parade route, and for recognising the genuine concerns and wishes of the residents of Somerset Drive. I believe that this will prove to be an important if tentative first step towards restoring community relations in the town.' Presbyterian Church Moderator Donald Patton calls for calm and praises Evelyn McDaid for asking for no retaliation over her husband's death. 'In stating unreserved condemnation of Kevin's murder, and disgust and shame that those who carried it out claim to be Protestants, there is no place for such acts in our society today, and no place for sectarian bigotry that sets people against one another because of different religious backgrounds or political outlooks.'[67]

CHAPTER 8

CUBS AND CUDDIES

On Saturday 23rd May disaster struck the band. In a freak accident, the Castlederg Young Loyalists' thunder was stolen on the way to the Ballykeel Loyal Sons of Ulster parade. The band was travelling as usual in a small convoy of cars. Near Ballymena, as one of the cars was turning off the main road, a driver coming around the corner in the opposite direction veered out of his lane and struck the Castlederg car head on. While the others in the vehicle, including Johnny the driver, escaped with minor scratches, bass drummer Ian Burke's left arm is broken and he could be out of action for the summer. With the band already struggling to keep up its ranks, the loss of a bass drummer seems almost like a deathblow as the calendar of parades reaches high season.

The struggle to muster a full complement of flutes and drums for parade has become a persistent problem for the band which has emphasised 'quality not quantity' in its recruitment. While its strong supporters will argue that the band is better in so many respects today compared with the raw Blood and Thunder of former times, there is a strong hint of nostalgia in their recollection of those days when recruitment was probably the least of the band's worries and there was a steady stream of 'cubs and cuddies' to swell the ranks and fly the flag.

Trevor Donnell, for instance, recalls a time back in the early 1980s when the Castlederg Young Loyalists band was one of the bigger Blood and Thunder outfits around: 'I remember a time in Omagh – the time we had the orange jumpers – and we were lined up for the parade. I think it was sixty-four fluters we had and fourteen side-drummers. We might have had four bass drummers at that time.' He knows the strong magnetic attraction of the big show especially on potential recruits to the Blood and Thunder bands. He was there once himself, he points out: 'The first flute band ever I would have come across was I think the Omagh Protestant Boys. It was either them or the Blair Memorial, but it was one of the Omagh bands anyway. They arrived here at a parade in Castlederg one time and it was something else entirely from what we would have had before. You see, you could have an accordion or a pipe band coming up the road and it would be fine, but then you would have a flute band – and it doesn't matter what flute band it is – and you see all the young people running out to see them. You can actually see them pushing out to get a look. I enjoy a pipe band and an accordion band myself, but it's always the flute band for the young people.'

Since his own days as a starry-eyed adolescent admiring the early Blood and Thunder bands, Trevor has been part of the establishment and development of the local band and his experiences are reflected across most of the marching bands that make up the best of the 'movement' in Northern Ireland today.

'From 1977 I've seen some changes. Back then a lot of people were just getting on the bus. I remember it was a double-decker bus we used to go in from here and there's not too many of them on the road now. A lot of the people going out, really you wouldn't have them in the band nowadays because they were going out to drink and have as good a time as possible, which was bad for the image of the band. They weren't going out for the [Loyalist] cause or for the parade or anything else; they were just going out for themselves. Nowadays, all the band members are going out to look good and to sound as good as they can. It's moved on now a terra [huge amount]. There's a few bands yet would be stuck back in the 1970s, but the time will come when they will have to move forward. Nobody wants them at their parade and we certainly wouldn't want a band coming full drunk to anything we would be holding. It just rises trouble like and gets all bands a bad name.

'I suppose with Blood and Thunder, though, the loudest band coming up the street attracts a lot of the younger people. The loudest band gets them, but I think that is wrong. We used to attract our members that way, with the noise we would make coming up the street. But bands are starting to get more into the music, rather than just putting out ten to fifteen side-drummers to make as much noise as they can coming up the road. I suppose the noise coming up the street does attract young people to come along and join though. It's just that we're trying to swing our thing more to the music element.'

The emphasis on musical quality rather than more volume has come at a cost, not only in membership numbers, but also in financial outlay for the small corps of young musicians who now make up the band. For many, the decision to form a Blood and Thunder marching band in the first place had the benefit of maximum impact for lowest outlay. In the early days of the Castlederg Young Loyalists, for instance, the drums were simply transferred from the old accordion band and the accordions were sold off to buy flutes for the huge increase in band numbers. Choosing flutes over other instruments at the time, meant that a band could be equipped and on the road for the least cost. Today, however, the move into more of a blend of melody flute with Blood and Thunder means that better flutes have to be bought and each of these costs between £230 and £240.

Meanwhile the numbers of young recruits with the ability to master the music has ebbed to a trickle, sometimes barely enough to keep the band on the road. The Castlederg Young Loyalists Flute Band, however, has made a virtue of necessity and adapted its particular musical and parading style to the small numbers available, with a unique tight formation. This is a sharp contrast to the usual Blood and Thunder parading style, which sets out to fill the available thoroughfare with bodies and sound. The tight marching style and almost terse musical delivery enhances the volume and impact, and has won many admirers for the little band from the Derg.

'We played a few times last year with only four flutes,' Trevor points out. 'We even got an award last year for a parade when we only had four flutes in it. It was a talking point [in band circles] for a long time afterwards, so it was.' He also points out that the quality of the band's flute music holds out against the decibels that the big traditional Blood and Thunder outfits can manage. 'We had a band up in Portadown one night and they might have had forty flutes coming down the street. We were coming up from the bottom of the street and the big band had to actually stop playing because they couldn't match us and we just marched on ahead. There is satisfaction in being in a small band, after being in a big band. I would rather be in a small one, because you get far more respect from the crowd even. There is respect for coming from Castlederg and coming with a small band.'

Back when he was a founding member of the band, the Castlederg Young Loyalists was the only show in town for youngsters attracted to the Blood and Thunder movement. It had sole and immediate access to the fertile recruitment ground of the local Castlederg High School. Within a few years there were Blood and Thunder bands in Newtownstewart and Donemana, also drawing from the Castlederg school's catchment area, but the Castlederg Young Loyalists still held sway in the town. Now the band must compete with the rival attraction of the Pride of the Derg band which has gained a strong membership since it was founded only four years ago, by maintaining big and brash Blood and Thunder and keeping its music to the tried and tested.

'You could say that they [Pride of the Derg] were formed out of our band,' says Trevor. 'It was started after a few boys in our band left when we tightened up and tried to bring in strict rules about no drinking and what not. Under the new rules that were agreed, nobody was allowed to drink before we paraded, but they could do whatever they liked after the parade. A few members didn't like this and they set up another band. They would call themselves a heavy Blood and Thunder band, and we would put ourselves in between because we would play a mixture of melody and marches and this sort of thing as well as keeping some of the Blood and Thunder.' Because the Pride of the Derg band also draws on the recruitment field of the local high school, Trevor believes that the parent band has to be more astute in keeping up its ranks for the years ahead. 'That was one of the reasons why I wanted to get the young people in on the committee. They can keep the contact with the school and pull new members in.'

Since the start, the level of co-operation with the school has been good, helped no doubt by the fact that the founding bandmaster Derek Hussey taught there. Today, the desire to explore a more challenging musical range has been helped by

'Old Boys' model the various uniforms worn down the years by the Castlederg Young Loyalists Flute Band at the 30th anniversary dinner in Omagh.

Substitute bass drummer Michael steps in and out in Markethill.

Davy Lowry, foreground, and other fluters show their style in Markethill.

Bandmaster Trevor Donnell has to hoist the big drum in Magheraveely.

Parading through disputed Ferguson Crescent with Castlederg police barracks in the background.

The band passes under the controversial paramilitary flags on Killeter Road.

Supporters shelter as the mid-July weather rains on the Castlederg parade.

Retired Catholic parish priest, Canon Tom Breen, gets ready for the Twelfth parade in Dromore.

Parading through Dromore on Monday 13 July.

Piles of band equipment in the finishing field after the Twelfth parade.

Young band members take a break after the Twelfth parade.

CYL Old Boys gather at the graveside of Norman McKinley and Heather Kerrigan during a special 25th anniversary ceremony.

The current band parades across Castlederg Bridge in memory of fallen members.

CYL Old Boys bass drummer Robbie McKinley parades in memory of his brother Norman who was killed by the IRA.

Laying wreaths at the cenotaph on the 25th anniversary of the deaths of Norman McKinley and Heather Kerrigan.

A tricolour flies over disputed Ferguson Crescent and a poster advertises the big Republican rally and parade in Galbally.

The Castlederg Young Loyalists pass through Ferryquay gate in the Relief of Derry parade.

The Castlederg Young Loyalists Flute Band leads the local Black Preceptory through Ferguson Crescent.

The band bannerette and standards.

Castlederg Young Loyalists watch local rival band, the Pride of the Derg, form ranks for the Last Saturday parade.

Bass drummer Ian strikes a pose before the Last Saturday parade in Castlederg.

Castlederg Young Loyalists take their place in the Last Saturday parade.

Fans crowd around for the finale of the band's annual parade.

Fluter Ryan Burke proudly wears the new band uniform for the band's annual parade.

The band's bass drum which
has its name, motto and the
local Orange Lodge number
on it.

Castlederg Young Loyalists drummers go thundering through Coagh on the final
parade of 2009.

Band members Judy, Gordie, Joanne and Richard on what may be their final parade with the Castlederg Young Loyalists.

Outgoing bandmaster Trevor Donnell and his young assistant Davy Lowry after the final parade of 2009 in Coagh.

Richard Donnell (right) teaches a younger Davy Lowry and another recruit for the Castlederg Young Loyalists.

Castlederg Young Loyalists with their parade awards in 1984.

The Eleventh night bonfire in Castlederg before …

… and after.

David Doonan, a music teacher in the high school who has even helped to arrange a few tunes for the local band. The collaboration has rubbed off on the young band members and while all those still at school are studying music, they have combined with student members of other bands – notably the Red Hand Defenders Flute Band from Newtownstewart – to form a school Blood and Thunder band. The collaborative effort, named the West Tyrone Young Defenders, has taken part in a number of competitions and parades, while its members retain their primary membership of their own bands. The dual experience has inspired further enthusiasm.

At the age of sixteen, Davy Lowry is the assistant bandmaster of the Castlederg Young Loyalists and he has just completed his GCSE in music, having done his practical coursework and test on a military march, 'Air Force Blue', which is now in the Castlederg Young Loyalists repertoire. 'I heard it first on the flute and it sounded well and then I brought it in here and we learned it along with "Lannigan's Ball", so we did,' says Davy. 'I play it as a rock piece on the flute along with a drum kit and a rock and roll electric guitar. I played it as a rock piece in the music practical for GCSE and it went very well too, so it did.'

Music is more than an academic interest for this young band member: 'I started playing the flute three years ago and it was in the band here I learned to play. There were different tunes I wanted to play myself and if the band didn't play them, I just learned them myself. I took to it, I suppose, and

I was very interested in it,' he says. 'I'm keeping music on for A Levels now and for my actual coursework for GCSE I wrote two pieces and recorded them using the same flute.

'A few other ones did it [music GCSE] this year as well and there was a fellow piped and there's another fellow fluted too and he used to be in this band as well. Having the school in the town really helps the band for recruiting new members and we have four or five now from the school.'

While the band has always drawn recruits from the local high school, the combination of their recreational interest in Blood and Thunder band membership and their schoolwork is relatively recent, Davy points out. 'It was mostly started this year,' he says, adding that a major influence is music teacher David Doonan who 'encourages you to learn different tunes, so it's not just the work that's laid out for the exams. He would encourage you to learn hard things as well.'

While his musical taste does not yet extend to the work of classical flautist James Galway, who once played in a marching flute band, Davy admits, 'I would listen to different classical pieces. "Highland Cathedral" is lovely on the flute and the "Titanic" tune, that's lovely on the flute too. But there's all these different tunes I would try out. You can play the "Galway Girl" on the flute too and I'm getting the notes of "Sweet Caroline". So I'd always be trying to play different sorts of things and I also play with a dance band the odd time. The band I play with, they're a local band and there's just a few of us in it with a drum kit. One of them is a relation and I know the rest of them through the school too.'

Musical exploration through the school also inspired the setting up of the West Tyrone Young Defenders Flute Band at Castlederg High and it only started this year because of a change in school rules. 'This year at school we were allowed to practise in the music room. Mr Doonan said, "As long as you're in the music room and you don't take the flutes out of the music room, it is okay, but if yous are caught fluting about the school and making a racket and all, you won't be allowed your flutes in the school again. So you can have the room as long as you only use it for music." Then at music [class] one day, we decided it would be a good idea to set up the school band. We had enough people in the school to get a band started, so we did. It's made up of this band and the band in Newtownstewart. This year we had nine fluters, three drummers and a bass drummer.

'We are thinking of entering a competition now, a band competition for different styles of school band and we would come under the fife band – because fife is just a different name for a flute. Derek Hussey is entering us, or at least he's thinking about entering us for the competition,' says Davy, who clearly appreciates the adult backing for the school band efforts and the vindication of the value of his involvement in the Castlederg Young Loyalists Flute Band as his main recreational interest. However, he's not just a music nerd; he is also an enthusiastic member of the local football club in

Killen, a small Loyalist village not far from his own home just a couple of miles outside Castlederg. He is also a junior member of the Orange Order, one of the very few in the band and certainly the only Orangeman under twenty years old in the band.

'I have been brought up with the music. My dad has always been in pipe bands and my brother used to be in another flute band. Dad was in Drumlegagh Pipe Band. I had the bass drum of it here one night. I've always been interested in pipe band music and flute music too. I could listen to the pipes all day. My dad didn't pipe or anything, though; he played the big drum.

'I wanted to join a flute band, so I said this to my dad and he said this band [Castlederg] would be the best band to join because of the way it's run. He says it's very well disciplined and the rules in the band are good because you're not allowed to drink at parades. I'm always left off at my door and I'm not running about the town at night with a band uniform on me drinking or anything. The discipline was what he really liked about this band. At the end of the day, nobody wants their children out drinking and running about, I suppose. Every night we'd be out parading I'd be left right home to the door and all, so it's great that way. You feel well looked after in this band.'

As the assistant bandmaster, he has had to take on some of the burden from Trevor Donnell, including ensuring that the band continues to care for its young members. 'I'm still very young, I suppose, and this is still a learning process. I was very surprised when Trevor asked me if I would take on the assistant bandmaster role. Obviously he recognises something in me. But I get on with everybody in the band and while people would have their own close friends, there are just different cliques and together we form the band. Everybody sort of has their own people they'd hang about with and they would have people they would ring about various things, like things to do with the band, but I get on the best with everybody.'

As he assumes leadership of the band: '[I] would like to see one or two more fluters but at the minute I think everything's just great. We're doing piles of parades and the annual [parade] is getting bigger every year. So we are definitely moving forward.' Blood and Thunder bands, of course, have exuded young male testosterone since the movement began back in the 1970s. However, young Davy sees no need to maintain the customary male profile of the band. He perceives no problem with widening the gender balance and he points out that Judy, the only female fluter now in the ranks and the very first in the band's history, has blazed a trail that he would wish to continue. 'So long as everyone in the band can play well, that's all that should matter.' On the wider issues that have formed the backdrop to the introduction and evolution of Blood and Thunder bands, young Davy has no strong opinions other than his belief that all bands should adopt the same discipline as the Castlederg Young Loyalists.

As a recent recruit of only three years, he has no experience of the communal friction that resulted in the Castlederg Young Loyalists being prohibited from parading through parts of their home town. Born around the time of the ceasefires, his own life has coincided with one of the longest periods of peace in Northern Ireland since its creation. The dark years of the Troubles and their huge toll on his own community are the stuff of history books. In fact, history is a subject that he loves and would like to teach after university which he hopes to attend in Northern Ireland, rather than moving 'across the water' after his A Levels, like so many other young Protestant students from Northern Ireland. 'I can do everything to become a teacher in Northern Ireland. Even after university, I think I can do everything in Northern Ireland and I don't want to be anywhere else.'

As far as he is concerned, the dispute over parade routes is primarily down to the unacceptable behaviour of Blood and Thunder bands in the past. 'It doesn't really bother me at all, but I suppose it bothers some people,' he says. 'There's people that think – aw, a flute band, that's just people full [drunk] and running about the place, like. But I haven't seen it yet, so I haven't, in the three years I've been here with the band. I haven't seen anybody full when they're fluting or drumming. There are still some bands that would not have the discipline though.' Among the more unreconstructed or traditional Blood and Thunder bands, he would place the Castlederg Young Loyalists local rivals, Pride of the Derg, which would not put as much emphasis on discipline. 'They also draw recruits from the school, too, but there wouldn't be a wile pile [significant number] of school ones in it. It's more people in their twenties and up, but there's one or two from the school. They wouldn't have the same discipline or standard of music though.'

He has a brother and sister, but neither has been involved in the Castlederg Young Loyalists. His brother was in the Pride of the Derg band about four years ago, but he left after a while. Davy suggests that his brother might still be involved if he had not 'joined the wrong band. He used to drum but he doesn't do anything now.' His sister, meanwhile, was in the colour party for the award-winning Killen Pipe Band. As Davy says, 'She used to carry the pole for them.'

While hoping that Trevor Donnell does not bow out of the band completely when he finishes his term as bandmaster, he accepts that his mentor has undertaken a huge and vital role in helping the band, and the Blood and Thunder marching band culture it represents, to evolve in recent years. That is a contribution he wants to continue. 'I think that, because it has been so well disciplined under Trevor, the band has done really well. There's other people would not know what to do to keep our standards up, so I would hope that Trevor will not bow out altogether.' On his own ambitions with the band, 'I know that if I did become bandmaster, I would certainly not be changing any of the disciplinary rules.'

The band discipline centres around showing up for practice and parades in which the Castlederg Young Loyalists set out to represent their community in the best possible light while maintaining and asserting their cultural traditions through the music they play. It is an activity that occupies every weekend from May through September and into October. For a teenage boy, it is a daunting schedule of total commitment during a time when others are simply relaxing and 'hanging out' during school holidays. Young Davy has no hesitation however: 'I enjoy parading so I do, so it's not as if I'm going to complain, "I have to go to a parade this weekend". I enjoy doing it, but I have other interests as well and stuff I'd be doing as well. But parades would come first, so they would. It's a lot of work at the moment, but we do get a lot out of it by being in the band. We get a lot of recognition and we are mentioned in the papers and all for the way we play [in Quincey Dougan's weekly *Newsletter* column]. Because we are a small band and play the way we play, we do get a lot of notice from other bands as well. We all enjoy that. We know we're not a big band and we're not really going out to be big and loud when we parade. We want to play well and look good. I wouldn't really care how loud we were so long as everybody is playing well.'

Thursday, 4 June 2009

If some bands are very slow to move on from the raw form of Blood and Thunder, so too are their critics. Commenting in the daily *Irish News*, a leading columnist describes Loyalist intimidation in the Antrim village of Stoneyford: 'Their preferred form of intimidation – because it was safe, handy and personally cost-free – was their own menacing presence in the form of Orange Order and flute band marches through the village. Like poisonous smog, kick-the-pope band music wafts regularly from the village Orange Hall and envelops the nearby homes of Catholics. Like peacocks, they strutted around the village on foot or patrolled in their own cars.'[68]

A week before, band members in Newcastle, County Down, arrived for practice to discover that the Orange Hall had been burned in an arson attack. It is the start of the regular high summer tit-for-tat when band halls and GAA clubs are the chosen prime targets.[69] Yet the fact that such venues continue to provide invaluable recreational resources for young people and develop their academic interests as well, is conveniently ignored.

Meanwhile, mustering the flutes and side-drums and finding a bass drummer on loan for each parade has become the preoccupation of Castlederg Young Loyalists, and much of each practice session is taken up with trying to contact absent members to see if they can make it to scheduled parades. This weekend is the big one; the Kilcluney Volunteers' parade in Markethill on the first Friday of June has become the pinnacle of the annual calendar for the marching band community. It is a date that nobody wants to miss. On the following night, the Castlederg Young Loyalists are scheduled to parade in the tiny border hamlet of Magheraveely, County Fermanagh, but will the band have enough members to parade with any dignity? Young Davy Lowry has an important Orange Lodge meeting he must attend, while among his fellow fluters Niall is working late and he certainly can't get off until they have 'red up' (tidied up) and Johnny has a party he must attend. Meanwhile drummer Davy is going to be away in England. This means there will not be enough flutes to parade, Trevor decides, so he will have to notify the Magheraveely organisers to explain the band's absence. 'It's a real pity because it's a good wee parade and they come to us without fail every year,' he comments, obviously reluctant to let this one go.

There is more luck with the big Kilcluney Volunteers' event in Markethill and a show of hands indicates that everyone who is at the practice will be there. That prospect cheers everyone in the gathering, but there is some fresh concern when Trevor suggests that there is no point in going early. He explains that while they have lined up two bass drummers who are prepared to help out, they will have to parade with their own bands before they become available. 'So what's the point of going early and standing about all night?' There is an immediate chorus suggesting they should go early to watch the parade. 'Aye and how do we get the band together when it comes time to parade, if people are away off up the town and can't be found?' asks Trevor, who then relates the story of a particular but unnamed band member who was up the town watching the parade last year and missed parading himself. 'He was standing there watching the parade in his uniform and then we come along … and then later he came scolding down the road after us. But it was his own fault, standing about and we didn't parade until about half-eleven that night, so he had plenty of time to check back with us and still see a lot of other bands.'

That prompts another story told by Nicky, a member of the CYL Old Boys band who has been coming along for drumming practice and to help as a marshal for parades. One year when the band was parading for the Twelfth in Omagh, he says, they arrived in the county town only to find that the bass drum was not in the boot of the car that was supposed to bring it along. 'Then next thing an Ulsterbus pulls up behind the car and the driver steps down out of it with the drum. He had seen it sitting there in the middle of the road when he came along and so he stopped, picked it up and brought it on with them.'

One of the band members who is particularly anxious to get along to Markethill early is Johnny, who says the Kilcluney Volunteers' parade is his favourite in the whole year because it is the biggest. 'They had 105 bands at it last year,' he points out. 'Now that's some commitment there because they have to go to all the bands that go to theirs, but they have the numbers and they can split the band into two or even three if they need to, whereas numbers is always a problem for us because we're a small band.'

Now twenty-one years old, Johnny has been in the band for four years. He had already left school when he joined up. 'My friends were in it and they talked me into it,' he explains. 'I suppose it was a bit like joining a football club, but it grows on you then and you stay. I started playing the flute because that is what they were looking for at the time. I suppose if they had been looking for drummers, I'd have done that. Anyway, now it's something I really enjoy doing and it keeps me out of the pub, too,' says Johnny, who reckons that he knows about thirty tunes on the flute that he can play to 'parade level' without the need for much rehearsal. Like others in the Castlederg Young Loyalists, he is always enthusiastic to learn more music.

When he joined the band, Johnny was already an apprentice electrician, and since then he has completed his time. However, the downturn in the economy, and particularly the building trade, means he is out of work at present, so he has a lot of time to practise his flute as he doesn't have the cash to indulge in other recreational pursuits of young men his age. Besides, his friends are in the band and Ian, the injured bass drummer, is Johnny's best mate. He shifts uncomfortably when he admits that he was driving the car when the accident happened that left Ian with a broken arm and out of action for the band. However, he quickly points out that he could not have avoided the crash. 'Ian got the worst of it but the car was wrecked.'

The forced absence of his best mate as the bass drummer, he points out, highlights the struggle with numbers, which is 'constantly a problem' for the band. That, he believes is largely because of the age profile of the members in what has always been a youth organisation. Given the time commitment to achieving the standards that all the members want in their performance, and the tight discipline it entails, there tends to be a bigger turnover of band members as they develop other interests in life. By their mid-twenties, most members of the Castlederg Young Loyalists drop out as they settle down to other things in life. While they are still in the ranks, they must abide by the rigid standards they have all agreed on. 'The discipline is not something I would like, but it is there to keep the band looking well,' says Johnny. 'It's there for a good reason and the band looks good because of its discipline.'

Looking good and sounding better is the agreed purpose of the band and Johnny, who is the first member of his family to ever become a musician, feels that he is representing his community well every time he goes out on parade with the Castlederg Young Loyalists Flute Band. That is also what keeps him involved. 'We're a young group here so we are and we're getting better all the time. I'll stick around for a lock of years anyway and see what happens. I really enjoy it, so it's no bother.'

The need to replenish the ranks and bring on the standard of music has prompted the Castlederg Young Loyalists to spread the net wider. Timmy, who undoubtedly is the band's star fluter, chief musical arranger and occasional piccolo player, comes from Cookstown, about fifty miles away, at the far end of Tyrone. He joined the Castlederg Young Loyalists because he was friendly with Andy, the drummer who had moved home from Castlederg to Cookstown but continues to play drums with the local band.

'I was with the Sons of William in Cookstown for sixteen years, but I wanted a change and I decided to join the CYL here,' says Timmy. 'I always liked this band, they're a small outfit, and I really wanted to help them out as well.' He has been in the ranks of the Castlederg band for four years now, but most times he does not attend band practices for practical reasons. However, he keeps in touch constantly by phone and he helps and advises on tune arrangement with Bluetooth recordings. 'I was out on my first parade with the Sons of William in Cookstown when I was only eleven and I'm thirty-three now and we're still going,' says Timmy. 'But we have a good wee band here and it's getting along the best despite all the setbacks,' he adds proudly.

Early starts seem to encourage longevity of commitment and involvement in Blood and Thunder bands. Quincey Dougan, for instance, points out that he joined the Kilcluney Volunteers when he was twelve and during his early twenties the band was his entire social life. 'There was not a social life outside it and if you were out at all it was in the band uniform. I met my wife through the band and other people have done the same.

'My own personal history is that I'm in bands and my family has been in the Orange and in bands since time immemorial. I have two brothers and two sisters. The two sisters are members of another local flute band and my two brothers were in Kilcluney with me. They're not in it now because one is living in London and one is living in Belfast, but it was part of you here in this locality and the number of families that have band involvement is huge.'

Quincey sees the evolution of the Blood and Thunder band movement reflected in his own life and development. 'When I was younger I would have been pretty wicked, like. You know, I was very staunch, very hard-line and very extreme in my political views. But time mellows us all and you take wee things on board. I started becoming involved in promotional work and my interest was that I wanted to do the best I could for my own band and get it everything possible and build up the parade in the town too. So then it went that I was involved in community dialogue, which was a big thing, and I was in Dundalk or up the country and I was sitting down with people from other, different backgrounds. For far too long, unfortunately, my side of the house would have viewed even talking to somebody as being compromise, but I never viewed it as compromise. You're there telling people what you are; you're there trying to explain. That's not compromise. So I have come through that community dialogue and I have done many talks on bands. I've done a degree and I've always tried to look at the bigger picture because I thought that was the problem with our side – that we didn't look to see the bigger picture. The degree that I started was in Borderland Studies from Dundalk Institute.

I have done the third year of it, but last year my daughter had a very bad accident and badly injured her legs. So that happened in September when I was to start my fourth year, so I never got back, but I'll be going again part-time from September.

'Borderland Studies is about examining borders in every area – borders in language, in music, in the mind, and that cleared up a lot of stuff. I'm a big history buff as well. Old newspapers are like gold dust to me. I have a house full of old photographs. But the downfall of Unionism has been that straight ahead narrow viewpoint; plus with the whole communications upsurge, it means that with increased information now we have to look at the world and where we are in the context of the whole world. You know, people look at 12 July and say, "What are you doing celebrating something that's 300 or 400 years old?" Right, so what about 4 July in America; what about Bastille Day in France? Why are they at it? What about every country in the world where they have a similar festival … but when it comes to here, I'm a relic. This stuff has to start being addressed collectively so it has,' says Quincey, who has been a moving force behind the Ulster Bands Forum where these issues are discussed, as well as the recently founded Confederation of Ulster Bands.

Meanwhile, the work of channelling the energy of young people away from destructive behaviour is a vital task, he believes. Involving them in the Ulster Protestant cultural traditions of the marching band movement is a vital component in that. Quincey points out that rather than needing social and political conflict to maintain their momentum, the Blood and Thunder bands thrive in stable politics. Yet social and recreational trends can have a huge adverse affect on the bands.

'When the whole rave thing took off, the bands suffered hugely because of the amount of young people that drifted off into the raves and the drugs culture that came with it,' he recalls. 'It was phenomenal how that rave thing affected bands everywhere. But we kept going. Most bands did so because they were their own small body and autonomous, they didn't have to answer to anybody else. It was the same thing with Drumcree: while some bands benefited from increased numbers, I don't think we did, not massively anyway and only temporarily. But we've kept going. You see my band is the same as other ones throughout the country: rain, hail or shine, and even if it's down to five men, there'll be one man there who will keep that going. Because if we have one guy in the band and his dad and his grandfather before him were in the band, and he's in the band from five or six and he has about thirty years done, someone like that does not let these things go.'

CHAPTER 9

MARKETHILL TO MAGHERAVEELY AND BEYOND

Friday, 5 June 2009

There is no Ulster final in the keenly competitive world of marching bands, but if there was, the venue would certainly be Markethill, County Armagh, and the date would be the first Friday of June. On that day, Markethill belongs to the local Kilcluney Volunteers Flute Band for its annual parade and everyone in the marching band world knows it is the place to be. For those who enjoy heaps of loud, colourful entertainment for a paltry, voluntary contribution, this is as good as it gets. Starting at 7.30 p.m. to finish before midnight, the music is as varied as the hundred and more bands taking part and they include pipe, accordion and silver interspersed through the best melody flute and Blood and Thunder. In wave after wave, the bands strut their stuff through this small Unionist town on the cusp of Nationalist South Armagh, with the majestic Mourne Mountains forming an impressive silhouette skyline to the south-east. Make it to Markethill on the first Friday of June and you suddenly understand the huge amount of time, effort and expense put into the organisation, practice and fitting out of these bands. For Markethill is the catwalk and success here can bolster a band throughout the rest of the year, because the ensuing enhanced reputation attracts more recruits and more bands to its own parade.

Kilcluney has one of the best-travelled marching bands and this pays off when favours are returned for this parade. From Dunloy in north Antrim, Kilkeel nestling under the Mournes, from north, south, east and west Belfast and the surrounding localities of Antrim and Down, from throughout Armagh and Fermanagh, from Monaghan over the nearby border and from Tyrone as far west as Castlederg, bands make it to Markethill to return the visit of the Kilcluney Volunteers to their own parades. On arrival they line up along Fairgreen Road to parade through the town, along Coolmilish Road and Newry Street to the junction of the main Armagh to Newry road, then back by the war memorial again, through the town centre, to the starting point. Along the way they pass four independent judges and an estimated 15,000 spectators who line the route, especially the throng at the bottom of Main Street where bands generally pause for the gallery. This creates a concertina effect; for while the start of the parade is carefully marshalled to ensure a suitable gap between the bands, the loop in the town centre means that as many as five bands can be within fifty metres of each other.

A small traffic island beside the war memorial provides a marvellous vantage point to see the bands at close quarters – their earnest effort, pride, physical strain and concentration. For listening enjoyment, however, this isn't the choice spot. A cacophony of tunes bounces off the ears, while the drums, especially the big bass drums pounded with extra gusto at this juncture, certainly give the sound effect of thunder on an early summer night. Yet judging by the delight of the individual spectators, including a constantly growing number of band members who have completed their parade circuit, this is precisely what most people have come for. And they have come along in droves, with parked cars snaking back along the approach roads. While the police offer general guidance and ensure those not attending the parade can get through the traffic jam, parking is self-regulated and very efficient. As each vehicle slots into place, the occupants hurry off into the town. Many are in uniform and carrying instruments, some struggling with big drums. As one friendly visitor remarks casually on the walk into the town, you would be 'more than happy that it's a flute you have and not anything heavier' on the final uphill part of the 1.2-mile route through Markethill.

As the crowds converge on the crush barriers, Kilcluney band representatives are there with collection buckets and donors receive a little paper sticker with the band's name and a 'thank you' so they will not be asked to contribute again. Most visitors, including band members, donate a pound coin or two, but many slip five pounds, ten or even twenty and more into the buckets. With the huge sale of souvenir DVDs of this event, this provides the band's budget for the year. The more visitors, the more cash. Kilcluney Volunteers do not need to worry on this score, for in the world of marching bands, this is the equivalent of Glastonbury or the Oxegen Festival. Bands make a point of being here and being heard. So arriving at the bottom of the courthouse hill is like straying into the embarkation preparations for the D-Day landings sixty-five years ago, except this has a festival flourish provided by chip and burger vans and stalls selling brightly coloured tat. Young men and women in uniforms dart here and there directed by marshals in bright red jackets and holding clipboards. Even at the relatively early (by parade standards) hour of 8 p.m., the show is well underway and the first bands are finishing up at the masonic hall with a final air before dispersing with military precision. Among the early birds are local pipe and accordion bands demonstrating solidarity with their neighbours in the Kilcluney Volunteers Flute. As bands fall out and others march into their place, some linger on to talk to friends and greet acquaintances, see and applaud other bands or queue up at the food vendors. All the while, the stream of arriving spectators trickles through, heading up the hill towards the town centre as successive bands spill over and down the other side.

8 p.m. Along Fairgreen Road – which Belfast actor Dan Gordon (who does the voice-over on the souvenir DVD) suggests should be renamed 'Fairorange Road' for the first Friday of June – the sheer scale and precision of the event is apparent. In wave after wave, bands march to the starting point where the marshal on duty delays them until the band ahead has gone about 100 metres. This allows the spectators – and the judges – to concentrate on one band at a time. A small boy stands beside his father, who says, 'Here's the True Blues coming now.' The Armagh city band moves into place for the off signal. The toddler, dressed in a blue hoodie and blue combat trousers has a small drum on a harness that sits comfortably over both shoulders and he holds two full-size drumsticks in proper drumming style. As the band sets off, he beats his drum in almost perfect time. His proud father used to drum himself with a local pipe band and recounts to me how his wee boy couldn't wait to get at it despite being only three years old. 'A real True Blue little boy,' I remark. As the next band moves into place, the drummer dad remarks on the older age profile of the colour guard, pensioners lined up in front of a young Blood and Thunder band. 'It's great to see the older generation so involved,' he says, seemingly heedless of the fact that most traditional Unionist activities have trouble getting young people involved. 'But it's a great event for any age, a real family occasion,' he adds, as an extended family group of parents, grandparents and children take up viewing positions just beyond.

8.30 p.m. The frequency of pipe and accordion bands has dropped off, with the big sounds of Blood and Thunder taking over. And in the clear evening light, the incredible acrobatic performance of the drum majors is on display as they show remarkable dexterity with band-sticks and even acrobatic skills as they somersault and tumble along. The red-headed drum major of the Cormeen Rising Sons of William proves a real crowd pleaser with his mighty flourishes. Children watch in awe and then try to copy the moves with their toy band-sticks. Also grabbing the attention of onlookers are the bass drummers and some clearly aren't bothered about conserving energy. Most of the big bands have two bass drummers to swap around at strategic pauses. The substitute usually carries a spare drumhead in case one is ripped from the heavy pounding. Particularly flamboyant is the bass drummer of the Pride of Prince William from Lisburn, who pounds the drumheads with his beaters while lunging from side to side of the road, his face drawn in a grimace of concentration. But there is no such cavorting from any of the drummers of the Mourne Young Defenders from Kilkeel, whose 'Drum salute' is high precision with the eight side-drummers juggling their sticks in perfect unison while not missing a beat.

9 p.m. Up the town, bands that marched briskly into the fray are beginning to flag as they crest the steep Main Street. Further back, outside the Victoria Bar, the Markethill Protestant Boys Flute Band pauses for cheers with a sustained bout from the bass drummer. The crowds are packed thickly here and family groups exploit every vantage point between cars, whose occupants remain aloof and clog up the route. Some cars also provide ready stores for young men and women who drink from bottles of beer and alco-pops. A few seem to have been at it for a while, and their raucous cheers and shouts seem out of place, yet are no different from a big football match gathering. Here, the team colours are red, white and blue, orange, purple and the green of Northern Ireland football tops. A novelty stall is festooned in blue Chelsea FC scarves, despite the fact that the only band from England here is from Liverpool's Everton Road.

9.30 p.m. The pubs are packed and the town centre convenience shop is doing a lively trade, even with its grocery aisles cordoned off. There is a queue of youngsters for soft drinks, sweets and savoury snacks, and a few patrons file to and from the off-licence in the rear. Outside, meanwhile, the war memorial provides a playpen for young children who run round and round the black marble plinth to the beat of the bands. 'Look not on this memorial with sorrow but with pride and try to live as nobly as those who served and died', the gold lettering advises. Respect for those noble dead is apparent as colour party vanguards lower their standards when passing. Bands returning up Newry Street finish tunes and remove caps, clasping them to chests in a brisk salute by the plinth before striking up again.

10 p.m. As daylight turns to gloom, the bands pour through to occasional cheers for some notable performance. The Liverpool band earns hearty applause, as does the Upper

Falls Protestant Boys, whose home in a tiny orange island in the green sea of West Belfast, is spoken of in hushed respect by bandsmen who have been there for the annual parade – due to take place tomorrow (6 June). They talk of the special atmosphere in terms that suggest West Berlin during the 1949 airlift. The continuous wave of bands comes thundering through and, every so often, small gaggles of camp followers come in their wake, supporting their bands, defying detractors and making their mark on Markethill.

11 p.m. Back along Fairgreen Road, a funfair is in full flow with flashing lights and electronic sounds. Nearby, a local mouldings factory is working overtime while the steady flow of bands makes its way along the route. At the starting-point, the Castlederg Young Loyalists Flute Band is ready to go but for the lack of a bass drummer. Despite all the worries, there are nine flutes and four side-drums on hand, besides the colour party of Kenny, Helen and Michaela. Trevor Donnell explains that the arrangements with two bass drummers have fallen through, but a young drummer now parading with the Dunamoney Flute Band will help. Everything now hinges on his turning up. Trevor is nervous. 'With a drummer from a different band, you never know how it will go. The band he is in plays slower and that won't work for us.' Castlederg's Young Loyalists bide their time. Flag girl Michaela says a few of them have been here since the very start of the evening, having left band member Niall off in Belfast for the ferry to England. Posing proudly with her banner, she is confident her band will do well in Markethill. 'We did this last year and we had a colour party of seven then,' she says. 'We had seven right up to about the Twelfth and then it fell off, but we are every bit as good now.'

11.30 p.m. Word has come through that the bass drummer has been waiting at the wrong place and is hurrying along now to join the band. Trevor says they'll get going just as soon as he gets there. The drummer arrives in a lather of sweat, with no time to change. Trevor consults starting marshal Quincey Dougan and then suddenly, the band is off, marching smartly along to the tune of 'Lannigan's Ball'. No bands simply take this parade in their stride and one knows instinctively, as soon as they start, neither does the Castlederg Young Loyalists Flute Band. Even in the panic of need, the elements have fitted together, the substitute bass drummer is working perfectly and obviously enjoying his second turn around Markethill, and the band are putting on the best display they can. Even the youngsters milling about the big funfair stop to pay attention.

11.40 p.m. Kenny takes a wrong turn and his colour party leads the band through the throng on the wrong side of the war memorial without a noticeable slowing of pace as the crowd parts like the Red Sea and the Castlederg Young Loyalists step into the Promised Land of the town centre. Strutting to the tune of 'Go Man Go', the Castlederg Young Loyalists head up the hill with the bass drummer holding up well despite rivulets of sweat disappearing into the folds of his out-of-place Dunamoney uniform. Over the brow at last and down to where other bandsmen burst into a round of applause as Trevor gives the final order and the band falls out.

12 p.m. The Kilcluney Volunteers headed off in the wake of the Castlederg band for their hometown triumph and can be heard in the background. This night belongs to them and the Castlederg boys and girls are more than happy that everything worked out in the end. The final leave-takings are made quickly and they head off up the road lugging their equipment for the journey home.

Saturday, 6 June 2009

If Markethill is akin to the glorious Twelfth for the marching bands, Magheraveely has to be the equivalent of the 'Scarva Sham Fight'[70] – a great night, but one not to be taken too seriously. In contrast to the efficiency and sheer scale of the Kilcluney Volunteers' event, Magheraveely's Pride of the Village parade on the following night exudes the rustic charm of a bygone era. Despite earlier worries, the Castlederg Young Loyalists have managed to find enough flutes to attend.

Set in a tiny hamlet with a population of 254 in the 2006 Census, Magheraveely is off the beaten track, two miles from Clones where I grew up. Even in the 1960s and 1970s, we recognised that the tiny Fermanagh hamlet on our doorstep was off the radar of the modern world – a small corner preserving social distance and Protestant proprieties along the sometimes deadly frontier.

It was here that Northern Ireland's Minster for Enterprise (and temporary First Minister) Arlene Foster spent her formative years. Little has changed since and those who turn up seem surprised when the parade actually starts just an hour behind schedule. It has a lot to recommend it to the 'last chance before midnight' Castlederg Young Loyalists Flute Band, who are invariably the penultimate band at parades. Yet driving from Clones past the landmark 'King Billy's Tree' at Knockballymore, change is apparent in the absence of the huge British army checkpoint of my memories that once guarded this approach. Now there is nothing to indicate a state frontier and the first evidence that I have passed into Northern Ireland comes when I reach the village bedecked in Union Jacks with a banner proclaiming 'Magheraveely Flute Band – Celebrating 80 Years 1929–2009'. This parade, with a Parades Commission notification of fifty-nine bands, 1,400 participants and an additional 1,000 supporters is to be the biggest event ever in Magheraveely, and it is happening unbeknownst to ninety-nine per cent of those living within a three-mile radius. On the Knockballymore Road a hand-painted sign directs traffic into a recently mowed meadow and a marshal on duty suggests it 'might be handier for getting out afterwards'. It is noticeable that the village, about a hundred metres up the road, is quiet, apart from the lonely skirl of bagpipes in the evening air. With the scheduled start only five minutes off, I check with the marshal. 'Och, you're in Fermanagh now, so we'll be going by Fermanagh time ...' He notes another car pulling into the field with a southern registration. 'Or maybe even Monaghan time,' he adds with a hearty laugh.

8.30 p.m. A leisurely stroll through the village takes all of five minutes, even with a stop for ice cream. The long wait begins but there is a relaxed air about the place, even among band members ambling down to the local Orange Hall, the designated starting point. Tea, sandwiches and traybakes are available there, but the main focus is the Oasis Bar, which is soon packed to capacity with patrons outside on the footpath and more heading through the entry to the marquee at the back for overspill and dancing. I am assured this will be 'heaving' by the end of the night.

Many bands have come from the Clones area. Angela Graham from Drum Accordion Band arrives with her daughter Catherine and they stop for a chat. Angela extends a warm invitation for the Drum 'picnic' on 15 July. The word 'picnic' is used in the southern border counties to describe band parades in isolated Protestant communities, while public attention focuses on the annual pre-Twelfth carnival in Rossnowlagh, County Donegal. We discuss the imminent end of Angela's job with the cross-border Clones Erne East Partnership because of the end of EU peace funding. There is still a huge amount of work needed to get people to explore and appreciate the cultural life and activities of neighbours from the other side.

With her experience, Angela remarks, 'Yes, it will happen, but you have to give people time, all the time they need ...' With that, she heads off to the Orange Hall.

9 p.m. Suddenly the silence is shattered by the staccato rhythms of Lambeg drums launching the parade to mark eighty years of the host band. The thunder is raised on Malacca canes wielded by members of the Lisnaskea Lambeg Drum Club, men with taut, muscular arms. Florencecourt Old Gate Flute Band is first out on parade, followed by small bands from Roslea and Wattlebridge, Aghadrumsee and Inver, all in Fermanagh, then from Drum, Cappagh, Druminan and other localities in County Monaghan. Interspersed among them are the big bands from Omagh, Cookstown, Lisbellaw, Keady and Killylea. The neighbouring Newtownbutler Border Defenders Flute Band is not here. A young representative was around earlier to explain that there has been a bereavement. However, word is that some bands at another parade in nearby Tempo will be coming later.

9.30 p.m. My name is called and I spot a Castlederg Young Loyalists uniform in the small crowd at the corner. Neil Johnston has been in touch with the others by mobile phone. 'They're in Maguiresbridge and should be here in about fifteen minutes or so,' he reports, just as several other Castlederg bandsmen arrive from Cookstown. 'I was talking to some of the stewards and they say we can just do the return part if we're late.' Meanwhile, in the small village atmosphere, nobody seems too put out by the lack of formalities. Down from the crossroads, two police officers are talking to a motorist. A man in a marshal's jacket nods at them and says, 'Wish them boys'd get away on from out of here.' I suggest they are just here to 'keep an eye on things'. 'We don't need them keeping an eye on anything,' says the steward, nodding towards the pub and winking, impatient to get to the real business of the night, once the formalities are out of the way.

10 p.m. The crowd outside the pub has ballooned onto the street as bands parade into the distance. A brief lull and then the Lambeg drums raise another roll of thunder to signal the return. Soon the ceremonial drummers reach the crossroads and a boy with a miniature Lambeg has joined them. The canes are splintering as the drummers stop and unharness their gear. Another couple of men step in, check the tension of the goatskin drumheads by pulling on the criss-crossed linen ropes and haul them on. One drum is decorated as if it has seen action down the years; the other is blank, perhaps on its maiden tour of Magheraveely. Harnesses are adjusted around necks and shoulders, and the drummers set off for the Orange Hall while their young apprentice tries to keep up. Soon the bands are following along in their wake, as the crowds grow. A family group edges to the front to inform some others that they have come from Tempo and the bands that paraded there are now here in Magheraveely.

10.30 p.m. Again the local bands are in the vanguard as lingering daylight fades on successive ranks marching out of the gloom. The Blood and Thunder bands from Montober and Lisbellaw, and the Omagh True Blues come along; the latter dressed in casual blue bomber-style jackets with a bass drum with the printed motto: 'Hit with pride, beat with passion'. Then more bands pass with drum majors doing acrobatic juggling tricks, pausing to play to the gallery outside the Oasis Bar. The bass drummers come into their own here to the delight of the crowd. In a minivan parked beside me, small heads keep popping up through the sunroof to check what is happening. Each time, the head seems to belong to a different small boy. One spots my camera, pops back down and, in an instant, four grinning small boys are peeking out of the roof with another smiling out from a side-window.

10.45 p.m. A deafening skirl brings Enniskillen's Pride of Erne Pipe Band into the central arena where the pipers form a circle around bass drummer Willie Smith. The crowd strains forward and others spill out the Oasis doors. Willie pounds the drumheads while wheeling and lurching around the circle in a Blood and Thunder performance – very different to the usual powder-puff drumming of pipe outfits. The delighted crowd demands more; the pipes are off again and so is Willie to roars of approval. The tune ends and the crowd calls for more, but Willie can't oblige. He slumps onto his drum, shoulders hunched and the beaters drop to his sides. The pipers form ranks and, as the crowd scampers out of their way, they march off. Willie recovers and picks up noticeably as he marches into the distance.

10.55 p.m. The crowd seems to lose interest and the

hubbub of conversation rises outside the pub as the remaining bands march past. New arrivals to the hostelry – most in band uniforms – push through to the facilities beyond. A man with a video camera has been recording the proceedings with the frequent co-operation of the stewards. Suddenly he springs to attention and says to me, 'Here's a great wee band coming now.' From the gloom the Castlederg Young Loyalists emerge. Kenny with the banner leads three side-drums, eight flutes and, right in the middle, Trevor Donnell pounds it out on the bass. The different style attracts the pub crowd which strains forward expecting another gallery performance. However, the Castlederg Young Loyalists thunder through. Barely around the adjacent corner, they halt, finish the tune and fall out to a breathless command from Trevor who seems shattered as he is helped out of the drum harness for several moments of deep breathing before he can chat. Yet he is clearly delighted the band was able to make it and he explains they had to wait for young Davy Lowry to finish his Lodge meeting and then traffic along the way held them up. 'But we made it in the end and that's what matters.'

11.10 p.m. The flutes are put away into the white belt pouches, drums are hoisted onto shoulders and the Castlederg Young Loyalists Flute Band ambles back to the pub where the host band performance ends in raucous cheers. Then, as the family groups drift off home, the remaining crowd filters into the pub to celebrate the 'pride of the village'.

Wednesday, 10 June 2009

East Bank Protestant Boys Flute Band host an annual fundraising procession along Derry's city walls with twenty-three bands, including the Castlederg Young Loyalists. Melody flute, Blood and Thunder and accordion bands are all present. The hosts finish the night with their 'outstanding' rendition of 'Killaloe'.[71]

Friday, 12 June 2009

A caller to my door seeks donations for new flags to be put up around our housing estate. I express disapproval of flags being left up until they wear down to dirty rags. He says these flags will be taken down at the end of summer, washed and put up again next year. 'We've got to put up the flags to keep the Taigs out!' says he. I pay my fiver and say nothing!

That evening, twenty-two bands of mixed genres from Fermanagh, Tyrone and Monaghan take part in Ballina-mallard Accordion's annual parade in the north Fermanagh village, but the day's largest parade is in Rathfriland, County Down, with fifty-six bands out for the local Pride of the Hill's annual parade. Another large Friday night parade, at which the Castlederg Young Loyalists are in attendance, takes place in Magherafelt for Dunamoney Flute Band, where 'the distinctive Curran Flute with their skeleton drums, the strong flautists of the Cookstown Sons of William Flute, the Giant's Causeway Protestant Boys who have recently had a new lease of life injected into the band, and the host bands themselves were all highlights of the evening'.[72]

Saturday, 13 June 2009

In Belfast, the Regimental Bands of the Ulster Volunteer Force are on parade in the east of the city, while the West Belfast Volunteers Flute Band host their annual event on the Shankill Road. Parades are also held in Dervock and Armagh city with the Armagh True Blues' event the biggest of the weekend, 'the entire town reverberating to the sounds of flute and drum'.[73]

Thursday, 18 June 2009

Castlederg Young Loyalists bass drummer Ian stops for a chat and tells me the cast on his forearm will be off in a couple of weeks. He hopes to get back to his big drum immediately and says he really has been missing it. Not half as much as the band misses him at the Orange Hall, where the practice has begun with two new band members, a fluter who left the band to join the Red Hand Defenders in Newtownstewart and has come back and will be travelling to Scotland with the band for the annual 'Glasgow Twelfth' parade; and a young trainee fluter. Every so often, bandmaster Trevor calls over to the former defector, 'Have you got that one, Stevie?' 'Aye it's just the new ones.' So the band takes extra time with 'Lannigan's Ball' for his benefit.

Yet finding temporary stopgaps for the big hole in the

heart of the band has become an urgent weekly task. While the band can make the parade in Keady tomorrow night, it seems certain it will miss four others the following weekend. Marching bands can ill-afford to snub neighbours, and missed parades have an impact on the band's own parade when favours are returned. This could seriously affect revenue. The Keady parade will feature Willie Smith from Enniskillen on the Castlederg band's big drum. He has already filled Ian's role in Derry. "He burst one of the drumheads and had to finish the parade with only the one,' says Trevor, who is reminded of a visit to Scotland years ago when he was the bass drummer. He burst two drumheads on the various parades around Glasgow and, on their final night back in the hall, the sole remaining spare drumhead broke as well. One of the big Scotsmen took the drum, put it over his head and danced about wearing it around his waist all night. He points to the bass drum now used by the CYL Old Boys, 'That's it there; that's the drum he wore that night.'

One final matter before the post-practice meeting breaks up is an invitation from Strabane District Council for band representation at a meeting about flags on the following Thursday in the Derg Valley Leisure Centre. The flags issue has raised concerns on both sides of the community, the invitation letter says, and it is proposed to set up a Flags and Emblems Forum to avoid provocation. 'I want you all to be clear about what this is about,' says Trevor. 'When some people saw this letter, they said the council was trying to stop people putting up our traditional flags completely. That's totally wrong. I'm told that they have no trouble with us putting up our flags. The problem is the flags that are put up and never taken down … and I'm talking about our flags, the GAA flags, and all the rest. We've no problem in trying to control the problem because we'll be putting up our flags at the end of June and we'll be taking them down again in September after our parade. And the same goes for the other side with GAA flags or the other flags.' He glances around the room. 'What do they put them up for? Is it the Easter Rising or something?' In fact, on the Nationalist side, flags are really only put up for GAA matches.

Friday, 19 June 2009

Castlederg Young Loyalists are among about four dozen bands lining out for the Drumderg Loyalists parade in Keady, County Armagh. Other parades draw a similar number of bands for Boveedy Loyalists in Kilrea, County Derry; Curran Flute, where twenty bands parade, also in County Derry; and Benburb Pipe with ten bands in County Tyrone.[74]

Saturday, 20 June 2009

The Pride of the Maine Flute Band from Ballymena, County Antrim, issues an unreserved condemnation of the unruly behaviour of an unrelated band during a parade in the town on June 6 when 'provocative' music was played and insults were hurled at Catholic parishioners outside their church in

Harryville. The apology is in the parish bulletin of the Church of Our Lady, and the Pride of the Maine band says the other band stopped off while returning from an event elsewhere. 'The organisers of the Pride of the Maine march condemn unreservedly the behaviour of the members of the other band and deeply regret the offence caused to their Catholic neighbours,' the apology states. The band also contacted parish priest Fr Paul Symonds, who describes the band's response as 'encouraging' and an indication of how much community relations have improved since the sectarian murder of Catholic teenager Michael McIlveen in May 2006. The priest is delighted that the annual Pride of the Maine parade on 6 June passed off without incident, with about seventy bands and around 2,500 participants following a route that passed close by All Saints Catholic church in the predominantly Nationalist area of the town. An observer says, 'The parade as it passed All Saints was conducted in a very respectful manner. The music was appropriate and of a non-sectarian nature.'[75]

Also on that day, fifteen bands take part in the Strain Lightbody Memorial Flute Band's parade in Newtownards, County Down, forty-five in the Finaghy True Blues parade in Taughmonagh, Belfast; Portadown True Blues attract forty-five bands to the 'Hub of the North' in County Armagh; Tullaghans Sons of Liberty Flute Band in Ballymoney, County Antrim, has almost fifty bands in its parade and Bellisle Flute has eight bands parading at Carrybridge, County Fermanagh. Meanwhile, a parade for the republican

Kevin Lynch Memorial Flute Band in Dungiven, County Derry, features three bands.[76]

Monday, 22 June 2009

The Orange Order rejects a call by Northern Ireland's deputy first minister to withdraw all its parades from 'Catholic areas'. Martin McGuinness made his plea at the annual Sinn Féin commemoration at Wolfe Tone's grave in Bodenstown, County Kildare, saying that while there were hundreds of Orange parades, only a few cause controversy and 'it is these I want to focus on'. An Orange Order spokesman says this is 'a disappointing attack on the Protestant community' and adds, 'they have totally failed to understand that parading is an integral part of the Protestant culture'.[77]

Wednesday, 24 June 2009

Armagh city hosts a parade by the small Allistragh Flute Band from the fringe of the city, with thirty bands taking part; Mosside Rising Sons of Ulster has a good showing of about thirty-five bands in County Down; and Desertmartin, County Derry, has another thirty-five bands for the joint parade of Desertmartin Accordion and Cranny Flute bands.[78]

Thursday, 25 June 2009

Parade in Orritor near Cookstown, County Tyrone, for Drumnaclough Flute Band has a turnout of about thirty bands.[79]

Friday, 26 June 2009

There is a huge parade of forty bands in tiny Mountnorris, County Armagh, for the John Hunter Accordion Band, most of whose members are directly descended from the eponymous founder. In County Down, thirty-five bands compete in the Ballinahinch Protestant Boys Flute Band parade; while in Armoy, County Antrim, the Pride of the Park parade has thirty-two bands; and in County Tyrone, Trillick Pipe Band is expecting nine or ten bands; while in neighbouring County Fermanagh, Lisnaskea Lambeg Drum Club makes arrangements for fifteen bands in its parade. Across the border in County Monaghan, Druminan Flute Band hosts its annual event with eight bands, including neighbours Drum Accordion as well as the Pride of Ballinran Flute from County Down, which both paraded earlier in Mountnorris.[80]

Saturday, 27 June 2009

The Kilkeel parade for Pride of Ballinran Flute Band, with thirty bands marching the route from the harbour to the town centre, has a strong showing of bands, both local and from County Armagh, with a good turnout of melody flute bands; Magherafelt hosts the thirtieth anniversary parade of Ballymoughan Purple Guards Flute Band who turned out sixty members in new uniforms along with a total line-up of forty bands for the night; and in Ballymoney, where Eden Accordion hosts its annual parade, there is a tally of some forty bands.[81]

CHAPTER 10

BYGONE DAYS OF YORE

One short grainy sequence stands out in the video footage included in the commemorative CD-DVD package of the thirtieth anniversary of the Castlederg Young Loyalists Flute Band. It is right in the middle of a two-hour film archive between successive scenes of the band at various stages of its history. In the other sequences, the band members wear different style uniforms as they parade behind ornate banners held aloft by tightly disciplined colour parties. In many sequences, they play martial hymns such as 'Onward Christian Soldiers' and are followed by orderly ranks of Orangemen, Sir Knights of the Royal Black Preceptory and well-matured Apprentice Boys of Derry. In others, they play Irish and Scottish airs and tunes from stage shows and films in an expanding repertoire. Most show the band parading through towns, villages and cities; others show them marching along country roads in summer sunshine to the emphatic strains of Blood and Thunder music. One lengthy sequence is of the Castlederg Old Boys and their inclusion offers the added entertainment of matching them to their youthful presence in other sequences as youthful members of the Castlederg Young Loyalists Flute Band. Yet not even the inclusion of the painful interview by BBC correspondent Fergal Keane with Kathleen Darcy, the widowed mother of the young bandsman shot dead by the IRA, stands out as starkly as the sequence that begins at '1:17:23' on the timer and lasts just under fifteen minutes.

It opens as a lone drummer gives a mustering beat on his side-drum and a group of boys and young men in fancy dress mill about in front of the camera (the Eleventh Night parade is a recreational event rather than an official parade, so band members wear casual clothing or fancy dress). The scene shifts to families in summer clothes strolling down an eerily empty street. In the background, a steel security fence seals off the town centre which has, in local memories, on a number of occasions been 'reduced to rubble' in IRA bomb attacks. A younger Kathleen Darcy walks with neighbours and friends, smiling happily for the camera.

Then four smiling young women stride confidently towards the camera in Priests Lane which runs between Young Crescent and Ferguson Crescent, the local interface where two roads branch off towards Castlefinn in County Donegal. The border is a mere couple of miles away and the huge, heavily fortified Castlederg police station dominates the junction opposite the old schoolhouse that has been turned into the Scholars Bar. The four young women wear bright T-shirts – one pink, one white and two lime green

– high-heeled shoes and summer cotton straight skirts hemmed about six inches above the knees. Their hairstyles are unmistakeably early 1980s – short, semi-permed bobs – and they carry flags resting in halter lanyards around their necks – the Union flag, Scottish Saltire, the Red Hand of Northern Ireland and an Orange standard. The flag girls fan out to fill the entire width of the street in the grainy video footage and they clearly are enjoying themselves enormously as members of the Castlederg Young Loyalists Flute Band in fancy dress outfits spill out in their wake, dancing and swaggering through the heartland of Nationalist Castlederg playing 'Here Lies a Soldier'.

Suddenly a lone RUC officer with a moustache is seen standing on full alert, his expression grim. Between the female colour party and the band, British soldiers in combat helmets and battle fatigues appear, guns at the ready. They take up firing positions around the pub and the police station, alert, watchful. More soldiers are positioned around a dark van facing back down the town towards The Diamond. One soldier has a Labrador dog on a short leash moving into position further up the Castlefinn Road at the Catholic church.

The music grows louder as the drummers and fluters move right past the camera lens. Two drum majors are twirling band-sticks while two boys, dressed as babies in improvised nappies and sucking dummies, skip through the ranks banging cymbals. The six side-drummers stride along, one dressed in a rabbit outfit, another as a light blue walrus and another as a clown. Behind them are three bass drummers wearing combat uniforms, berets and dark glasses, giving it their all. The fluters, also in costume, are jubilant as they march down Ferguson Crescent towards the Killeter Road. Some kids on bicycles, a lone police officer and a few mothers with babies in push-buggies follow in their wake. As they pass, two teenage girls notice the camera. One waves, and they all move along, leaving only one heavily armed RUC officer to hold back a car at the mouth of the Kilclean Road.

Scene shift, and the band emerges from The Diamond into Main Street and stops between the Derg Inn and the Castle Inn. The thunderous drumming which has provided a link to the previous scene recedes and the haunting strains of 'The Road to the Isles' becomes audible. Marking time, the flag girls shift jauntily from one foot to the other, hips swaying. They move into a tighter formation with the drummers, turning their backs to the camera, dancing to the tune, as the fluters march in circles around them. The fluters are in clown outfits, fancy dress women's garb and one puny figure wears a caveman outfit. The crowd of spectators gathers closer and several onlookers take photos. A toddler comes out to dance and another grim-faced policeman moves slowly from right to left across the foreground.

The scene shifts again and band members, reformed into ranks, shout out a jubilant 'Yeow' as they march jauntily through a throng of supporters at the side of the Derg Arms.

The young 'caveman' leans back and howls to the heavens. Scene shift, and the drum majors perform their stick acrobatics and the two youngsters in fancy dress wearing 'nappies' and banging cymbals prance through the now stationary ranks as they thunder out 'Derry's Walls'. As the camera pans slowly, palls of thick dark smoke are seen billowing through the air from a raging bonfire in the near background with frantic flames leaping about its surface. A close-up shows that many fluters, as well as the bass drummers, wear paramilitary-style outfits. The camera moves back to the colour party, shoulders and hips moving to the rhythm. As it moves away, one of the flag girls lowers her pointed flagpole and gives the drummer in front, dressed in a bunny outfit, a slight poke in his cotton-tail. There is a shrill whistle and a renewed chorus of loud 'Yeow' cheers from off camera and the band is back into marching formation.

The camera now moves through the ranks of the fluters, more combat jackets are now apparent and a bearded figure in an Ulster Constabulary uniform is talking to another man, a young Derek Hussey. Then a lone shrill whistle and Hussey's voice calls 'Quick march'. To the beat of a side-drum, the ranks move off with a defiant roar. Back they march through the town once more and with the black smoke rising through the twilight, the houselights suggest that Castlederg is ablaze as the band prances along in celebration. The whistle gives two shrill blasts and the sequence draws to a close on a line of drummers facing the flutes with bandmaster Hussey leading them in 'God Save the Queen'. The curt 'band dismiss' and the ranks are broken.

For an outsider, these video sequences provide a remarkable insight into the past of the Castlederg Young Loyalists Flute Band. At first, the episode seems no more than the simple, unbridled pleasure of local people engaged in a small town public celebration of their heritage. Yet this is actually a glimpse of an event never witnessed by the overwhelming majority of people living in Castlederg at that time. This is an exuberant and triumphal celebration, an annual ritual that once brightened the life of a small frontier Loyalist community during a very dark period of its history; a public event asserting territorial control of the town that involved huge security operations by the police and the British army with the implied assurance that such favoured treatment could go on forever. For make no mistake about it, the episode captured in this short film documentary belongs to the Loyalists of Castlederg and most of their Nationalist neighbours went out of their way to avoid it. Far from a mid-summer carnival for all, it is a unique visual and audio record of an occasion that still marks the high point of that community's annual calendar; yet it can never again be celebrated in a similar manner.

The contrast between then and now is stark and, even looking back over the short history of the Blood and Thunder bands, those who were most deeply involved at the start acknowledge the distance they have come. The Castlederg

Young Loyalists founding bandmaster Derek Hussey recalls the days of the band from the start in 1977 when 'quite a few bands were formed around that period of time'. Some believe that setting up a Blood and Thunder band is 'relatively cheap and easy'.[82] However, in most cases it involves huge community effort and at least the nodding approval of the local Unionist establishment. In Castlederg, the Bridgetown Orange Lodge called a public meeting to discuss the imminent demise of the Lodge's accordion band. Before having its own accordion band, Bridgetown had a pipe band attached to the Lodge; and even before that, there was a flute band.

'So in a way it was getting back to the original,' says Derek Hussey. 'Flutes had to be bought and, in fairness to the Lodge, they allowed the band to take the accordions which could then be sold off to buy some Miller-Brown flutes, but after that there was some fund-raising to buy the first flutes. There were the usual draws, dances, collections around the doors and many had collection cards and initially the band was very well supported by the public. Band practices were held in Bridgetown Orange Hall, although we weren't a Lodge band. We were very much attached to Bridgetown Lodge and the Lodge allowed the band to be financially and organisationally independent, provided that they were prepared to provide the Lodge with music on the Twelfth and any other occasions that they needed. And we also developed a relationship with the local Black Preceptory as well as the local Apprentice Boys.'

The original bandmaster says that his appointment was a matter of convenience rather than any specialist musical contribution he might make to the band. 'When the initial public meeting was held, I was originally elected band treasurer. But it just so happened that I knew some people from Omagh, particularly members of the Omagh Protestant Boys [Flute Band] and their fluters and their drummers came down to help us out at the very beginning and they were very beneficial to the band. I presume that because I was the guy who knew the fellows from Omagh, I was initially appointed bandmaster.'

Initial band numbers were relatively modest. 'At the very beginning when we started practising, you are talking around the thirty to three dozen and, as the band developed, it built up until we had on our dedication night [Saturday, 22 October 1977] … I am not sure of the exact figure but it was something like forty-two flutes, a couple of bass drums and ten or twelve side-drums and a couple of cymbal players. It was a big band but big bands would have been the vogue at that time.'

While the band was a secular organisation, it was unmistakably Protestant from the outset and the hymn sung at that dedication ceremony was one that has encapsulated the consciousness of Ulster Protestantism during the years of conflict: 'O God our help in pages past / Our hope for years to come / Be thou our guard while troubles last / And our eternal home.' At the dedication, the band played 'The

Ramblin' Ulsterman' a prelude perhaps to the years to come when the band would 'blast' its tunes 'all o'er the land', in the words of its own 'Castlederg' anthem sung by Derek Hussey on band recordings.

In the early days, of course, funds were sparse. The initial band uniform was chosen for simplicity and practicality, as well as availability at relatively short notice. Derek Hussey recalls, 'The first uniform was orange jerseys, white shirts, black trousers, a large purple dicky bow, and a purple beret with an orange plume. The orange jerseys were sourced locally in a factory just outside Castlederg, which sadly is no longer there. The trousers were from a local clothes shop; the dicky bow, plus the berets and plumes, were indirectly from Scotland via a shop in Belfast. In my time, I can clearly recall one, two, three uniforms, but I finished as band master in 1993 or 1994 … around that time … and I can think of quite a few other uniforms since then. I would imagine the band are moving towards double figures in the uniforms they have had.'

Big numbers and uniform dress created a collective identity for the young band members, but a more lasting bond was forged in blood with the murders of Norman McKinley and Michael Darcy during the first decade. The sense of British identity was nurtured on the road, well beyond the much more limited calendar of parades back in those early days. Derek Hussey believes that it benefited enormously from trips 'across the water', which confirmed that the culture being created through the band movement had resonance there too.

'Our first trip across to the mainland was in 1982,' he remembers. 'We were engaged by a women's Lodge in Motherwell to do the Hamilton Parade in Scotland for their Twelfth. Then, in 1984 – there was a gap for a year – then we went to Cambuslang for the first time and there was quite a relationship built up with that particular part of Glasgow for various parades and essentially for the Scottish Twelfth. The band has since been across to Scotland on many occasions and indeed not just for parading but going across for concerts and such like.

'We also travelled to London with the Apprentice Boys for its Londonderry protest. That was back during the original attempt to change the name of the city of Londonderry. That was some occasion. We travelled across on the ferry, bused down to London, and bused back again, but it is something that many members of the band would remember for quite some time … parading in the capital city. Thinking back, we had a very strong band that went to London and we received great praise, not alone from those who were participating in the parade, but from people who just happened to be in London, had seen the parade and were very impressed with ourselves and indeed all the participants in that parade.'

Times move on and so has the band, he notes. 'There have been quite a few changes. I suppose initially the description of our band would have been an out and out Blood and

Thunder band. What I have noticed of late is that you have a band that has developed with great decorum, great discipline, playing tunes in a slightly different style to what we would have done. But times do move on and I give great credit to those who are currently in the Castlederg Young Loyalists. Now the deportment of the band, the style of music is something that is to be envied, not alone in our own area but throughout Northern Ireland and beyond. You give credit for that to the members of the band, but of course the band does need leadership. Trevor Donnell provides that leadership and I give full credit to him.'

Nigel, webmaster of the Castlederg Young Loyalists Flute Band and a former member of the Red Hand Defenders Flute Band in Newtownstewart, also has vivid memories of the early days. 'I remember the bands starting,' he says. 'I remember going to 12 August in Londonderry with my father and I wouldn't have been very old and there was at that time a mixture of bands – you know, pipe bands and accordion bands – and there was a few old-style flute bands; Sion Mills had one of them flute bands and they looked more like bus conductors than anything else. Then I remember this big band coming from Belfast and this band from Scotland and they were massive. I remember standing there in total awe and the reason was that these boys were so good. They just had black trousers and white shirts with the necks open and most of them had black glasses on them. There was something sinister about them to a young boy, but it was attractive all the same. That would have been the very early 1970s, maybe even 1971, because it was one of my earliest memories.'

Nigel's vivid memory of his first encounter with the Blood and Thunder band scene is familiar to most Loyalist men of his age in Northern Ireland. For these bands have been 'without question, the most distinctive development in Loyalist political culture since the 1960s' and they breathed 'new life into the established tradition'.[83] They formed a bridge between modern youthful style and the world of mature privilege that was disintegrating, particularly for those Protestants who felt under threat or isolated from the centre of strength and power.

'I was reared just outside Strabane,' says Nigel, 'a totally Republican town, a town you weren't allowed to go into because if you went in you probably wouldn't come out again. But I remember the word going around that they were starting one of these bands in Donemana and it was termed as a "Kick the Pope" band. I was going to a school in Strabane so there was a lot of boys coming in there from Donemana as well. This was about 1974 or 1975 and I would have been about ten or eleven. I remember thinking, "Right I'm going to go for this band" and I remember going home and telling my father that I was going for this band in Donemana. I remember it well because my father would have always been a bass drummer and he was in a pipe band in Castlefinn in County Donegal – because that's where he had originated, you know, in County Donegal. In later life, he had been in Tullywhisker Pipe Band, but at that stage he was no longer drumming. He was just involved with the Orange Order in Tullywhisker; so on the Tuesday night he says to me, "Right, so you want to join a band. Come along with me and I'll sort this out." And the next thing I know I'm landed in Tullywhisker Orange Hall and I'm handed a practice chanter and I'm training to be a piper. I thought, "This is not for me. I'm not going out with a skirt on me for people to laugh at." It went on for a while though and you know, sometimes I look back on it and I regret not sticking with the pipes, because I can play them a wee bit but not a lot.

'So when the [Castlederg Young Loyalists] band started in the town here, for some reason I really didn't know anybody from around this area because, where we lived near Strabane, the crowd that went to the school all came from the other side of the town – from Donemana and Artigarvan and all over that area. So all the people I would have known were from that part of the country. I didn't know so many people from up around here. So when the band was starting up here in 1977 I never gave it much thought at that stage, to be quite honest with you. And then about two years after that, the [Red Hand Defenders] band was started in Newtownstewart. My father knew a couple of the people involved and I was older then, so I got involved and,' Nigel laughs, 'Tullywhisker's loss was Newtownstewart's gain. Well, Tullywhisker I'd left anyway because even at eleven years of age, it just wasn't for me … My brother was taken to it as well and he's still at it and I was taken to band practice for years, but I never got a skirt.

'But the flute bands have taken over because in the old days you could come along and pick up a few tunes and you were out marching with the band. You wouldn't do it now with the way these boys are playing though. If you had gone to two or three band practices back then, you could have drummed in a parade. And really, if you could have fluted two or three tunes they'd put you away into the middle somewhere. If you ever watch a parade you can tell. You'd see this wee band going up the street and they'd have ten flutes and then you'd see a band coming down the other way and they have maybe fifty in it and there would be no difference in the volume of the tune they'd be playing.

'But there is no comparison between the bands now and the bands then. Then you would have sat in an Orange Hall all year learning the bagpipes, which is no easy task, and for what? The Tullywhisker band would have done the Hospital Parade in Castlederg, which was on every year to raise money for the hospital. That was always a couple of weeks after the Twelfth, around the 24 or 25 July. They would have done the Twelfth, of course, and then you did the Hospital Parade and then Black Saturday … and that was it. When the flute band culture came on the scene, you were parading every weekend because every time a band started up it had its own annual parade and it became more and more a cultural thing. Because you had a reason to parade on 12 July – there's some people would argue that you didn't have – but then when you started to have the annual parades, you started to have the competitions as well, you know. You'd have the best Blood and Thunder, best melody flute, best drum corps, best appearance and all the bands started to become competitive.

'You know, you'd have bands there that would be better one year than we were, but you would be watching them and finding out how they were doing it, and you would go out the next time to make sure they weren't better or to make sure that you were better. And that attracted many young boys into it because now it wasn't a case of sitting in a hall all year and learning to play an instrument to go and do maybe two parades. It became a community and a culture and you got the young people interested and involved. When I was in the band, I got to know people from Ballymena, Antrim, Omagh, Londonderry, Craigavon and all over. Every time on a Friday or a Saturday, you would be meeting up with them and maybe having a drink with them. That sort of culture, that sort of community, never existed before the bands. That was very strong and it's very strong yet and that's a great draw for young people to be involved.'

Besides the camaraderie, the emerging culture and the thrill of the drums, there were other reasons why the Blood and Thunder bands gained such ground among Loyalist youth in the polarised society of Northern Ireland during the late 1970s and 1980s. Their edgy, in-your-face assertion of identity was a response to the surge in robust Republicanism that coincided with and followed the H-Block hunger strikes of 1981. As Sinn Féin's new political direction eroded the Unionist hegemony in the institutions that had thrived on Nationalist abstentionism, the bands became the secular face of Unionist youth against the cultural confidence of Nationalism.

'In the early days there would have been a fair bit of justification for the bands' reputation for trouble,' admits Nigel, 'but unfortunately people do not move on with their opinions. This band would not justify any negative reports at all. Trevor has gone out of his way to try to move things away from that. But thirty years ago, you know, it was a crowd of young boys out for a bit of craic. It's a completely different world we're living in now. Them young boys playing in there in the band tonight, they're part of a Loyalist flute band and they know their culture; they know where they came from and everything that happened in this town and they know their history. But [during the Troubles] we were going out to parades maybe having buried one of our mates a few days earlier and, even if you wouldn't know the place you were in, you would know this was the Republican area of it because the police would have it blocked off. It was easily identified and maybe if the police had stayed away out of the road you wouldn't have known.

'People say it was wrong and you shouldn't have been doing it, but when you're seventeen or eighteen you are easily influenced and, as I say, maybe a few days earlier you would have buried a mate you ran about with. You know, it's very, very easy to become bitter, but it's even easier to become blindly bitter. Because when I was growing up several people close to me were murdered – there's thirty on the website and I knew them all, but some of them were good friends. When one of them was killed, I didn't know who had killed him. The only thing that I did know about them was that the killers were Catholics. So when you were walking up the street and you were meeting a couple of Catholics walking down, you would be wondering, "Is that one of them?" That was a very, very unhealthy way to be thinking but it is how you found it, because we didn't know any better. It became almost a part of our culture at that time. There maybe was more of a reason then why people were going out to band parades for divilment more so than there is now. Now it's more the marching band, the old military-style marching band and it's much more about the music for them boys there than it was back then. Jesus, you had boys going out with a flute playing A, B, B, B, A, then maybe they'd forget the second verse and they'd still be walking along waiting to play the bit they knew. But you know, it's totally, totally different now from what it was, which isn't a bad thing.'

Nigel believes that vital work is being done by the Blood and Thunder bands in fostering and nurturing cultural identity and community pride among Loyalist youth. This work could be jeopardised by opposition to the bands that is rooted in sectarian stereotypes and by official compliance in political correctness. The huge number of parades now held to generate the revenue needed to keep bands going could be curtailed by more recognition and funding, yet Blood and Thunder bands are largely denied support. 'Trevor has applied for grants every year for the past ten years, but there's a non-acceptance in the government that, in this country, there's some things that are either one religion or the other,' says Nigel. 'They take in an application from a flute band looking for money towards drums, say, and they look at it and say, "Right, is there any Catholics in the band? So right then, it is not cross-community." To me, that's discrimination. Maybe they would call it positive discrimination but it's still discrimination.'

Breaking down the sectarian barriers, he argues, can only be achieved by recognising difference and conceding that cultural measuring-sticks do not come in one handy size. It also requires people to recognise, support and even applaud the huge change that is taking place in the cultural activities of Ulster Protestantism while retaining the core beliefs of their legacy. 'You know, there's a lot of people want to live in the past,' Nigel says. 'It's this attitude of zero tolerance. Yet there's very few people in this town that didn't know someone, or had a relative or someone close, that was lost. There's one of the pages on the band website where I listed out all the things that were done against the Protestant people of this area and, you know, there were some pretty low ones. One in particular I remember is a woman and her two wains held all night waiting for him [the husband] to come home – he was a night-shift worker – and the boy joked and laughed with her and told her what he was going to do and all. Now I thought that was as low as you can get. But of those that were killed, there were four in one band. That typifies this area because, if you go down to Tullywhisker [pipe band], it also has four members who died in the Troubles – Winston Donnell, Kenny Smyth, Tommy Harron and Kenny Brown. The band here may be only going since 1977, but it has a huge legacy to live up to, a history that can't just be obliterated to suit political correctness.'

For his part, Quincey Dougan says that while the Blood and Thunder bands are a recent cultural phenomena, they reflect the rich history and traditions of the Loyalist people of Ulster in all manifestations, both good and bad. 'The story of the band that I'm in for twenty-four years shows this. There's been a band here [in the Kilcluney area of Markethill] for more than a century and there is a record of a brass band and a pipe band. The flute band was formed in 1949 and it was just Kilcluney Flute Band and nothing else back then. From 1974, the name changed. The membership wanted to change the name and they changed it to Kilcluney Protestant Boys and that was a direct result of what the people in the band wanted. So they decided the name needed to be changed and then later on the name changed again to Kilcluney Volunteers. Some people would automatically take a paramilitary inference from that, but there's an Orange Lodge called Kilcluney Temperance

Volunteers and there would be many folk memories in this area even yet about the [original] Ulster Volunteer Force and even the Volunteers of 1798 who were put down by the militia – the majority of those militias were Orangemen. The story is told that there was a company of Kilcluney Volunteers raised way back in 1795. This volunteer thing is a very strong memory, right from the year dot. There's still folk memory here right from the 1641 rebellion and our band standard is a memorial to 1641 when Kilcluney church was burned right to the ground, so it was. Again, I wouldn't downplay the fact that the name's inclusion of Volunteers at that time [in the 1970s] would have had a resonance in the period … because they were turbulent days. I don't think anybody would try to hide the fact that there was some influence of the [modern] Ulster Volunteer Force. These are truths we have to admit and there is no point trying to gloss over them. We have to be honest about all this stuff. I'm not a believer in flowering things up. If you tell a lie, it'll be found out.'

Quincey believes that the congregational, rather than hierarchical, nature of Protestantism has influenced bands. 'I suppose one trait of the marching band movement – and it is something that has kept us back, which is a shame – is the fact that there is an honesty there and I think it comes from core Protestantism and the nature of the Reformed religion as it has developed – the honesty and the individuality. It is this thing that you just didn't give a damn what anybody thought. We don't care, because we know we are not doing bad. We're right and to hell with them! This has been to the bands' – and to an extent to Unionism's – detriment to a large degree. But bands are bands first and foremost.'

The legacy of the past, when typical Blood and Thunder band members were deliberately provocative and often engaged in civil unrest, has overshadowed the development and progress in the band movement and the good work done by most of them, Quincey believes. It has also disguised the fact that the level of musicianship ranges to the very top. 'We had a guy on our books that studied music in Oxford, so we did. There are many good musicians in bands, you know. There is a stigma though that hasn't recognised the B Flat flute as a musical instrument, which is absolutely ridiculous if anybody analysed it. James Galway came out of a flute band and there's a hell of a lot more too. But we have sixty-nine men on the books at this moment. You know there's a hell of a lot of people fluting. To learn any instrument takes dedication and it takes a commitment and I would challenge anyone to do what we do all the time. You know, males from age twelve to eighteen are the hardest ones to work with and we're sitting down teaching hundreds of them instruments every week of the year. Who else could do it?'

The appeal down the generations has been more than learning a musical instrument, however. 'There's a sense of belonging that you get with the band that you can't get in other circles. Even take Markethill, the amount of people that came through the ranks – shop owners, business owners, people that're working in all different aspects of life from street-cleaner to multi-millionaire – the amount of them that came through the ranks of the Kilcluney Volunteers over the years is just absolutely amazing. It was nearly a rite of passage to come through your local band. But then this area has ten bands – that's just in the Markethill district, which is very much a band-orientated part of the world so it is.'

Having been involved in a Blood and Thunder band for almost a quarter of a century, since he was twelve years old, Quincey has seen first-hand the evolution of the movement into modern times and how that has been missed or deliberately misrepresented. 'It is incredibly misunderstood and there is this overarching perception about Blood and Thunder bands and it's there even within Unionism. The Orange views bands as trouble and there would be a lot of schism with the Orange in many places. A lot of bands are independent bodies, whereas in the 1960s the band was part of the Lodge. You know we meet in Kilcluney Orange Hall; we parade with Kilcluney Orange Lodge on 12 July. If there are other functions or anything else called for, we work with the lads in the Lodge. But we're an independent body and if we want to do something, we do it, we don't ask anybody's permission, and we don't go cap in hand. That is the case with most marching bands and particularly with the bands playing Blood and Thunder music.

While many older people disapprove of the Blood and Thunder bands because of their reputation for bad behaviour and 'wrecking the place', Quincey points out that most of them are very tame compared to many pipe bands drawn from an older generation. The pipe bands, he says, have 'the hardest-drinking men in the country' and this is apparent at big events such as the world piping competitions at Glasgow Green. Yet he relishes the cross-generational aspects of the parades, where older pipe band members compete alongside the teenagers of the Blood and Thunder bands. Quincey says, 'We get on in the marching bands even if some don't see that.'

The separate development of the bands has seen a parting of the ways in other aspects, notably in the crossover membership between the bands and the local Orange Lodges. 'When I joined the band, it would have been sixty per cent. Young men would have come out of the band and into the Lodge but that's a thing that has changed over the last decade. I suppose, post-Drumcree that has ceased to be the case. Whereas the majority of bandsmen went on to become Orange Lodge members, now the majority of those who are in bands would not become Orange Lodge members. The Orange Order to some people has taken this image of being an old man's organisation, whereas for a while it wasn't and you had to be there, you know,' says Quincey, who views efforts by the Grand Orange Lodge of Ireland to entice young members with initiatives such as its comic character, Diamond Dan, as 'about thirty years too late'.

'What we want to do is open minds. We don't want to change and we're not going to change but when a band walks down the road and there's somebody standing at the side of the road that takes exception to it, then they're not taking exception to what they see, and they're not taking exception to what they hear; what they are taking exception to is what they're reading into it. It is what they are thinking and what is going on in the subconscious about what is the motivation for this. They're thinking about agendas; they're thinking about strategies. But bands don't have agendas and bands don't have strategies. Bands work from one night to the next and there's no pre-planning. Catholics would have had this perception that when an Orange Lodge meets, they are plotting the downfall of Rome, but what they're actually talking about is the price of sheep, for God's sake. That's what they are doing. It's all about what is happening this weekend and about Orange dances. They don't give two shites about what is going on in Rome … and neither do the bands.'

CHAPTER 11

FROM TWELFTH TO GLORIOUS TWELFTH

Friday, 3 July 2009

DUP Minister Arlene Foster expresses dismay at the intolerance shown by Republican protesters at a band parade in Newtownbutler, County Fermanagh: 'Sadly, in marked contrast to the dignity shown by those supporting the bands, a small rump of Republican protesters felt the need to yet again show their intolerance towards our proud culture and identity. Those who attempted to block the parade route, and then proceeded to wave foreign flags from the sidelines, only show their bigotry and prejudice.' About sixty police officers were in the village for the parade involving fifteen bands which local dissident Republicans in the 32 County Sovereignty Association describe as 'nothing more than a provocative sectarian coat-trailing exercise to stoke up tensions in the area'. Ms Foster says the Border Defenders Flute Band deserves credit for exemplary behaviour: 'The event was a huge success, with an excellent showcase of our proud marching band tradition.'[84]

On the same night, Bushside Independent Flute parade in Ballymoney had twenty-four bands, and in Newbuildings, outside Derry city, the Pride of the Orange and Blue Flute had twenty-nine bands on parade.[85]

Wednesday, 8 July 2009

Pride of the Village hosts a parade of twelve bands in Beragh, County Tyrone, with Omagh Protestant Boys standing out and Castlederg Young Loyalists also present. In Ballymoney, County Antrim, the Stranocum Flute event has thirty-three bands.[86]

Thursday, 9 July 2009

It was to have been the final practice for the CYL Old Boys band, which would disband formally after the special parade to mark the thirty-fifth anniversary of the deaths of murdered comrade Norman McKinley and his fellow UDR victim Heather Kerrigan, killed in an IRA attack on 14 July 1984. But as the veteran bandsmen gather, it becomes clear that they enjoy the fellowship, the memories and the familiar tunes of yesteryear. Some are not willing to let that go, so by the end of practice it is agreed they will convene after the anniversary ceremony and decide what to do.

Earlier, a meeting of the younger Castlederg Young Loyalists discussed plans for the biggest weekend of the year. Tomorrow, the band will travel to the Gortagilly parade in

Moneymore, County Derry, convening the following evening for the traditional Eleventh Night tour of Castlederg. They will then play a concert at 'the field' in Newtownstewart during the bonfire celebrations. With the Twelfth parade on Monday, and the anniversary event the following day, there is a brief respite in the schedule, which follows hot on the heels of last weekend's trip to Scotland. The young band members are still on a high from that expedition which began on Friday and lasted until they got home on Monday.

But while parading is what the band does, the immediate concern is a whip-round for a few cases of beer to share on Saturday before going on to Newtownstewart. 'There is more to this band than parading,' says bandmaster Trevor. 'We need to socialise and spend time together too. So while it is against our rules to drink alcohol before performing, we are going to make an exception to that rule for this weekend, but it will only be a few beers, mind you, here in the band hall after we have paraded the town.' There is no disagreement on that score, but a discussion of what beer to buy leads to a chorus of suggestions. Kenny is on the phone already checking out what is available at Tesco in Cookstown where he lives. He comes back with a price, roughly £11.95 a case for four cases. Johnny says ASDA in Omagh is doing a deal of three cases for £20, which leads to other recommendations, but Kenny is not budging and, since he has been nominated to get the beer, his preference will prevail.

Band members are reminded about punctuality for the Saturday evening parade around the town at 7 p.m. to comply with the Parades Commission's rules. Trevor adds that he is still awaiting a 'determination': 'I was talking to the sergeant and it seems there is a problem about the [UDA and UVF] flags at Millbrook. They thought maybe we [the band] had put them up, but they have nothing to do with us. I don't know who put them up, but that seems to be the reason we are still waiting for our determination.'

I refrain from disclosing that my contribution in the recent door-to-door collection may be partly to blame. Some things are best left unspoken and, despite my best efforts, I seem to be embroiled in the flags issue anyway.

Friday, 10 July 2009

A series of seemingly co-ordinated attacks carried out by nameless vandals on Catholic churches and a GAA club in County Antrim raises tensions ahead of the Twelfth. It follows attacks on Orange Halls elsewhere in Northern Ireland. Catholic churches are attacked with paint in Ballymena, Portglenone, Ahoghill and Cullybackey. Headstones in cemeteries adjacent to some of the churches are also attacked and daubed with paint. A car is driven into the grounds of a GAA club in Ahoghill and set on fire. Protestant churchmen, the Orange Order and Unionist parties condemn the attacks.[87]

Saturday, 11 July 2009

12.30 p.m. A large tricolour flag is suspended above the exit from the main Lifford to Sligo road at Ballintra in County Donegal where a Garda is directing traffic for the annual parade of the Grand Orange Lodge of County Donegal. Two junctions down, the traffic slows to a halt and I back into a parking spot beside another car from which a man and woman have emerged. As I get myself sorted, the woman gets back into the car and turns it around. I remark that it will be handier to get out afterwards and the man says that is what he has been telling her all along. I ask her if she has a 'back-seat driver' and she says that if there is a murder here today, I'll know what it is about. Such banter is what Rossnowlagh is about and I wonder, as has been suggested many times since this demonstration became a popular benchmark for liberal commentators, if this romanticised presentation of an arcadian Twelfth is the future of Orangeism and the public celebration of Ulster's Loyalist culture?

Ahead on the small coastal road that heads straight for the beach and the Sand House Hotel, the focal point of the Donegal Bay resort, people are shuffling along from their parked cars towards a makeshift village where there is a huge display of Union Jacks and other regalia amid bilingual road-signs, holiday homes and caravans. Here, people sit on lawn chairs and at picnic tables. The hucksters are out in force, their stalls an Aladdin's Cave of loyal regalia. The ubiquitous burger vans and ice-cream vendors form a tunnel all the way to a junction where another road sweeps off towards the hill beyond where Orangemen and their bands are gathering. The age profile here is different to band parades, with many retired people and mature couples; young families are in a minority and teenagers a rarity. There is a relaxed, pastoral atmosphere; it has the feel of a historical pageant rather than a demonstration of a living culture. I take up my vantage at the junction where Gardaí are chatting to people in the crowd.

1.10 p.m. A man at the booth beside me has started to preach in a voice that soars above the babble of conversation. From a Baptist church in east Fermanagh, he tells us in great detail, with the aid of a whiteboard display, the meaning of the symbols we will see on the banners. He tells us of the Open Book (Bible), of Jacob's ladder and more, and he remarks that he has never met anybody who did not want to go to heaven. I resist the temptation to say that I don't want to go just yet. He tells us of another 11 July when he was preaching in Moira in 'the North'. Meanwhile, crowds shuffle by, including 'dudes' carrying surfboards which seem totally out of place amidst the regalia of Ulster Protestantism. Cars inch their way towards the hotel, many drivers with bemused looks on their faces. One of the preacher's colleagues hands me a leaflet. 'There probably is no God', it proclaims provocatively on the front page. I pocket it for later.

1.30 p.m. Fifteen minutes after the parade was to start, senior Orangemen are coming up from the Sand House

Hotel. They include Brethren from Ghana, Africans in Orange collarettes and chains of office. There are also Canadians, including a couple of ladies resplendent in white dresses. The Orange dignitaries are shepherded along by the Grand Master of the Leitrim County Orange Lodge to a shuttle bus operated by the host Ballymagroarty Orange Lodge and supplied by a firm from Cookstown.

1.45 p.m. Lambeg drumming in the distance creates a rustle of expectancy. People who have been waiting patiently suddenly find themselves at the back of a crowd of new arrivals staring into the near distance, where banners flutter in the breeze. Over the course of the next five minutes there is much jostling: a woman in a red jacket keeps encouraging her companions to press forward. 'You'll not see the bands from there,' she calls back as the throughway for the parade shrinks further.

1.50 p.m. A smiling man in a brand new suit, Orange collarette and white gloves carries the first banner for the Donegal Grand Orange Lodge. Lines of dignitaries follow him, the lay and clerical leaders of the Orange Institution from all over the world, followed by a group of Orangewomen in clothes more reminiscent of 1950s middle England than a Donegal beach resort. Then comes the Churchill Silver Band followed by the various representatives from counties south of the border – Leitrim, Monaghan, Cavan and Dublin/ Wicklow, and then the districts of Donegal. Lodges from Fermanagh and other northern counties follow and, finally, the local host District Lodge from Ballymagroarty, which seems huge until an adjacent onlooker points out that it is supplemented by other Orangemen who have come by themselves to walk.

Between all these marching men and women are the bands, of course, with accordions and pipes to the fore. Many seem curiously quaint, like the Newtowncunningham True Blues which is made up of older men and young girls. There are some sizeable flute bands too – Magheraveely Pride of the Village from Fermanagh, Lissarley from Monaghan, Omagh Protestant Boys and Moygashel Sons of Ulster from Tyrone, and Curran from Derry, but they seem noticeably subdued in their performance here, as this is a sedate, rural parade. A clear favourite among tunes is the children's hymn, 'What a Friend I Have in Jesus'. Others favour martial airs such as 'Onward Christian Soldiers'. Only the bass drummer from Curran Flute Band provides a swaggering, thumping performance and even then only for the briefest moment. Even the Enniskillen Pipe Band's energetic Willie Smith is subdued today. There are few claps and cheers; one of the few comes for the Omagh Protestant Boys melody flute as it swings through the junction. This comes from a young woman in a Magheraveely band uniform who paraded earlier. 'That's all I wanted to see,' she announces and heads off with her friends.

3.15 p.m. As the parade ends, dark clouds roll in. In the queue at the two mobile toilets, a smartly dressed young woman waits patiently with her Highland Terrier dressed in a little Orange sash. I decide to break for the border and, as I inch my way into the exiting cars, raindrops on the windscreen presage another summer downpour in Rossnowlagh.

6.55 p.m. Back in Castlederg, cars pull in quickly and decant band members who put on their tunics and prepare instruments as the start time approved by the Parades Commission approaches. A few smiling police officers wait at the junction of McCay Court and four parade marshals with bright yellow bibs take up positions front and rear. Bandmaster Trevor Donnell gives the order and at the stroke of 7 p.m. the Castlederg Young Loyalists Flute Band is off through the almost deserted streets of its hometown playing a jaunty Irish jig. In the vanguard are the bannerette and the Battle of the Somme flag of the old Ulster Volunteer Force battalions. Approaching the Diamond, the second tune is 'How Great Thou Art' and the band loops around High Street into Priests Lane. The tune ends and an eerie silence descends, punctuated by a single drumbeat. Police officers guard the roundabout between two pubs favoured by Nationalists. As the band passes the police fortress at the corner of Castlefinn Road, a man in a Tyrone GAA rain-jacket hurries towards the supervising sergeant: 'Hey Davy, Davy, they're carrying a UVF flag.' The police officer seems nonplussed and the man repeats his protestation. 'I could see it clearly around there,' he says, pointing back along the route. A couple of other young men in GAA jackets stand looking on with surly expressions as the band passes in virtual silence. The tension is palpable as the band moves beyond Ferguson Crescent into the Killeter Road. Right until the final hours, the Parades Commission had withheld permission for this route, which has long been the subject of controversy. Sinn Féin, in the guise of the late councillor Charlie McHugh and West Tyrone MP Pat Doherty, has claimed this is a Nationalist district where residents don't want Loyalist parades.[88] Unionist politician Derek Hussey asserts the band's right to parade through the commercial area to the town's largest Loyalist enclave in Millbrook Gardens. Councillor Hussey says he carried out a door-to-door survey some years back and the majority of residents were not Nationalist and none objected to parades. Yet there have been clashes between supporters of the rival claims in the past, the last involving a visiting band which deviated from the designated parade route.

7.10 p.m. Ferguson Crescent is deserted, business premises are closed and the houses no longer occupied by residents to protest or delight in the passing parade, still muted but for the single drumbeat. On Killeter Road the band strikes up with another traditional air, 'The Ulster Girl', the tension lifts and the Castlederg Young Loyalists Flute Band marches off towards the contentious flags. Turning into Millbrook, the bandsmen are back firmly on home territory. Several members live here and residents are gathered in front of their homes or on the street corners to see the parade. Robbie McKinley, one of the four marshals, waves in acknowledgement. As the band marches off to the far end of the estate, a woman standing on her small front patio remarks on how good it is to have the band parading through Millbrook: 'You know, I can't remember the last time we had a band through here.' In the near distance, the thumping reverberation of Blood and Thunder bounces off walls as the band reaches the turning point and starts the homeward procession.

7.35 p.m. The band swings back out onto Killeter Road past a lamp-post with three flags, the Union Jack on top, a UVF flag next and then a UDA flag. Nobody gives them a second glance. The band strikes up with its signature 'Castlederg' medley of tunes as the rain gets heavier, coming down virtually in sheets. Trevor calls ahead to marshal Robbie McKinley to tell the police they'll be shortening the parade route. He and other band members seem tense again as the single drumbeat brings them back through Ferguson Crescent, the roundabout and the roads where cars are parked tightly along the footpath. Again, the junction is deserted except for the men in Tyrone GAA jackets as the small parade moves into Priests Lane where an armoured police Landrover is parked. In the caged turret observation post at the corner of the police fortress, a face peers out at the passing parade.

7.45 p.m. Back on High Street and turning for home, the band strikes up a jaunty air and there is a noticeable air of relaxation. A respectful pause at the cenotaph and then the thunder of parading back along Main Street, past small clusters outside the Derg Arms and Castle Inn, and the proprietor of the Indian takeaway who stands in his doorway. Then around the corner to the formal dispersal at the Orange Hall. Robbie McKinley points out to a policeman that it looks like 'typical Dromore Twelfth weather'. The band members head in for a couple of beers and some post-parade fellowship, before heading off to Newtownstewart for the bonfire.

7.50 p.m. Up through the town, the streets are quiet until, from the church opposite the police station, the congregation emerges from Saturday evening Mass. Clearly the parade did not disturb their pre-Sabbath worship and most were probably unaware it even happened.

8.45 p.m. Summer rain falls in a torrent on the big stack of wooden pallets in Parkview Court, Castlederg, beside the ruins of the local castle. Three poles jut from the top of the bonfire, each with a flag attached. One is partly obscured by a Sinn Féin poster for MEP Bairbre de Brún, defaced with a moustache and horns protruding from the forehead, that is attached to it. One flag is the Irish tricolour, hanging limply, while that on the tallest pole is a Fermanagh GAA flag. There are five other Sinn Féin posters and one SDLP poster for European candidate Alban Magennis attached to the poles. One Sinn Féin poster shows the West Tyrone team with de Brún and party leader Gerry Adams. Scrawled on it are the words 'Is this Charlie?' a reference to the late local councillor. Another poster has a scrawled speech bubble coming from de Brún's mouth with the letters 'POTD' for Pride of the Derg, the rival Blood and Thunder band organising tonight's Eleventh Night festivities. Cars patrol the site to make sure no one lights the bonfire ahead of time, pulling into Parkview Court, turning and heading off through the town before the next pulls in and does the same. At the Derg Arms on the corner of Main Street, people in cars wait for something to happen while a group huddles for a smoke at the front door.

9.30 p.m. Half an hour after the Pride of the Derg band was to have commenced its outward parade, scattered spectators are gathering along the rain-drenched route. Some huddle under umbrellas, while others take advantage of the glass-topped awning that covers the entire footpath outside Kyle's Arcade across from the war memorial. A woman and her grandchildren play up and down the covered footpath and young people chat and greet passing friends. A man emerges from the adjacent Methodist church, greets a neighbour and they discuss briefly the newly installed minister who hails from Lisbellaw in County Fermanagh. The churchman climbs into his car and drives off. Another vehicle comes along and, with difficulty, backs into the spot. Finally, and reluctantly, the car behind it makes more room. A woman holds a baby out of the window of the vehicle to see the children running up and down.

9.45 p.m. The thunder of drums sounds in the distance and people begin to move from the shelter over to the top of Main Street. Through the gloom the colour party of four

253

strides along in close formation, with a phalanx of eleven side-drummers leading two bass drummers and a flute corps of more than twenty. They fill the entire street and play popular Loyalist tunes. The entire band is in civilian clothes, heads uncovered in the pouring rain. They march up to the end of the Diamond and come back down the other side before drawing up to the crowd which has suddenly expanded to several hundred. Band members turn towards the crowd, scanning the faces as they play basic Blood and Thunder airs, with none of the embellishments the Castlederg Young Loyalists Flute Band incorporates in its repertoire. A voice calls out 'Volunteer' and the band strikes up again with what sounds to me like Phil Coulter's 'The Town I Loved So Well'. The crowd seems delighted and as the band marches off towards the bonfire site, people follow along happily.

10.10 p.m. The Pride of the Derg Band comes to a stop, still playing as shadowy figures splash fuel onto the pyre of wooden pallets. Flames spread quickly as the band moves off to the side. The music stops while attention focuses on the bonfire. A crowd gathers along the high wall at the back of the Derg Arms and Derek Hussey comes across from the Castle Inn. He chats to a police officer who says the crowd will disperse quickly once the flags have burned. Somebody raises one of the Sinn Féin posters and holds it up to the flames, ensuring it catches. Figures dance around as the flames lick out towards them.

10.30 p.m. The bonfire is now at its height and there is a small cheer as the Irish tricolour and the Fermanagh GAA flag are consumed, flaring brightly before disappearing into the general conflagration. Already some onlookers are beginning to disperse, leading children home through the rain. Soon it will just be the die-hards and the drinkers.

10.50 p.m. Heading home through Castle Park, the row of trees shielding Parkview Court seems to be on fire as the glow dances around them and licks the sky. The band has started up again. As night deepens and the rain persists, the thunderous reverberations can still be heard clearly from Millbrook Gardens. The Blood and Thunder music around the bonfire celebrating the glorious arrival in Ireland of William of Orange is an affront to those who oppose all Loyalist parades. For those who support them, the leaping flames and thunderous music signals that the Union and all they hold dear is safe for another year on the eve of the Twelfth.

Monday, 13 July 2009

Noon – At a roundabout junction of the main Omagh to Enniskillen road on the edge of Dromore, an Orange-sashed marshal for the West Tyrone Twelfth parade – delayed a day because of the Sabbath – and a police officer are deep in conversation with retired Catholic parish priest, Canon Tom Breen. The affable old man, dressed in black with a Roman collar, leans for support on a fold-up chair. A quartet of teenage boys wearing junior Orange sashes comes by. Canon Breen greets them and soon they are all chatting, until the Catholic priest moves off to a frontline vantage point on the corner of Johnston Park on the route to the field. Almost immediately he is engaging neighbouring spectators in conversation. At flag-bedecked houses people settle down with refreshments for the biggest event in their village since the recent Fleadh Cheoil Thír Eoghan festival of Irish traditional music. A succession of feeder parades pass through the junction on their way to the Omagh Road starting point. Under cloudy skies with intermittent sunshine, the burger stalls are doing a brisk trade as the crowd gathers. There is an air of good-humoured expectation for the day that marks the zenith of the marching season for Loyalist Ulster. It is broken only by a brief squabble in a passing family, which turns to acute public embarrassment as other spectators turn away. The protagonists slope off and conversation turns back to more important matters. An elderly couple wonder aloud if it is time for a cup of tea from their thermos flask or whether they should hold off for the parade of sixty Lodges with fifty bands passing. The Dromore parade includes the districts of Sixmilecross, Strabane, Fintona, Omagh, Killen and Newtownstewart. Meanwhile Tyrone's biggest parade, with seventy Lodges and fifty-four bands, is held in Coagh for districts from the east of the county; and a smaller Twelfth parade in Fivemiletown caters for the Clogher Valley districts of Fivemiletown and Annahoe.

1 p.m. Dromore Twelfth weather brings a shower and I find shelter in the doorway of Dromore Credit Union on the main street where the crowd stands under lines of big bright umbrellas. A grinning man approaches from the other side of the street and identifies me by name. He is the chairman of St Dympna's GAA Club here in Dromore, out to watch the big event, and he identifies other Catholics in the crowd. There is no objection in this Nationalist village to an Orange parade. The local pubs – the Central, O'Connors and Carron's Corner Bar – are doing a brisk trade, as are the local shops open for bank holiday business.

1.15 p.m. The rain holds off as the Omagh District Lodge parades by in the vanguard, followed by the Killycurran Pipe Band and the Killycurran Faith Defenders Lodge. Next comes the Blacksessiagh No Surrender Lodge with their banner of King William in iconic pose on his white horse. Their pipe band is followed by the Gillygooley Sons of William Lodge with another pipe band, Cappagh Guiding Star with yet more pipers and then Mountjoy Faith Defenders Lodge and its pipe band.

1.40 p.m. The street fills with sound as the first Blood and Thunder band rounds the corner. Children suddenly pay attention as the Blair Memorial Pride of Omagh Flute Band fills the street. Two young bandsmen among the ranks of about forty are wearing sashes to demonstrate membership of the Orange Order and following the band is the Omagh No Surrender LOL 850 with a banner depicting an older man identified as the late Brother Tom McClay. My GAA friend explains that Mr McClay was well known for his involvement in the 'B' Specials drawn from the local Protestant community in the 1950s and 1960s. Even among those willing to tolerate and even welcome a major demonstration of Orange culture, there are memories that nurture sharp differences. Next along Dromore's Main Street are the Reformed Faith Defenders, a junior Lodge from Omagh whose banner depicts a young man tied to a rock as the waters rise around him with the legend 'My faith looks up to the Lord'. The junior Orangemen are followed by a senior Lodge from Omagh and then more Blood and Thunder from the Omagh True Blues with a three-man colour party and a young drum major performing stick acrobatics. Just one of the young bandsmen sports an Orange collarette. Edenderry Temperance Lodge from Omagh district is next, with a pipe band and King William banner, followed by the Sixmilecross district banner leading Brackey LOL and its King William banner. Then the third Blood and Thunder band comes along, Pride of the Village from Beragh, followed by Beragh Lodge and its King William banner, then Seskinore Pipe band and its Guiding Star LOL with a depiction of Britannia. The sequence is repeated until Newtownsaville Lodge comes along in the wake of an accordion band, and following them is the Omagh Councillor Allan Rainey on a big orange tractor drawing an almost life-size model of his local Orange Hall. On the back of the trailer, a metal frame accommodates two Lambeg drums being flayed with curved Malacca sticks. One of the drummers wears a sash, while another man in suit and sash sits on a chair. As the float passes, the crowd is distracted by the burst front left tyre of Councillor Rainey's tractor. Then it's back to a succession of pipe bands, King William banners and occasional accordion bands as more Lodges pass along the street from Tyrooney, Cloughfin and Gortaclare. Newtownstewart comes along with pipes followed by the Blood and Thunder of the Red Hand Defenders, and the more sedate flutes of Sion Mills, with pipes from Ardstraw, Strawletterdallon and Plumbridge filling the gaps. The rain is back before another unidentified pipe band comes through wearing capes over their kilts and then it's time for Killen district with the Castlederg Young Loyalists Flute Band, in whose ranks bandmaster Trevor and his assistant Davy both wear Lodge collarettes over the band uniform. After that it is back to the skirl of the pipes from Kilclean, Kirlish, Killen, Killclooney, Tullywhisker and other localities, before the accordion bands from Aghyaran and Barron, and some final blasts of Blood and Thunder from Donemana's Pride of William and the Pride of the Derg bands, the latter back in full red uniform after last night's civilian attire. Finally the parade is brought to a conclusion as the Trillick Pipe Band leads the host Lodge 208 to the field. In a lull from the rain, the crowd disperses, many heading for the beer gardens and others setting off for the 'Field' out the road.

3 p.m. In a cordoned area of the big, recently mowed meadow, the band equipment is stored under flags and banners. Bass drums, side-drums and pike-shaped flagpoles form brightly coloured mounds around the expanse. It is as if a great army has decamped and left behind its equipment. Here and there, teenage band members linger and a group from the Newtownstewart Red Hand Defenders plays with spray cans of hair dye. A lone young boy in a kilt lifts a pair of drumsticks and plays a quiet beat on a side-drum. A couple of young girls in pipe band uniforms link arms as they pass the boys with smiles and glances. Down a slight incline, a long trailer stage accommodates about a dozen Orange dignitaries and members of the Blacksessiagh Accordion Band as the Blue Thistle Highland Dancers from Drumquin and Newtownsaville Social Club Lambeg drummers end their performance and the religious service begins. Three rows of folding chairs in front of the stage are sparsely occupied as Orangemen shelter under brollies and others look out from parked cars. The main speaker, Deputy Grand Master of the Grand Orange Lodge in Ireland Edward Stevenson, takes to the podium: 'The Twelfth is a very special day in the culture of Northern Ireland and I am delighted to be with you here in Dromore, in my home county of Tyrone. It is also a day when we commemorate the Battle of the Boyne, fought all those years ago along a river bank now in the Irish Republic, near Drogheda, and we give thanks for the civil and religious liberty we still have today as a result of that victory.' The rain increases in intensity and a few more forsake the platform for the adjacent tent in which Fintona Presbyterian Church offers tea, sandwiches and traybakes for £4, and soft drinks at 50p. Across the road and just opposite the field, Kenwell's yard has been temporarily turned into the 'Castle Inn' offering bar and toilet facilities. Here the traffic is thickest and the police are trying to keep it moving along. A car stops as an elderly passenger is greeted warmly by a passing family with young children. A police officer vents his fury at both car occupants and pedestrians. 'This is not a place to park,' he exclaims crossly in an English accent and the car moves off reluctantly, before halting again about 20 metres further along. The conversation resumes and the policeman rushes over to berate them again. The woman announces for all to hear, 'No, you're not being allowed to talk to your Nana today.'

Back down the town, the burger stalls, ice-cream vendors and pubs are doing a roaring trade as groups flit about meeting and greeting. Progress along the street is slow as groups chat. The sporadic bursts of rain cause some to scatter for shelter, but others just draw flags, hoods or anything to hand over their heads and giggle through the downpour. This is Dromore, after all, and it always rains here on the day of the Twelfth parade.

Tuesday, 14 July 2009

7.20 p.m. Car parking is at a premium as vehicles pull up for passengers to climb out into the rain. Band members form ranks – Castlederg Young Loyalists, the CYL Old Boys and the Kilclean Pipe Band. Others don Orange sashes and line up behind the Old Boys, where bandmaster Trevor Donnell has taken his place as lead drummer under the direction of his old bandmaster Derek Hussey, who is in the ranks of the fluters. Already many of those present have been out in the Corgarys to the exact spot where Norman McKinley and Heather Kerrigan were ambushed and killed twenty-five years ago today. Among the gathering at the IRA ambush place were two surviving members of the UDR patrol who recounted their memories of the horrific event, friends and relatives of the victims who placed flowers, members of the Old Boys band who played with Norman and members of the current band. 'It was very moving,' says Trevor, 'especially for these young people here who knew nothing or very little of that time and that event. As a band, we had to mark the twenty-five years for Norman, who was one of our drummers and for Heather, who wasn't really a member of the band, but she carried one of our flags on several occasions. I remember Heather being with us at a Belfast parade back then.'

7.30 p.m. Two flag girls take up positions at the head of the Old Boys and on the bandmaster's whistle, they move off. Behind them come three long lines of Orangemen from local Lodges, marching in step. Behind them, the Castlederg Young Loyalists band strikes up and moves off at a suitable interval. Finally, the Kilclean Pipe Band moves off to a skirl that fills McCay Court, out onto Main Street and over the bridge. The procession moves briskly along the road, which is still wet but bathed in summer evening sunshine. Clusters of spectators look on from the car park of the Free Presbyterian Church and other vantage points. The bands play hymns as police keep the traffic at bay and the long column wheels onto Drumquin Road at Castlederg High School. Traffic is halted just beyond the cemetery, but suddenly a group from the Omagh Wheelers cycling club whizzes through the cordon and comes pedalling fast towards the Old Boys Band which has spread out to fill the entire road. At the last minute, the cyclists split into two single file columns and take to the opposite footpaths.

7.50 p.m. A long single file of Orangemen moves along the narrow path between orderly rows of matching headstones towards the gravesides of Heather Kerrigan and Norman McKinley. The Kilclean Pipe Band comes through the gates and to a single drumbeat makes its way past the imposing hewn granite monument that marks the grave of Lieutenant-Corporal Paul Samuel McMahon of the Royal Irish Regiment, 'dearly beloved son and brother', who was born on 10 December 1979 and died of natural causes on 6 January 2009, the latest member of the crown forces to fill this small town graveyard.

8 p.m. The Kilclean pipers have taken up position at the back of the huddled congregation as the words of Psalm 111 are recited:

In the Lord I take refuge.

How then can you say to me:

Flee like a bird to your mountain.

For look, the wicked bend their bows;

they set their arrows against the strings

to shoot from the shadows

at the upright in heart.

When the foundations are being destroyed,

what can the righteous do?

Family, friends and bands lay wreaths as the pipes play 'Abide With Me' and Derek Hussey steps forward. 'They shall not grow old as we who are left grow old,' he intones. 'At the going down of the sun and in the morning, we shall remember them.' In one voice, the crowd responds, 'We shall remember them', and disperses in silence to re-form ranks. This time, the pipers lead the Orangemen, with the Old Boys next and finally, the current band. In tight procession, they make their way back across to the war memorial on the Diamond.

8.30 p.m. The crowd parts around the war memorial and the Castlederg Young Loyalists Flute Band marches through and takes up position. With standard and flags lowered, they play a hymn. Then Robbie McKinley and a brother of Heather Kerrigan step forward and lay wreaths at the base of the cenotaph, before stepping back into the crowd. Robbie wears his Old Boys uniform of bright orange shirt with his collarette draped over that. Tears well in his eyes; he wipes them away with his hand. Again the invocation is recited by Councillor Hussey and this time the rumble of response, 'We shall remember them', echoes through a huge crowd. The Castlederg Young Loyalists Flute Band then leads the way around the Diamond and back to McCay Court. The Orangemen follow, then the pipers and finally the Old Boys. After playing 'God Save the Queen', the bands fall out on command and the Old Boys are called into the hall for a decision on their future. On an evening of poignant memories of fallen friends and the fellowship of marching along hometown streets, it seems unlikely that the Old Boys will fade away.

Thursday, 16 July 2009

8.30 p.m. In Bridgetown Orange Hall's band room, a small group is chatting beside the tables used for drumming practice which are covered in an array of the recent trophies the band has won, while the flags and standards have been arranged around the walls to maximum effect for the Twelfth celebrations. Trevor tells us the Old Boys voted to continue so that they can parade at the annual parade each September.

Friday, 17 July 2009

Could there possibly be anywhere more aptly named for a gathering of marching bands than the village of Drum? On a clear and sunny, if chilly, July evening, twenty bands parade up and down the main street, past Stewarts' shop and post office,

Andersons' tavern and the Orange Hall that has pride of place at the heart of this community. The crowd applauds through the performances, older people meet and greet, chatting in clusters around garden seats and behind yellow tape to reserve parking and viewing space, while children play around a huge old tree and on the trailer stage. Among those who have come to Drum for the evening is Stormont's Minister for Culture, Arts and Leisure, Nelson McCausland. Considered a Democratic Unionist Party hardliner, he is a long-time Ulster-Scots activist. The Ulster-Scots Agency has provided funding for this event and there is even a crew present from the Irish-language television channel TG4 to record a vibrant Ulster Loyalist community. If ever proof was needed that band parades are not staged merely to threaten or intimidate, then Drum surely provides it.

The only thing that seems out of place, even bizarre to those outsiders who come to what locals call the 'Drum Picnic', is that it is situated in the very heart of County Monaghan. Drum is south of the border, part of a strong Ulster Protestant community consigned to the Free State by partition in 1921. Drum and surrounding localities cherish their Ulster Protestant identity and adhere to the traditions maintained at gatherings they call 'picnics' to avoid unwanted attention. Slowly emerging from the fear and trepidation induced by the Troubles, their vibrant Ulster Protestantism survives in one of the 'lost counties' and for the first time the parade has been opened to outsiders and publicised.

8.30 p.m. Stormont Minister Nelson McCausland greets a quartet of Ballinamallard Accordion bandsmen from Fermanagh and enquires if they 'come down here every year'. 'No this is our first time,' replies one of the bandsmen outside the Orange Hall. At the side of the Orange Hall, a burger stand has been set up with a price list posted on the wall for '100% Irish Beef burgers' at £3 or €3.50 with drinks at £1 and all proceeds to Drum Accordion Band. Angela Graham, who sits on the board of the Ulster-Scots Agency and is a leading member of the local band, points out that this is the first time burgers have been available. Drum would not usually be on the itinerary for chip vans, she notes, so in previous years the fare was confined to teas and traybakes, which are still available inside the Orange Hall. 'We try to do something different every year to bring it along,' says Angela, who has been spearheading efforts by the Clones Community Forum to help local Protestants and their traditions emerge from the shadows. 'We invite people to come along and we also ask people we think might be open to this experience and appreciate the value of it. We get some funding now through the Ulster-Scots Agency which is itself funded by the Department of Arts, Sports and Tourism in Dublin and the Department of Culture, Arts and Leisure in Northern Ireland. Last year we invited Minister Éamon Ó Cúiv to come along, so this year we invited Minister McCausland and he accepted immediately, we are very pleased to say.' Such ministerial affirmation from both jurisdictions is clearly important to a community that has kept its head down for almost eighty years until the recent outreach in the aftermath of the Good Friday Agreement.

8.45 p.m. On the stage outside Andersons, the Roughan Silver Band from County Fermanagh is entertaining the growing crowd with show tunes. Children play around the old tree, while toddlers and babes in arms are admired by friends who have not met in a while. Nobody seems impatient, being content to stand and chat. A large car glides down the village street with two Gardaí inside. There are a few nods from the crowd, a casual salute or two and the car moves down to the end of the street, turns and comes through again, not to be seen for the rest of the night.

9.05 p.m. The crowd further down the village has parted to the sound of a hymn played in march time. Soon the blue tunics of the Drum Accordion Band come into view stepping briskly along, but with no banner or colour party before the phalanx of twelve button accordions followed by the bass drum, cymbals and two side-drums in the rear (the bands of Monaghan, Cavan and Donegal do not carry flags). To friendly waves, the host band takes over the village, closely followed by the Brookeborough Flute Band from County Fermanagh, again with no flags or colour party, but with the drum corps out front. Then, also from Fermanagh, come the Ballinamallard Accordion band and the Roughan Silver Band, as well as the Aughadrumsee Flute Band.

The local Druminan Flute Band is next, followed by Inver Flute, Cooneen Pipe and Rosslea Accordion bands, all from Fermanagh. Lissarley Flute Band from the Newbliss area is next, its playing style nearest to a Blood and Thunder outfit among marching bands from south of the border. Then it's the John Hunter Accordion from County Armagh, Mullaghboy Accordion from County Cavan and Clontibret Pipe Band from County Monaghan. South Fermanagh's Pride of the Village from Magheraveely with their banner provides some Blood and Thunder next, followed by Cappa Accordion from Monaghan, Billyhill Accordion Band from Cavan and then the local Coragarry Accordion taking up the rearguard on the outward journey.

9.40 p.m. With the light beginning to fade, the Drum Accordion Band comes marching through on the return leg of their parade. All the bands who have been through already follow, with the addition of the local Killyfargue Pipe Band and Doohat Accordion LOL 264 Band. That brings the turnout of bands to nineteen, as the crowd applauds and then relaxes as night descends.

10.10 p.m. The host band parades once more up through the village but this time wheels right at the Orange Hall and through the gates of a small field. Finishing a rendition of 'Abide With Me', the band forms a guard of honour and, as each succeeding band comes through the gate, the Drum hosts applaud. Then a thunder of drums comes up through the crowd as a newly arrived big band halts at the Orange

Hall, with the second banner of the evening. This is borne along by the Tamlaghtmore Tigers from Ardboe, Tyrone, who have arrived late and are now moving out of the way to allow the other bands to complete their leg. From tune to tune with barely a pause, the drumbeats roll and the band marks time. Gradually, the marching feet move sideways through the crowd until a channel is secured and they march briskly and assertively onto the wide pavement outside the Orange Hall. As the remaining bands parade to the field next door, the Tamlaghtmore Tigers mark time on a single drumbeat. Finally, they launch into a couple of concluding tunes to rapturous applause and cheers from younger members of the audience. If Drum needed a concluding drum-roll before settling back into its sedate annual picnic mode, the visitors from Ardboe provided it.

Saturday, 18 July 2009

The twenty-seventh annual parade of the Portrush Sons of Ulster Flute Band attracts thousands of spectators, including many holidaymakers and tourists, who watch thirty-three bands. Blair Memorial Omagh led off the parade on their first visit to town, with Drumeagles Young Defenders Flute Band, Ballymoney, Castlederg Young Loyalists Flute Band, Maghera Sons of William and Derryloran Boyne Defenders, Cookstown among other bands on show.[89]

Friday, 24 July 2009

A night of parades for Blair Memorial in Omagh, Belfast's Pride of Shankill Flute Band and in County Monaghan for Doohat Accordion Band near Newbliss village.[90]

Saturday, 25 July 2009

The South Belfast Young Conquerors Flute Band parade at Donegall Pass sets off at 2.45 p.m. Later that evening, the annual parades take place of Dunloy Accordion in Ballymoney, County Antrim, and in Lisbellaw, County Fermanagh, for the Defenders of the Rock Flute Band.[91]

Wednesday, 29 July 2009

Tyrone's Ditches Pipe Band parade takes place in Poyntzpass village near Newry.[92]

CHAPTER 12

WALKING THE WALLS

Wednesday, 5 August 2009

Sixty bands parade in Cloughmills, County Antrim, for Crown Defenders Flute Band.

In Dungannon, County Tyrone, Ballymacall True Blues Flute Band annual parade has thirty-five bands.[93]

Thursday, 6 August 2009

Attention turns from Kenny's new tattoo to Richard, who regales fellow band members with his plans to extend his own tattoos up his left arm and onto his chest. Pointing to a vacant patch on his forearm, Richard says he plans to get that done after the marching season. Tattoos are highly desirable among band members, as attendance at any parade would indicate, where bare arms covered in designs that reflect oriental fashion as much as adherence to political allegiances and football clubs can be seen. So discussion of tattoos fills the gap in conversation at Bridgetown Orange Hall while Trevor makes calls. As much as ever, band practice involves juggling of numbers with name-calls, head-counts and phoning and texting of those not present. With a sufficient muster, arrangements can be made about who will drive and who they'll pick up. Trevor remarks, 'It doesn't get any easier.'

This weekend is important – a parade in Kilkeel on Friday, then out with the Apprentice Boys in Castlederg on Saturday morning and on to the Relief of Derry parade. Trevor has a taxi run to the airport before Kilkeel, but he'll have room to bring people home. How many fluters? A headcount totals eight for Friday, fewer for Saturday. Neil Johnston thought the Apprentice Boys parade was the following weekend so he switched shifts. Is there a colour party? In Kenny Sproule's absence, who will carry the bannerette? Judy says if there are enough flutes, she could step out with the bannerette. Trevor makes a mental note of it all. Occasionally something is keyed into a mobile phone, but seldom written down. Somehow it works out. However, some things do need to be written down and local political activist Ryan Moses stops by to fill in forms for grants for new uniform trousers being measured for tonight. The band files down into the big hall to be brought down – or up – to size.

Friday, 7 August 2009

Maynard Hanna of the Ulster-Scots Agency is talking to friends on the corner of Greencastle Street and Harbour Road in the centre of Kilkeel when a tiny band comes thundering along with only five fluters.

'Where's that band from?' one of the men asks.

'From Castlederg,' Maynard replies.

'Boy they've had a good run,' observes the other as heads in the crowd turn to the distinctive style of the tight little outfit from west Tyrone. And they did indeed come a 'good run', for Kilkeel is about as far from Castlederg as it is possible to travel while staying in Northern Ireland, a journey of ninety miles that takes two and a half hours through Omagh, Armagh city and Newry on a Friday evening, with the parade scheduled to start at 7 p.m. for the Mourne Young Defenders.

After driving a taxi run to Belfast, Castlederg Young Loyalists' bandmaster Trevor Donnell arrived early and has been waiting for his band to arrive. While chatting occasionally to Maynard and a mutual friend from Scotland, he is frequently on his mobile phone checking where the cars are along the route.

Kilkeel is big band country, a Unionist enclave on the coastal plain where the Mountains of Mourne sweep down to the sea in largely Nationalist South Down. Surrounded by communities in which young men find their cultural expression in Gaelic games, Kilkeel's Loyalist youth flocks to the Blood and Thunder scene. Maynard Hanna, former organiser of the local Schomberg Ulster-Scots Association and now Belfast organiser of the Ulster-Scots Agency, names eight local marching bands. The biggest are the Blood and Thunder outfits of Mourne Defenders, Pride of the

Valley and the Pride of Ballinran, all turning out tonight in Kilkeel. 'There is huge support in this town for the Mourne Defenders,' observes Maynard. 'When they come home from the Twelfth, you would have 5,000 supporters waiting to see them parade though the town. I don't know if there is another band with that level of support.'

Started in 1976, the Mourne Defenders band has been making huge efforts to banish the negative reputation of Blood and Thunder bands. Its impressive drum corps stands out for precision routines. Its choice of music ranges from traditional Orange tunes to show tunes and even a few Johnny Cash numbers. Bandmaster George Balance says, 'It's a very big commitment. We would have youngsters who would practise for maybe two, three, four years before they would get to go on the road. There's a wee guy in the drum corps. He's been practising two and a half years and he's only thirteen. The standard of the drum corps is so high now, you need to have musical ability with the sticks. When we first started, anyone could pick up a pair of sticks, but the skill is so high now we are doing pipe band drumming and it's not everyone who can grasp that.'[94]

Scottish Blood and Thunder enthusiast Bobby Totten, who organised the Castlederg band's visit to Cambuslang in early July, points out that the Mourne Defenders Band has won many fans across the water, not least at the 2005 Lord Mayor's Show in London when they marched with the British army's London Regiment. Even before that, the

Mourne Defenders took part in the Kendal Street pageant in Lancashire, second in size as a community festival only to London's Notting Hill Carnival. Those engagements involved honing the band's marching skills and long sessions were spent at local football pitches working on drills that were taken from the Boys' Brigade manual.

Bobby, meanwhile, has come across on the ferry from his home in Scotland for his sixth time this year. 'I'm over and back all the time. I just love coming over for the bands,' he says, although it soon becomes clear that his favourite band is the Shankill Road Defenders from Belfast with their distinctive drum major. 'I joined them way back in 1964 when I left home in Scotland and came over here,' Bobby says. 'I had been in a band in Scotland, but this was where I wanted to be involved in the bands. Mind you, we were nowhere near as good as these lads are now.'

Like many in the Scottish band scene, largely concentrated in Glasgow, both of Bobby's parents come from Northern Ireland. He recalls childhood visits to his mother's home in Belfast's Sandy Row where he heard the legendary William Hewitt playing the Lambeg drum. His early education in Ulster Loyalist music stayed with him and he is regarded as an expert on bands. When one less than exemplary outfit passes in Kilkeel, Bobby winces visibly and remarks that one of the fluters is out of tune: 'It's the fellow there second from the left in the back row.' Bobby then remarks that he is being kind to the bands tonight and he usually has more cutting remarks about those who are not trying to raise the general standards of marching bands. Nor has he any time for the big bands that think too highly of themselves. 'But I suppose the thing to always remember is that no band comes to one of these parades to play badly. They are all out there doing their very best ... for some, maybe their best isn't good enough.'

Meanwhile, Maynard Hanna talks in a torrent, skipping from anecdote to observation to declaration, and from denigration to affirmation. He is a larger-than-life Ulster Scot, here in Kilkeel to promote a new book from the Ulster-Scots Agency.[95] Yet while heaping praise on the bands, he lets loose a tirade against the media in general, and the BBC in particular, for its refusal to feature the marching bands except on the very rare occasions when there is trouble. He recalls that for this year's Scarva parade, the BBC just did its stock short report on the Sham Fight where actors portray King Billy and King James (with the obvious victor), and followed that up with a traffic warning about a Highland games event in north Antrim. 'I heard afterwards there were 1,000 at the Highland games and there were 125,000 at our parade and the BBC couldn't even acknowledge that and yet the following Sunday they were showing hours of GAA [Ulster Finals] to sicken us when anybody who wanted to watch that could get it on RTÉ.'

Alleging a firm bias against Loyalist culture, Maynard says the media is stuck in the past when it comes to Blood and Thunder bands and Ulster Protestant identity. There is no comparison or equivalency, he maintains. 'There's a Republican flute band near me … and it's really pathetic to see them parading. They don't know how to play music; they don't know how to march; and they have two bass drums and they're not even on the same beat. They don't know how to play together. That is because parading and doing it well is our thing … It's all in the way people dress and the respect they show; how they move together. This is what we are good at.'

10.25 p.m. The Castlederg Young Loyalists band has rounded the bend to a short burst of applause from spectators outside Alfie G's bar. Though few in numbers tonight, the band responds to the encouragement and the five fluters fall in behind the small colour party to parade in circles around the drummers. It's about style and presentation, but it also helps to know how to play.

Saturday, 8 August 2009

9.45 a.m. The final notes of 'The Ulster Girl' fall silent and the Castlederg Young Loyalists Flute Band parades through Ferguson Crescent to a single drumbeat. In their wake are local members of the Apprentice Boys of Derry in crimson collarettes. The small parade marches briskly past a few police officers in bright yellow jackets and a couple of civilians, one of whom – a local Sinn Féin activist – talks into a mobile phone. In the foreground, two Irish tricolour flags billow from telegraph poles, while a huge billboard advertises National Hunger Strike Commemoration events on 14

August. Its background is another tricolour. Ahead is the big observation tower of the local police station, a military fortress with armour-plated walls and steel grilles through which a shadowy observer is just visible. The band marches up Priests Lane, turns right and strikes up the marching tune of 'Killaloe'. In less than five minutes, the high-tension event is over without incident. The band parades home and prepares for the Maiden City.

12.05 p.m. At the heart of Derry city, council workers are erecting 'spit barriers'. Huge interlocking devices with the bottom half made of steel grilles and the top of Perspex, they create a tunnel along Ferryquay Street into the Diamond where a wide gap is created around the war memorial with normal crush barriers – a no man's land between footpath and parade route. The see-through part of some of the spit barriers has been discoloured by what looks like yellow dye. They do not invite closer inspection even by the steady stream of curious people. One tough-looking pair, with the sinewy swagger of battle-hardened street warriors, ambles along inside the spit barriers. They regard clusters of police with barely concealed contempt, but drop their voices when they become suspicious that I am being nosy. At the Diamond, they greet another young man sitting on a bench. A group of young bandsmen passes. 'You can almost smell the bastards,' says one of the street warriors as they amble down towards Shipquay Street to the Guildhall.

The spit barriers were requested by David Ramsay,

Chief Marshal of the Apprentice Boys of Derry, for the huge parade to commemorate the relief of this city of many names. He says marshals at the recent Twelfth parade were put at risk when they tried to prevent parading Orangemen from retaliating after spectators spat on them.[96] Meanwhile, Apprentice Boys Governor Jim Brownlee has been heartened by cross-community support for the Maiden Festival that now incorporates the Relief of Derry parade. 'This past week the Maiden City Festival has offered its own celebration of diversity, respecting the many differences in cultural expression that make life interesting,' says the governor. 'People from all over the world have joined with the people of this city, from all communities, at lunchtime and evening events, listening to music and learning though drama and living history. Living with deference to difference is essential to civil and religious liberty, tolerance and respect. It would be a poorer world if we were all the same.' He adds that those who wish to provoke, to abuse and to spoil the 320th commemorations of the Relief of Derry 'respect neither their neighbours nor their fellow citizens and should be castigated as the sectarian bigots they are'.[97]

12.30 p.m. The mood is lighter back at Ferryquay Gate, the one the original Apprentice Boys slammed shut in December 1688 in defiance of the massed forces of King James II.[98] A police sergeant is advising a couple of visitors with Dublin accents on the best vantage point: 'This would be a good spot where they enter the walls, but you'll probably be scunnered with every band playing "Derry's Walls", unless that's what you want to hear,' he remarks obligingly. They thank him and move down Carlisle Road. Further along the street, notices on the top of the spit barriers warn the bands that they are entering the cenotaph district: 'Stop playing, keep marching from next point'. Although the overwhelming majority of shops are closed, those that are open have a steady stream of visitors. They spill in and out of the Richmond Shopping Centre and the Foyleside Centre, many seemingly oblivious to the huge parade. Some wearing Glasgow Celtic tops walk past others wearing Glasgow Rangers tops. No bother.

12.40 p.m. A digger front-loaded with spit barriers trundles down to where the tunnel of barriers ends. There is an audible groan. One of the workmen talks to the people seated there on lawn chairs and to a man in an Apprentice Boys collarette. There is a cheer as the digger reverses. However, within a few minutes, it is back and this time the workers are in a police huddle. But there is another signal and the digger moves off without unloading its extra barriers. Meanwhile a group with two big Lambeg drums on the city walls over New Gate keeps up a steady tattoo. The crowds gather and men in matching ties congregate behind the Burntollet Sons of Ulster band at the mouth of Artillery Street. Tour groups arrive and a Hispanic family poses for a photo. A middle-aged Apprentice Boy takes off his collarette and drapes it around the shoulders of one of these visitors, while a band member obligingly takes a photo of the entire family.

1.15 p.m. The Relief of Derry parade is in full flow after the initial colour party and the Black Skull Fife and Drum Band from Glasgow lead the way through Ferryquay Gate. From Artillery Street, the Burntollet Sons of Ulster lead the Parent Branch of the Derry Apprentice Boys into the heart of the city in a tradition whereby the local Apprentice Boys wait inside the walls for the 'relief' forces. Parent Club members have already attended the morning service in the nearby Church of Ireland St Columb's cathedral. After they depart, the next wave in the Relief of Derry enters from Carlisle Road followed by the Clogher Protestant Boys band. Then three more Blood and Thunder bands, followed by ranks of men in suits and collarettes and then Avril's Glory Accordion Band from Liverpool. It's quickly back to Blood and Thunder after that with the Kilcluney Volunteers followed soon after by Tamnamore Flute Band.

1.45 p.m. The parade has taken on a distinctive character, remarkably different from Orange parades on 12 July. For a start, there are a large number of visitors, many from abroad, drawn to events in the Maiden City Festival which has a cross-community programme. Another distinction is the music – here Blood and Thunder is king: Ballymacall True Blues, Lower Woodstock Ulster-Scots, Aghanloo Flute, Pride of the Valley, a steady stream of Sons of Ulster, Sons of William, Young Conquerors, Young Loyalists, True Blues, Defenders and Prides of young lions playing their hearts out and swelling with pride as they pass through Ferryquay Gate and breach the siege of Derry to smiles and applause from onlookers.

2.10 p.m. A young drum major in full Guards uniform carrying a ceremonial mace leads two flag bearers: one wears the uniform of the Ulster Defence Regiment, the other the uniform of the 'B' Specials. Older people in the crowd applaud heartily while younger spectators and visitors seem puzzled. The Pride of the Raven from East Belfast follows in a thunder of percussion, augmented by cymbals. 'Still Marching On' boasts a motto on their bass drum proclaiming that they have been doing so since 1968. The uniforms are a reminder that exactly four decades ago, in 1969, the Relief of Derry parade sparked a riot that became the Battle of the Bogside. A decision to send in the 'B' Specials prompted London to deploy troops on the streets of Derry in Operation Banner, which lasted almost forty years.[99]

2.20 p.m. After flute bands from Dunamoney, Articlave and Lurgan, the Castlederg Young Loyalists Flute Band comes thundering through. I follow in its wake towards the cenotaph; extricating myself from the crowded corner of Market Street; negotiating past the Anchor Inn where several men are being checked by doormen; then moving along Ferryquay Street around huddles of police and against the flow of shoppers; then past the crowd outside the HMV music shop; and through the security barriers at the top of Shipquay Street and the barriers at the key intersection of Butchers Gate. Here, I'm held up by an exchange between a police officer and three young women draped in Loyalist flags who want to view the parade from 'over there'. They nod to the far side where people move up and down to the Bogside, saying that's where they were for the St Patrick's Day parade. 'So what's the difference?' asks one of the trio, who is very heavily pregnant. With considerable patience, the officer suggests they find somewhere more amenable. 'Like up there,' he points to Bishops Street, where there are no spit barriers and where the bands resume their music. I sidle through with a sympathetic smile for the young policeman.

2.30 p.m. The parade has halted in London Street where at The Tavern a packed gallery has gathered with flags. A middle-aged woman in a bright-pink singlet dances extravagantly to the Blood and Thunder music of the William Strain/William Lightbody Memorial Flute Band from Newtownards. She tries to gather an Apprentice Boy into her embrace. He squirms out of range and then checks several times to make sure nobody has taken a photo. The woman continues her solo reel while carefully balancing her plastic drinks' beaker. Other men in collarettes clap but keep their distance. In the packed narrow street, the bass drummer is giving his all. In a lull between tunes, the bands fore and aft take up the slack. Finally, the parade is unclogged and the bands come thundering through, among them the William King Memorial from Fountain Street with a bass drum proclaiming them 'All Ireland Champions' and a list of honours encompassing all the years of the twenty-first century. Named after a father of four who was kicked to death in 1969, the William King Memorial was to the forefront of the August 1996 Apprentice Boys parade, which followed negotiations with Nationalists that helped to quell what had been up to that point the most violent marching season in years.[100]

The band gets a huge response parading home through New Gate into the Fountain, the last Loyalist enclave on the west bank of the river. Here on a patch of waste ground, a stall selling Loyalist regalia obscures the spent ashes of a bonfire and a gable proclaims, 'Londonderry West Bank Loyalists Still Under Siege – No Surrender'. The writing on the wall, painted kerbstones and flags flying proudly from lamp-posts instil renewed vigour to the visiting bands. On a doorstep, a small boy with drumsticks beats out the pulsating heart rhythm of his community on the circular lid of a floor-light. Still the bands pour through: Craigywarren from Ballymena; Cairnalbana Flute from County Antrim; Pride of the Valley from Kilkeel; Moneyslane Flute from South Down; Pride of the Hill, Rathfriland; Young Defenders from Lisburn; and Hillsborough Protestant Boys. Along Kennedy Street, where deserted buildings give way to neat terraces in shades of dusky pink, happy residents enjoy the parade and a few drinks.

The procession wheels into Wapping Lane, where a big mural features the old city streetscape with a picture of King William pointing the way with drawn sword. Underneath, another scene shows the old prison with the words from Phil Coulter's song 'The Town I Loved So Well': 'past the gaol and down behind the Fountain'. Another pause as the Hillsborough Protestant Boys arrive in bright Orange shirts and blue tam o'shanters. The bass drummer beats furiously on a bloodstained drumhead. His tattooed arms fall limp as the tune ends before he unharnesses and rests the big drum on the ground. Again the blockage is released and the bands move on, with Pride of the Village from Beragh next, followed by Skeogh from Dromore, County Down, Churchill from Derry, Gortagilly from Moneymore and the Omagh's Blair Memorial. Down past Georges Street, Aubury Street and Henry Street, where residents sit in rows, the bands march, before spilling out onto Abercorn Road where the old Tillie and Henderson factory once stood in defiance of Karl Marx, who cited it in *Das Kapital* as a prime example of modern capitalism.[101] The parade skirts the big roundabout with its sculpture of two figures reaching out for a handclasp and sets off across the huge double-decked Craigavon Bridge, passing bands still spilling across from the Waterside as they commence the circuit.

2.30 p.m. At the top of Tillie's Brae, a visiting American couple is clearly enjoying the parade. They focus on the bands coming down from the City Walls. Every so often she nudges him to indicate a good photograph. They are from Washington state and only arrived yesterday, with Derry their first port of call before heading down towards Kerry.

They had no prior knowledge that this huge parade would be taking place. No other tourists they met were aware of it either. 'Can't believe it is such a secret, but we're delighted we get to see it,' she says. I suggest it is like a 4 July parade back home. 'No way, that is never as good as this.'

2.45 p.m The flute bands spill out and expand ranks to fill the road space – the Robert Graham Memorial from Crawfordsburn, Sons of Ulster from Moygashel; Dervock Young Defenders; Killymuck Sons of the North and then the Loyal Sons of Benagh from Newry. As the latter band passes, I make an unconnected remark to the American visitors and we laugh. Suddenly, there is a thunderous collision with the crush barriers beside me and a Benagh bandsman is being hauled back by three of his bandmates. Sinews protrude in his shaven head and he has a small smear of blood on one cheek; his face drawn in a furious grimace as he struggles against restraint. Beside him, another bandsman retrieves the spare drumhead he flung to the ground. One of the accompanying Apprentice Boys steps in to remonstrate and a few police officers move quickly to stand around the American couple and me. The bandsman is quelled and as his band sets off in ragged fashion, he comes inside the crush barriers and lopes off across Craigavon Bridge, obviously tired and emotional, while the Apprentice Boy who chided him keeps a close eye on his progress. A female police officer reassures the Americans and the incident is quickly forgotten as the Giant's Causeway Protestant Boys come along, followed by the local Pride of the Orange and Blue from Newbuildings, Ballyclare Protestant Boys with a stout Apprentice Boy in a huge Ian Paisley mask waving heavily tattooed arms, Upper Bann Fusiliers and the East Bank Protestant Boys with DUP politician Gregory Campbell, Stormont Minister for Culture until the recent reshuffle, marching proudly home. They are followed by Ballykeel's Rising Sons of Ulster, Warkworth Purple Stars from Belfast, Aghalee Young Volunteers, Sons of Kai from Rathcoole who are named for the 'Great Dane' footballer of Glasgow Rangers in the 1960s, Kai Johansen,[102] Pride of the Orange and Blue Auld Boys from Newbuildings and Hillview Flute from Belfast's Shankill Road. In a continuous flow, they parade across the bridge spanning the wide River Foyle as the final bands head up Carlisle Road back towards the fabled walls of the Maiden City.

3 p.m. The Pride of the Maine thunders into the Waterside to applause. With two bass drummers beating in tandem, they march up Spencer Road towards Irish Street. Already, busloads are moving off towards Strabane. Others linger at burger vans and hostelries. Each contingent steps off the bridge with smiles of relief, having finished their parade. The Whitewell Defenders are followed by the Steeple Defenders, then the Lord Carson Memorial and the Cullybackey Maine Defenders, with the Shankill Fusiliers followed by the Sons of William from Kells, Pride of William from Donemana and the Eglington Accordion, before the Red Hand Defenders from Newtownstewart. Twirling band-sticks are launched into the air and spectators wince with relief when they are caught cleanly. Youngsters throw more cautiously and often scramble to retrieve their stick from the marching feet. Then above the thumping drums and whistling flutes, the skirl of bagpipes heralds the Newtowncunningham Pipe Band from County Donegal. In sharp contrast to Dromore's Twelfth, this seems to be the only pipe band parading today; nor is there a single brass or silver outfit among the 130 bands walking the walls of Derry. But the pipes immediately give way to the Portadown Defenders' flutes, followed by Boveedy Flute from Kilrea, the Rankin Memorial from Ballygawley and the Major F.H. Crawford Memorial from Ballymena. Then, as the last of the Apprentice Boys cross the bridge, a huge banner in the rear proclaims 'Christ Jesus Came into the World to Save Sinners'. Even that is not the last word as a final trio make up the rearguard, a bald man in front wearing a Liverpool FC top and playing a traditional fife with two men behind strapped into huge Lambeg drums, their canes beating relentlessly on the taught goatskins. In their wake, spectators straggle across from the Cityside. Over at Carlisle Road Presbyterian church, chairs are stacked and canvas awnings dismantled after a busy few hours of teas and traybakes. The Americans from Washington hurry off to download photos and recharge their camera at the hotel. 'We were told they'll be coming back at five,' they report excitedly. A group of six young people dressed in Union Jack T-shirts and Northern Ireland flags marches down Hawkins

Street from the Fountain towards the bridge; one clutches a bottle of Buckfast wine. Suddenly the parade route is deserted except for police officers relaxing alongside the spit barriers and a clutch of news people around the cenotaph talking on mobile phones. A reporter with an English accent tells her news desk not to hold space: 'No, nothing really. I only saw one arrest … and that was a steward!'

4 p.m. Down at Sandino's Café Bar a man is working on some oriental art designs in front of one of the huge windows in this haunt of the liberal and left with a reputation for cross-community cultural exchange. It is a place where Nationalist, Loyalist and those with neither identity mingle. I join a friend for a pint. No, he hadn't seen the parade; the thought of doing so would not cross his mind, despite the interest of visitors. 'Don't they even care that they've closed down the entire city centre on a Saturday?' he asks, finishes his pint and heads for home.

5 p.m. Bustle again around Ferryquay Gate as Glasgow's Black Skull band draws nearer and louder. The police presence seems considerably heavier for the return parade of the local Apprentice Boys clubs and their accompanying bands after those from elsewhere have gone home. There are no lines of spectators and those not parading walk alongside their band of choice. Police reinforcements are dressed in boots, flak jackets and peaked caps with chequered bands, facing protesters who have raised a banner, backs to the parade. A woman in a summer frock gives a two-fingered salute to the a group of anti-parade protesters who have gathered, laughing as she saunters by. The bands, Apprentice Boys and supporters come at a hot and heavy pace – Burntollet Sons of William, Star of the Roe, Hamilton Flute, William King, Churchill Flute and then Pride of the Orange and Blue followed by their 'Auld Boys' band, and finally the East Bank Protestant Boys.

The atmosphere is tense and police officers look my way constantly. Some younger supporters are excited by the prospect of confrontation and break into a canter as the parade hurtles through the tunnel of spit barriers. Finally, the police cordon breaks and they move through the Ferryquay Gate as two heavy-duty police Landrovers take up the rear. A small group suddenly runs up the far footpath and through the barriers, shouting in Scottish accents. There are sounds of a brief altercation above the music. Then a man in handcuffs is led back down the street by two police officers. As they pass, one of the arresting officers says to the captive, 'Just because they're protesting doesn't mean you can run at them shouting "Wankers"!' An older woman, clearly incensed by the anti-parade protest, remonstrates in a middle-class accent: 'You're supposed to be our police, after all. We pay you with our taxes.' The young PSNI officer, a model of patience, replies, 'Indeed, and we are very grateful to you and all the other taxpayers, but we have to maintain the peace.' More police come through with a young woman in handcuffs. As they take her up Prince Arthur Street towards police vehicles, she calls in a Scottish accent to the arrested man. Just then, a Chinese couple and their young daughter coming around the corner are confronted by ten police officers dealing with two troublemakers. They hurry by, nervous. The big parade has been and gone, to the huge relief of Derry.

Sunday, 9 August 2009

PSNI area commander Chief Inspector Chris Yates says the behaviour of a small number of band members and those opposed to the parade should not 'detract from the good work that has gone on to normalise these events'. Twenty-six people are being questioned following trouble on Saturday night in which two police officers were injured and petrol bombs and other missiles were thrown. The trouble flared at Butchers Gate, Magazine Street, Fahan Street and Memorial Hall close to the Bogside after the Apprentice Boys parade had concluded. The police said that a 'substantial quantity of alcohol was seized during the day' but the parade itself passed off 'largely peacefully'.[103] Nine people charged are due to appear in court.[104]

Monday, 10 August 2009

MP for East Londonderry and former Minister for Culture, Gregory Campbell claims the trouble was 'orchestrated by Republicans'.[105] 'After such a successful day it is very disappointing that Republican thugs decided to unleash their criminal attacks on the police and property on Saturday night after the parade had concluded. The overreaction I witnessed at the weekend was on the part of deeply sectarian and bigoted individuals who had prepared petrol bombs for rioting and who have tarnished the name of Londonderry by their criminal behaviour.'

Brendan Duddy from the City Centre Initiative said Saturday's parade was 'terrible for the town': 'It's absolutely expected that it turns out like that, and the bottom line is that we've had enough of it.' Sinn Féin's Raymond McCartney says, 'Residents, particularly in the Waterside, feel that they're being hemmed into their homes from early morning until teatime. The town closes down – even though some people would say there's access – and then you have the aftermath.'[106]

Six men are charged with public order offences and two other males with possession of a petrol bomb. Their ages range from seventeen to forty-eight. All are due to appear in Londonderry Magistrates' Court. Another teenager arrested on Saturday night is charged with breaching his bail conditions and seventeen others arrested are released without charge.

Wednesday, 12 August 2009

There is a big turnout for Burntollet Sons of Ulster parade in Claudy, County Derry, with the King William Flute from the Fountain in Derry city leading off twenty-six bands.

Also on Wednesday, the Tamnamore Flute host a 'small but enjoyable parade' near the Armagh/Tyrone border.[107]

Thursday, 13 August 2009

The leader of the Pride of the Orange and Blue Flute Band is fined £750 for spitting at Nationalist protesters. Jason Moubrey from Primity Crescent in Newbuildings admits acting in an offensive and provocative manner after his actions were caught on CCTV and he was arrested during the parade in Derry city centre. Fellow Loyalist bandsman Trevor Simpson from Duncastle Park, Newbuildings, also admits acting in a provocative manner. A drummer in the Pride of the Orange and Blue Flute Band, he admits assault, acting provocatively with his drumstick and disorderly behaviour. The two bandsmen are aged thirty-five and thirty-eight respectively.[108]

Meanwhile, Ulster Unionist Councillor Derek Hussey condemns the theft of Loyalist flags from housing estates in Castlederg. An estimated thirty flags were taken from lamp-posts in Millbrook Gardens and other flags removed from Killen Park. Local Sinn Féin Councillor Kieran McGuire denies that Republicans were responsible, but adds that the flags include Loyalist paramilitary emblems 'put in people's faces to annoy'.[109]

Friday, 14 August 2009

Portadown Defenders Flute has fifty-eight bands on parade with an independent tally putting participants in all bands at 1,500.[110]

Saturday, 15 August 2009

Cloughfern Young Conquerors Flute Band hosts an after-noon parade with nineteen bands in Belfast's massive Rathcoole estate.

The Rising Sons of Ulster hold a parade with thirty-eight bands at the same time in east Belfast.

There is a Saturday night parade in Dunmurry for Queensway Flute Band with forty bands and in Ballymoney for Drumeagles Young Defenders Flute Band with fifty-four bands.[111]

Sunday, 16 August 2009

Galbally, a tiny village in mid-Tyrone, comprises a church, a pub, a grocery shop with a post office and a few dwellings. It is dominated by the local GAA grounds, just as Cappagh, only a mile away, is dominated by an imposing monument commemorating local IRA activists killed in the conflict. These include the eight 'Loughgall Martyrs' of 1989 – half of them from the village – whose ambush by the SAS in 8 May 1987 was the IRA's 'worst single setback during its modern history'.[112] Less than four years later, on 3 March 1991, three IRA members and another local man were shot dead here by the UVF.[113] This is the Republican heartland of Ulster and today, two sinister figures in paramilitary combat uniforms and balaclavas move along the hedgerows wielding 'semi-automatic rifles'. Around the bend of a small country road, two men carry a huge black banner demanding 'Smash

H Block'. In the background, there is a steady chant of 'IRA, IRA, IRA'. Two lines of youngsters move into view carrying large photos of the 1981 hunger strikers. Next there's a tramp of marching men and the colour party appears dressed completely in black with gloves and berets that have Easter lilies pinned to the front left. They carry the Irish tricolour, Starry Plough and flags of the four provinces. Behind are two columns of marching men and a couple of women in similar dress, then two rows of young men and women, members of Ógra Shinn Féin, in white shirts, green berets and bright orange neckerchiefs held by toggles. Then come three long columns of men – with a few women – in white shirts and black ties, moving more casually than those who preceded them. They chatter and some move with faltering steps. Behind, another large banner is carried, this time in white with 'Civil rights, Equality, Freedom', and underneath in bigger lettering 'The Struggle Continues'.

The parade proper begins with Sinn Féin politicians – Michelle Gildernew, Gerry Adams, Martin McGuinness, Michelle O'Neill and Francie Molloy. After that, family groups predominate: young mothers pushing buggies while other children gambol alongside; people strolling down a country road in sunshine, drifting in and out of company. By the time the first band comes along behind another colour party, the parade style and tone has been set as casual. The Martin Hurson Memorial Flute Band, named for the local IRA hunger striker, is in green paramilitary fatigues

– combat trousers, black boots and berets. Some of the eight fluters wear dark glasses.

The next banner commemorates IRA hero Fergal O'Hanlon, followed by another group of people in open-necked shirts and GAA tops, strolling casually. Then comes another band in black paramilitary uniform and a big banner for Sinn Féin Átha Cliath (Dublin SF) with IRA figures in the background and behind this is another banner held low to the road in Republican fashion for the Patrick Cannon Cumann, Donaghmede.

They are followed by young girls in dark green jumpers or white shirts, with tin whistles and three accordions, a bass drum and three side-drums. The band is not identified. A couple of Sinn Féin banners follow, held low, with a large group of casually dressed people in its wake. The Kevin Lynch Memorial Flute Band from Dungiven, also named for an IRA hunger striker, comes along in paramilitary black and dark green. It has four side-drums, two bass drums, which are not in sync, and eight fluters. Youngsters skip in its wake, while adults walk alongside. A long banner follows with pictures of the hunger strikers. Another banner and another band in black berets, followed by yet another band dressed in black with black drumheads and eight flutes, again unidentified. Then another banner, more people strolling along, and a tiny band – the Volunteer Ed O'Brien Republican Flute Band from Loch Garman, Wexford – behind three flag-bearers with five fluters preceding the bass drum and then two side-drums.

A big banner proclaims 'Monaghan salutes our TD Kieran Doherty Hunger Striker' and then another colour party leads a band with four side-drums, a bass drum and nine flutes playing 'Dirty Old Town'. This is followed by a large crowd of strollers and then a banner from Aughnacloy. The Volunteer Joe Cahill Republican Flute Band from Glasgow is next, wearing yellow polo shirts and dark trousers, with a colour party of seven, four side-drums, a bass drum and thirteen fluters stamping along in front of a banner that says, 'Carlton Republicans Remember the Hunger Strikers', with three flag-bearers and about two dozen men and women in matching white shirts and black ties in three columns. After this are two more banners, including the Volunteer Billy Reid Sinn Féin Cumann with a bunch of young women waving flags, including the Basque red, white and green union flag, the Palestinian flag and others.

A helicopter buzzes over the crowd as a huge tricolour is carried along, held horizontally (and upside down), then comes another band with a black drum, eight flutes and no name. A large banner in black and amber from the Loughmacrory GAA club, Cumann Peile Naomh Treasa, is followed by a large group carrying small black placards with the names of hunger strikers and a band in uniform black with berets and a banner saying: 'Fuair siad bás ar son saoirse na hÉireann' (they died for Irish freedom). Next comes the Joseph Mary Plunkett Accordion Band in yellow shirts with black ties and black caps with yellow plumes playing a local tune, 'The Mountains of Pomeroy'. One of the two side-drummers is craning back constantly to see what is coming behind, as if he cannot believe what he sees. It is a small truck covered in camouflage netting and two men marching alongside – one dressed as an RUC officer, the other as a British soldier. On the back, a paramilitary figure aims a big machine-gun at the Cookstown Sinn Féin contingent and behind them a succession of banners and casual paraders from other Tyrone Sinn Féin cumainn.

This blatant disregard by the Republican flute bands for the standards of dress and decorum demanded of Loyalists and laid down specifically in Parades Commission guidelines, prompts a trawl through the websites of such bands including the Martin Hurson Memorial Flute Band, Tyrconnell Martyrs Republican Flute Band and the Kevin Lynch Memorial Flute Band. The last accompanies a biography of the hunger striker with a little cartoon character urinating on the Union Jack and Red Hand flags. Other Bebo pages represent the South Derry Martyrs Flute Band, Tam Daly VSM Republican Flute Band, Dan Darragh Republican Flute Band from Ballycastle, the VSM Republican Flute Band from Calton, Glasgow, Liverpool Irish Patriots Republican Flute Band and Dunloy Fallen Comrades have similar tasteless features and frequent comments of a highly sectarian nature. The Strabane Martyrs Flute Band page features a colour party leading a chorus of 'The IRA', wearing paramilitary uniforms and dark glasses, while Banna Fluit Naoimh Phadraig from Cuil Chaoil (Kilkeel) has the little cartoon character who urinates but misses the Ulster flag. Finally, the Internet trawl also turns up a notice about the Eoin Roe Republican Flute Band starting in Portstewart, County Derry, stating that most of its members are from the local Eoin Roe Gaelic Football Club and that its uniforms and a practice hall have been donated by a local business. None of the Republican bands have an official website, with balanced content.

As a result of complaints about the blatant disregard for Parades Commission guidelines, there was a police investigation, a Parades Commission meeting, a GAA inquiry and parliamentary questions about this parade. Sinn Féin claimed it was 'street theatre' and not a paramilitary parade, but was put very much on the back foot for quite a while by the reaction to it.

Friday, 21 August 2009

Ulster Unionist parades spokesman Michael Copeland says Sinn Féin has 'double standards' after complaints made when the Parades Commission upholds a decision to allow forty-one Loyalist bands to march through Rasharkin, County Antrim, with the warning that paramilitary-style clothing must not be worn; flags, bannerettes and symbols relating to a proscribed organisation not be displayed; and musical instruments must not bear any inscription or mark of a proscribed organisation. The UUP politician says these parading guidelines were breached on Sunday, 24 March 2009, in a Republican parade through Rasharkin to commemorate IRA man Gerard Casey when 'party tunes' were played outside a Sunday School class.

'I can only presume that those objecting to Ballymaconnelly's parade are blind to the hypocrisy of their own argument,' says Mr Copeland. His remarks are dismissed by Sinn Féin's Daithí McKay, who points out that Republicans only hold parades where 'they are wanted'. The Sinn Féin man says, 'The parade in March was respectful, dignified and it was in memory of a local member of the community who was killed during the conflict.'[114]

Also on this day, the Robert Graham Memorial Flute Band hosts thirty bands in Bangor in a free-flowing event, while in south Antrim, the Ballyclare Protestant Flute Band has over twenty bands on parade and in Killylea, County Armagh, the annual parade of Pride of the Frontier Flute Band, Drumhillery, had thirty-four bands.[115]

Monday, 24 August 2009

The *Belfast Telegraph* reports a furious row in the wake of the republican parade in Galbally, with the disclosure that a member of the Dungannon District Policing Partnership took part in paramilitary style dress. He is Ruairí Gildernew, brother of Sinn Féin Agriculture Minister Michelle Gildernew, whose father is a Sinn Féin councillor and chairman of the local policing partnership. DUP Culture Minister Nelson McCausland criticises the GAA for allowing its grounds to be used for the paramilitary event and SDLP Deputy leader Alasdair McDonnell calls on the GAA to investigate this use of its facilities.

CHAPTER 13

HOME AND AWAY

Thursday, 20 August 2009

In the end it comes down to putting on a good show, especially at home. So there is a buzz of excitement at the Bridgetown Orange Hall, even if bandmaster Trevor is absent. Drummers are drumming; fluters fluting and the colour party, greatly expanded, is going through its paces in the main hall. If the band has struggled through the season, the crisis appears over in the lead-up to their annual parade. Almost as important are other home parades, including that of the rival Pride of the Derg band this Saturday. Fluter Johnny says the band is going to Lisburn for an early parade but will be returning to 'keep them happy'. This is about keeping up appearances for local standing and recruits. A good display is vital and the expanded colour party should provide that. Flag-bearer Joanne is confident: 'Last year we had eight in the colour party; the year before that we had eight as well, and next year we should have eight again.'

Saturday, 22 August 2009

Lambeg Orange and Blue Flute Band have forty-four bands in their Lisburn parade where the Castlederg Young Loyalists are among the first to parade 'with their tight style continuing to impress'.[116]

Back home in Castlederg, the Pride of the Derg parade takes place in rainfall and, for the second successive time, the rival Blood and Thunder band parades the town in a downpour before a large crowd. Led off by the Aghyaran Accordion Band, the event quickly becomes a display of straight-up Blood and Thunder. Clearly a big hit are the Shankill Protestant Boys who invest a huge amount of aggression into a performance from mostly middle-aged men with shaved heads, thick necks and lots of Loyalist tattoos. The percussion is relentless, as is the rain; and, right on queue, the Castlederg Young Loyalists arrive home from Lisburn to parade just before the host band takes centre stage. With a colour party of three, the Castlederg Young Loyalists play tightly and step along briskly while flag-bearer Joanne with her toddler son in her arms waves proudly from the footpath. Without pausing, the band parades on to the finish and applause. In its wake, the Pride moves like a lumbering beast around the circuit of the Diamond and stops for a gallery performance as the crowd cheers their performance.

Thursday, 27 August 2009

'I tried mine on at home and it looks great,' Trevor Donnell says, clearly chuffed with the new white trousers and hat that – with the existing tunic – make up the new uniform of the Castlederg Young Loyalists Flute Band. 'It's supposed to look like a US Marine officer; at least that's what he says,' the bandmaster explains for my benefit, referring to the uniform supplier from Lurgan. 'I suppose his job is to talk it up though,' he adds, with a touch of Castlederg realism. He clearly wants to unveil the new look at the earliest opportunity. Others are more inclined to wait for the annual parade. 'You couldn't wear them out to the field this Saturday anyway,' says Judy. 'They'd be ruined.' Trevor agrees and suggests that the band members ensure the legs of the trousers are very carefully measured so they are not dragging and the suppliers should do any alterations. 'We have to be very careful with them and make sure everyone changes out of them as soon as we're done. At £65 a pair for those trousers, it would be a very expensive outlay for just the one day,' he remarks, again pointing out that the new hats also cost £65 each. He remarks on a band member who had the new trousers measured and altered for her exact fit and then quit the band. 'Aye, I got a text from her as well,' says Michaela in the colour party, 'but she said was going to get the sack from work if she didn't put in the hours and she couldn't take any more time off.'

Trevor replies, 'I wish she had thought of that and told us before we went and had the trousers made to her size. You know I asked her if she was going to stay with us and she told me she would. I quizzed her about it and I said it was no good just being in the odd time. That's her out already and with Andy out for I don't know how long, we're two down already and we haven't even worn the uniform yet.' Andy, he explains for those who have not heard, has been in a serious accident over in England. Part of a crane he was working on fell on him. 'The specialists are working on him and trying to save his leg,' says Trevor, while a Get Well card for the band's side-drummer is circulating among the group. 'It's very serious.'

Friday, 28 August 2009

Fifty-two bands parade through Newry in the thirtieth anniversary parade of the South Down Defenders. In the village of Kells, County Antrim, twenty bands parade for the local Sons of William Flute Band.[117]

Saturday, 29 August 2009

11.45 a.m. Judy with her flute and Joanne with the bannerette are being arranged into a pose by a photographer from the *Newsletter*, who tells them the photo should appear in a special pictorial feature on Tuesday. One of the band members remarks that this is the same photographer who had them all posing for a photo on 12 July. 'Not a sign of it in the paper, though,' Trevor Donnell adds.

The group stands beside the stack of its drums, flags and banners during a dry spell on an otherwise showery and blustery 'Last Saturday' when members of the Royal

Black Preceptory come together for their traditional 'walk' which is in Castlederg this year. I ask Kenny and Trevor, both Orangemen, to explain the difference between their institution and the Black. 'The Black would be more Bible-based,' says Trevor. 'Aye they have to go to lectures,' Kenny adds. Members of the Black refer to each other as 'Sir Knight' and it is only open to Orangemen of several years standing. Today, Sir Knights from Omagh, Strabane and Castlederg districts are on parade with twenty-three bands. Nearby, groups of men in dark sashes hold banners which portray Biblical rather than historical themes. The Castlederg Chosen Few banner, borne aloft proudly to the field beside Castlederg High School, has a puny David wielding his sling against mighty Goliath. On the back, Moses parts the Red Sea for the fleeing Israelites as the Pharaoh's army pursues. Earlier still, the banner was paraded through the town with the usual restrictions around Ferguson Crescent.

'Let's take a dander back down to the hall,' somebody suggests and the band members set off. Around the field, clusters gather around their own stacks. At the Pride of the Derg a young boy with a large tattoo on his right forearm kneels, takes up drumsticks and begins a rhythm on a side-drum. Around the field, others take up the beat. Other bands arrive through a gate with an archway raised by Killen Star of Bethlehem Preceptory. At another entrance, the *Newsletter* photographer arranges a pose by a small blond boy in band uniform. His proud father looks on, smiling broadly.

12.30 p.m. Out on the Castlegore Road, final contingents are making their way to the field. A man in a black collarette hoists himself onto the low garden wall beside me asking, 'Is this dry, do you think?' I point out that it is quite wet still but he settles himself down anyway. 'Och, I have to sit for the knees are killing me,' he says. 'Do you know, this is the first time I've been out on the last Saturday when I wasn't piping?'

He then relates how he was a member of the Ardstraw Pipe Band for thirty-nine years, as well as the UDR Pipe Band based in Omagh, which became part of the Royal Irish Regiment band. He loved the regimental band life. 'When I was quitting it, because of the knees, they said they'd have to get a few extra people to do the work. I says you never passed a bit of remarks when I was doing it all.' He talks of the band and the constant scramble for members, for uniforms and for instruments. 'You'd never be off the phone with one thing and another. There's always something has to be phoned about. And you know the young ones in the band? They think it just happens when they are there,' he says. He was with the regimental band for a week in Cyprus when they played at various events. He also went to the School of Piping in Edinburgh four times, where the instructors were tough enough to make him rethink his love of bagpipes. One in particular was very strict: 'But he loved a few drinks afterwards and he always headed out with the Paddies as he called us,' says the Sir Knight with the bad knees.

12.40 p.m. The bannerette of the County Tyrone Grand Black Chapter is borne aloft to the field followed by eighteen grandees with their district bannerettes of Castlederg, Strabane and Omagh. They march proudly in dark suits, bowler hats, collarettes, aprons, gloves and cuffs, waving to onlookers. All have neatly folded umbrellas and a chaplain carrying a Bible is the only one without a bowler hat. At the gate, the dignitaries line up for a photo with the man from the *Newsletter*. Photographers from local papers join in and Strabane Councillor Jim Emery urges his colleagues to smile. I notice all the shoes, bar another chaplain's, are shiny, but they will have to cross the mucky field to the flatbed stage later.

Meanwhile, fluters Neil and Timmy have returned to the field and the others filter back in pairs and groups. Flag-bearer Michaela is among the first and she talks of school next week when she will enter 'Upper Sixth', taking music, technology and maths for A-Level. She plays the clarinet and saxophone, and I ask why she doesn't take up the flute. 'Maybe when we have more for the colour party I might do that,' she says brightly. 'It could be easier maybe than the clarinet and maybe if we get the colour party stronger I can start to take lessons on the flute.' She joins other band members who are looking over the hedge at the Pride of the Derg forming ranks on the road. Mention of their annual parade prompts a remark that some of 'the POTD crowd' made comments about the Castlederg Young Loyalists not being welcome. 'I don't care because I'll just be friends with everyone. It's their problem if they want to act the hard men.'

1.20 p.m. The muster is completed while Derek Hussey in his black sash smokes a cigarette and returned bass-drummer Ian adopts an exaggerated pose for a photograph. Then it's off again, wheeling out of the nearest gate between twin Union Jacks and off into the town. The band plays 'How Great Thou Art' with the Black men's banner swirling in the rising wind. At the bridge, people huddle under umbrellas or scurry for shelter from the heavy rain. The band goes thundering through the adjacent roundabout where the head of the parade waits for the last contingents before it re-crosses the bridge. Then up around the Diamond, the reverberations of Ian's bass drum sounding even louder at the point where the telegraph poles have Irish tricolours on top and the only spectators are a few smokers outside a pub. The band leads the local Black men on out the Upper Strabane Road before doubling back to complete the full circuit of the lower town. Meanwhile, the crowd heads back towards the field where the bands and Black men are heading as the rain-spattered breeze billows the big ornate banners of preceptories with equally ornate names – Omagh Olive Branch, Newtownstewart Ivy Leaf, Plumbridge Ark of Safety, Mountjoy Burning Bush and almost last, but not least, the Castlederg Chosen Few stepping out on home ground behind their favourite band.

Thursday, 3 September 2009

Local piper Bill is clearly enjoying the evening with the young bandsmen. He has been invited to add a novel variation to familiar tunes such as 'Highland Cathedral'. For much of the weekly practice session, Trevor tries out ways to show the flutes, drums and bagpipes to best effect. Bill apologises several times for mistakes, adding that he is finding it difficult to avoid adding his usual 'grace notes' to these airs. By the end, the arrangements have been agreed and Bill is given a copy of the band's last CD to go over the tunes. The Castlederg Young Loyalists will play them during the intermission of a concert by a Scottish group in Bentley's nightclub near Magherafelt, on Saturday night after a daytime parade in Belfast of the Regimental Bands Association. 'So can you meet us here at 10.30 on Saturday morning?' Trevor asks Bill, having called to confirm the bus from Castlederg to Belfast, then to Magherafelt and home late. 'Aye, if I can bring my cows along with me!' Bill laughs. 'Better again, maybe you can help me milk them. There's only seventy-five to do because twenty are dry at the minute.'

Friday, 4 September 2009

In Carrickfergus, County Antrim, the Ulster Grenadiers Flute hosts its annual parade of thirty-three bands; while in Lurgan, County Armagh, the parade and competition hosted by the Upper Bann Fusiliers Flute, on a new route finishing at the Mourneview Park home of Glenavon Football Club, includes twenty-five bands.[118]

Yet the grand finale of the season is when the Omagh Protestant Boys band fills the centre of Tyrone's county town with hundreds of uniformed band members combining colour parties, drum corps and woodwind sections all marking time in perfect step and playing in unison. As a spectacle it is impressive; as a musical experience it is exhilarating. Yet most people in the largely nationalist vicinity choose to ignore the event completely. In local hostelries along adjacent John Street, off-limits for band parades, the event barely registers beyond the attitude that it must be ignored at all costs even if it is hugely entertaining.

Not that the Omagh Protestant Boys event is completely ignored, for on a cool but much appreciated dry evening, a relatively large crowd has gathered at the junctions of Market Street, Drumragh Avenue and the Dublin Road. In a parade of more than forty bands, the percussion is cranked up here, making a cacophonous din at times. Yet that is what most spectators seem to enjoy. The sound is infinitely more tolerable only a few metres away at the large glass obelisk with its embedded Tyrone Crystal heart at the spot where thirty-one lives were ripped away in the bombing atrocity of August 1998. As the colour party of the Castlederg Young Loyalists approaches, Michaela lowers the ornate bannerette and her two companions lower the band's standards in silent homage to all those who died horrifically at this spot. The momentary gesture draws applause.

Further up the street, where the crowd peters out, the

most spectacular part of the parade is staged in front of only a dozen or so spectators at the wider public space at the top of High Street. This is where the bands do a u-turn, or simply backtrack through their own ranks, and parade back down the town.

As the courthouse clock inches just past 11 p.m. – the time the parade is to have been completed – sounds of heavy drumming rolls towards us and, next thing, a band is coming and coming and coming. First is a big vanguard colour party with bannerettes and band standards. Then drum majors and tipstaffs with elaborate sashes and staffs, the drum corps and the big bass drums and finally the ranks of fluters and other woodwind instrumentalists. On the side, marshalling bandmasters keep the show on the road as the mixed uniforms can now be identified by the drums as Omagh Protestant Boys, Skeogh Flute and Pride of Ballinran, both from County Down, Lisburn Defenders and Sir George White Memorial of Broughshane, both County Antrim, and the Ballymacarret Defenders of East Belfast. They reach the courthouse and in a drill movement that looks like it was practised many times, the ranks fold in on themselves and march back down. By the time the colour party reaches Bridge Street and begins marking time, the bandsmen have occupied the full open space at the heart of Omagh town. After a few tunes, the giant band is off on parade once more, moving around the corner to a burst of applause.

Saturday, 5 September 2009

The annual parade of the Regimental Bands Association takes place on Belfast's Shankill Road with bands from every county and more than a dozen visiting bands from England and Scotland. That night, Annalong's Silver Star Flute has a good turnout of bands at its parade in County Down.[119]

Thursday, 17 September 2009

'We've been parading with five and six flutes all year and now we don't even have enough uniforms to go around,' observes bandmaster Trevor Donnell. The band is in the throes of last-minute arrangements for its annual parade and there is a final discussion on whether they should wear the new uniforms. In the end, it will come down to the uncertain weather. But with more bodies than new uniforms it is decided that the colour party will parade in the dark trousers and hats, while the others will don the US Marine whites.

Saturday, 19 September 2009

8.10 p.m. On a small trailer stage outside the Castle Inn, the Singing Diggerman (aka Andy Lowry) sings 'The Pretty Little Girl from Omagh', before dedicating his next song to Amy Rose who has 'come all the way from Newtownstewart'. A couple take to jiving on the footpath in front of his stage, and the woman may well be Amy Rose, who came all the way to enjoy the carnival atmosphere of neighbouring Castlederg on a clear, crisp, autumn evening. God and Ulster smile on the Castlederg Young Loyalists Flute Band as the minutes tick down to the annual parade and band members jiggle collection boxes in the crowd. At the mouth of Meetinghouse Lane, Alan Feathers advises me to make my contribution in his box because Johnny, collecting across the way, has none of the tiny stickers that will identify me as having paid already. He proffers a sticky paper circle and says, 'That's the centre of a Polo mint.' To friendly greetings I head off to the main car park, the rallying point outside Bridgetown No Surrender Orange Hall. Bandmaster Trevor Donnell is walking through McCay Court wearing his CYL Old Boys shirt and obviously pleased with the dry weather. He reports that the band won the 'Best Small Band Blood and Thunder' shield at the Moneyslane Flute Band parade in Rathfriland last night.

8.25 p.m. At the car park, men in kilts are warming up their bagpipes in short bursts of musical scales that die off in a groan. Others are entering and leaving the Orange Hall where they are handed a typed document outlining a code of conduct: 'In order to achieve a trouble-free parade, we would appreciate the co-operation of all visiting bands that they do not react to any provocation by Sinn Féin/IRA at the top of the town (if any are there) as any reaction will only affect our parade next year. We request that no bands stop to play to the crowd as with time restraints, we need to keep the parade flowing smoothly. We would appeal to all bands to encourage members of the Blue Bag Brigade to refrain from following bands up the town and getting involved in confrontations with the PSNI and Republicans (again if any are there).[120] From 10 p.m. all bands will be re-routed around the Diamond. A social function will follow in the Castle Inn. There will also be a function in the Derg Arms just across the road from the Castle Inn; both functions are for band funds. The British Legion Club will also be open to all bands/band members. It is situated in Main Street, opposite the Ulster Bank. The Waterside Bar at the bottom of the town at the bridge is also a Prod bar. The street-drinking laws are in force in Castlederg so don't be getting yourself a £50 fine. Lastly, we hope all bands enjoy their time in Castlederg and have a safe journey home.'

8.35 p.m. Back up the town, the Singing Diggerman is belting out 'The Galway Girl' and 'Horse it into ya, Cynthia, fer you're the girl for me' to smiling faces and tapping feet. Meanwhile, a pair dressed as Barney the Dinosaur and a dwarf-type figure trundle a trolley laden with crisps and other treats. As they stumble into traffic bollards, a couple of youngsters help themselves. 'Barney' removes his headgear, the youngsters slink into the crowd, and the costumed pair march on with a lightened load.

8.50 p.m. Men in high-visibility vests take up position at the corner of the Diamond leading onto Ferguson Crescent, where several police officers are standing as the evening fades and spectators huddle in the shadows. The Singing Diggerman has wrapped up for the night. As the hour turns, strains of music are heard. Then along comes Robbie McKinley in his marshal vest leading the Aghyaran Accordion Band. Brawny men in kilts of the Sinclair Memorial Pipe Band from Newtownstewart follow, ahead of the first Blood and Thunder band – Pride of the Village from Stoneyford, County Antrim. As the big drums approach the Diamond, cavorting children cease their running and hurry over to watch. Next up is the West Tyrone Young Defenders Flute Band, made up of pupils from Castlederg High School who are also members of the Castlederg Young Loyalists, and the Red Hand Defenders from Newtownstewart. Behind a colour party of younger children, the four side-drums, big drum and eight flutes belt out 'The Sash' as they round the Diamond instead of following the route out the Upper Strabane Road (host bands usually shorten their own route because they are involved in marshalling, etc.). Next is the Tobermore Loyal Flute Band and then the CYL Old Boys resplendent in orange shirts and parading along to the applause and cheers of onlookers. The Old Boys also turn for home on the Diamond, pulling up behind the Young Defenders who are giving it all they can to compete with the bands coming up Main Street. Four bands are now stalled in the Diamond area, including the Star of the Erne Pipe Band with Willie Smith giving his all once again on the big drum. A man in a County Donegal Rangers Supporters Club jacket nods at the West Tyrone Young Defenders: 'Wish they'd shut the fuck up 'til we hear the pipes.'

9.30 p.m. Main Street has become Blood and Thunder Alley with five or six bands squeezed along this short part of the parade route. The sounds bounce off the three-storey buildings from the East Bank Protestant Boys followed by Montober, Drumconvis, South Fermanagh and the Blair Memorial. However, when the Omagh Protestant Boys march briskly along the return route, an older woman outside the Spice of India takeaway remarks with certainty, 'They're the best band here tonight.'

9.45 p.m. Back to Blood and Thunder as the shop-front windows reverberate to the pulse of Burntollet Sons of Ulster, Tamlaghtmore Tigers, Pride of the Derg, Cormeen Rising Sons and the Border Defenders from Newtownbutler, followed by South Down Defenders, Red Hand Defenders, Magheraveely, Moneyslane, Drumnaclough, Moygashel Sons of Ulster and Maghera Sons of William. Then come the Omagh True Blues, Cookstown Sons of William and Kilcluney Volunteers. The colour parties lower their standards at the war memorial, with only the Union Jack held upright. As the Newtownards Volunteers, Downshire, Rising Sons of the Valley and Pride of Ballinran are followed by the Mourne Young Defenders and Dunamoney, an older man standing nearby asks, 'Are they going to keep coming all night? How many bands are there anyway?' By my rough count, the parade has far exceeded last year's thirty-five bands and, yes, they still seem to be coming. But as 10 p.m. approaches, some stewards at the Ferguson Crescent junction move to form a cordon that closes off High Street. Under the Parades Commission stipulation, bands on the outward route after 10 p.m. will not go along Hospital Road, Young Crescent and back along William Street. However, there is a minor stand-off when Gortagilly Coronation Flute Band refuses to turn back. Finally, the stewards relent and Gortagilly becomes the last band to complete the entire circuit of the Castlederg Young Loyalists' 2009 annual parade. As other bands merge the two routes, a man who looks like an official observer talks urgently into his mobile phone.

10.10 p.m. Bands keep coming – Pride of Prince William from Lisburn, Castledawson's Star and Crown, Drumeagles Defenders and Ballymacall True Blues. Neil Johnston passes by in his marshal's vest, blowing into cupped hands, and says he is going back to his car to warm up before the host band parades. As he moves off, a returning band with a bass drumhead identifying the Cormeen Rising Sons of William passes. The bass drummer helpfully rotates to show that the obverse has Ballyrea Boyne Defenders on it and it is clear the Cormeen drumhead has been 'borrowed'. The seemingly endless parade continues with the Craigavon Protestant Boys, Drumderg Loyalists and the Portadown Defenders. And then silence as the Clogher Protestant Boys Flute Band turns into McCay Court shortly after 10.40 p.m.

10.45 p.m. A woman hangs up her mobile phone and hurries over to Trevor Donnell: 'The Randalstown band is on the way. They're only five minutes from here and they want to parade.' Negotiations ensue with a police officer as people pass by, some heading home. A man outside the Castle Inn asks if the Castlederg Young Loyalists will parade. Most relax and relish the prospect of more to come. Around the two most popular pubs, the crowd grows to six or seven deep on the footpaths and spills onto Main Street itself. Some talk of the imminent arrival of the Randalstown band and the fact that the Castlederg Young Loyalists won't parade before them. Young band members stand around chatting; one young man gallantly drapes his tunic around the shoulders of his blonde girlfriend and then stands shivering beside her. Others dressed in short-sleeved shirts seem oblivious to the cold as they drink from plastic beakers. Necks crane up and down the street for signs of action. Then a cordon of parade marshals moves in to form a solid cordon. The crowd swells further and moves in tightly towards the protected zone.

11.05 p.m. Behind a three-member colour party, the Randalstown Sons of Ulster Flute Band advances and comes to a halt at the cordon. A voice in the crowd asks who they are as four side-drummers rattle out some Blood and Thunder beats that almost drown the nine flutes. When they belt out 'The Sash', however, many in the crowd sing along. Then abruptly, the Randalstown Sons of Ulster disperse.

11.10 p.m. Approaching from the gloom, Kenny leads an impressive main colour party of seven, with four junior flag-carriers behind. The Castlederg Young Loyalists Flute Band takes firm control of home turf to cheers and applause. The tune ends, the pacing stops and the colour party swivels smartly to face the drummers kitted out in the new white trousers and white caps. A new young bandsman carrying bagpipes across his shoulder is dressed in the old uniform, while Ian and Michael, the substitute bass drummer borrowed again from Montober, wear all white with short-sleeved shirts. The band launches into a medley which includes 'The Sash'. Some try to sing along, but the band has already switched to 'How Great Thou Art', belting it out with lots of Blood and Thunder. A voice behind chokes with emotion: 'God, they're a great wee band.' Others obviously agree, as cameras flash and each tune is greeted with cheers as the band performs crowd favourites including 'Killaloe', 'Lannigan's Ball' and 'Go Man Go'. Then it's into 'Barnrocks' and 'Highland Cathedral' with the young piper joining in. The cheers erupt with added fervour. Finally, bandmaster Trevor rolls out a beat, the others join in and the fluters take up 'God Save the Queen'. On completion, Kenny calls out the order, the band wheels to the right, snapping to attention before falling out to a huge sense of triumph as people disperse.

11.25 p.m. Back at the Orange Hall, band members are changing rapidly and packing away drums and other equipment. Trevor asks how many bands there were and I estimate it at just under fifty, far exceeding anything staged before in the town. In a cluster outside, the young piper is the hero of the hour.

11.35 p.m. On Main Street, the British Legion and the

surrounding pubs are packed to the gunnels. There is virtual silence around the Diamond, apart from the cars passing through on their way home. A group of police officers heads back to the station where a Landrover is pulling in through the big armoured gate under the observation deck. One policeman is whistling jauntily. The tune is 'Killaloe':

> We're the Irish Rangers,
> The boys who fear no danger,
> We're the boys from Paddy's land.
> Yo! Shut up you buggers and fight.

Yet nobody is in the mood for a fight. This is a night of music and celebration, but for only one side of a still divided community in a small border town with a big sound.

CHAPTER 14

MARKING TIME

Thursday, 24 September 2009

A letter in the *Ulster Herald* takes issue with complaints by Sinn
Féin Councillor Sean Begley about the 4 September parade
of the Omagh Protestant Boys. It suggests the complaints
demonstrate the 'sham' of Republican support for the Good
Friday Agreement: 'Why does he not just come out and say
plain and simple, that Republicans of West Tyrone do not
want a Protestant about the place?' asks the letter-writer. 'To
even imply that there was a detrimental effect to the economy
of the town on the evening in question, when we consider the
crowds of people that flocked to Omagh to see the parade,
is simply laughable. And to then complain that the parade,
which lasted only two and a half hours, went "five minutes"
over time, really does highlight how desperate he is to find
anything to justify his anti-Protestant stance. Furthermore,
he expresses concern that these parades seem to be growing
larger. Surely this is a positive move, or would he rather that
the many young people who devote so much of their time

pursuing their interest in the marching bands, would instead congregate on street corners and engage in some kind of anti-social behaviour?' The letter suggests 'the real crux of the matter is that Mr Begley and his ilk can't stomach the fact that the Unionist section of our community have such a rich culture steeped as it is in a military tradition, which today manifests itself in the form of these impeccably turned-out marching bands'. In a final blistering put-down, the letter concludes, 'This Republican mindset is hardly surprising when we consider that the sum total of their military achievements, as evidenced by the "street theatre" display in Galbally a few weeks ago, consist of little more than masked men skulking behind a hedge before shooting their victim in the back and then running away.'[121]

As if in response to other Republican protests, meanwhile, a big pile of flags has accumulated at the top of the stairs in the Castlederg band practice room. They were taken down the previous Monday, explains Ben, one of the young band members. 'We always put them up in June and then take them down on the Monday after our annual [parade].'

Thursday, 1 October 2009

The band is rehearsing some tunes for a charity concert in Newtownstewart on Saturday, the first indoor engagement over the closed season. Alan Feathers wants to start practising new tunes. He rattles off an air on his flute, but can't remember what it's called. A voice pipes up, 'That's what do you call it, the

Soldier's Song.' The hall erupts in laughter. Trevor explains, 'Maybe you're thinking of "The British Soldier", but I don't think that's the tune.' Feathers continues to try out various tunes. 'This one is called "Itchy Fingers",' he says, his own fingers skipping merrily. He stumbles and starts again, slower. 'If you play it slow, it's wile dead,' he says. Some like the tune, but baulk at the rapid fingering. 'If yiz start practising it now, you'll have it up to speed by next March,' says Trevor, who points out that there are five engagements before he steps down as bandmaster. It is as if he has already started to sidle out of the role he began as a fresh-faced young drummer at the band's inauguration in 1977. He then reveals big news. 'Listen, I've been contacted by the Apprentice Boys. They want us to lead out the Parent Club in the walk around the walls, if yiz are up for it.' A few nods. 'Listen this is a great honour. It's just bands from Londonderry itself that get to do this. The only outside band ever asked to do it before was Black Skull from Glasgow, but we'll be the first Northern Ireland band from outside the city. I know if it had come up when I was your age, I'd have been jumping to do it and it wouldn't matter what else I had on that day. It's not many bands that can say they've walked the walls because there was a good bit of them closed off for years during the Troubles. So what'll I tell them?' There is some hesitation and mumbles until Trevor presses and Johnny says they'll do it. 'Right then,' says Trevor, 'I'll give them your name, Johnny, and they can phone you if the band doesn't show up.'

Friday, 2 October 2009

7 p.m. Band members sort uniforms, lug drums, break down flags and bannerette, and put them into carrier-bags and arrange who will travel in what car to the final parade of the year in Coagh, about fifty miles away at the far end of Tyrone. Bandmaster Trevor has gone earlier on a small bus with a group of friends, relinquishing authority for final arrangements on his last parade as bandmaster. Young Davy Lowry assumes control as assistant bandmaster and when Michaela asks if the flags have been packed, he tells her that's the responsibility of the colour party. Finally, cars loaded and locked, Johnny revs his engine, reverses sharply into a parking space and climbs into another car with his mate Ian. Other engines are gunned and the band pulls off in a five-car convoy.

7.45 p.m. I'm in the final car with Neil Johnston, the big drum, flags and an assortment of bags, hatboxes and other paraphernalia. As the convoy breaks up with traffic delays and different speeds, we settle into a relaxed conversation about his Christian faith and how he incorporates that with his love of Blood and Thunder. He tells me he has now switched from Kilskeery Free Presbyterian to the Independent Methodist congregation in Irvinestown because he was involved in its youth ministry. He talks openly of his fundamental Christianity, of a lecture he attended on Creation and how he enjoyed the part about Noah's Ark. Yet there is no hint of proselytising and he never intrudes on my own beliefs. The band, meanwhile, is his vital social outlet. 'I don't go out to bars any more,' he explains, 'so apart from church and work, I don't have other opportunities to meet people of my age. I suppose it would be different if I had a girlfriend, but I have a lot of time now that I like to spend with the band and that's where my friends are. It's like that in a band; it is where you meet your friends. I must say, I love it. I would miss it terribly if it wasn't there.'

8.30 p.m. Past Omagh and well down the Cookstown road after several delays, Neil remarks that the others have probably arrived in Coagh. But since we carry the big drum and the flags, they can't start without us.

8.45 pm. Finally from a maze of small roads, we drive right up to a main junction of the parade and park up on the grass verge so the drum won't have to be carried far. Although we are first here, Neil dons his tunic as bands stream by right in front of us in the final blast of the Blood and Thunder season. The Aughnacloy Sons of William parade next weekend is the very last, but because they did not attend Castlederg, the Castlederg Young Loyalists will not be there.

9.15 p.m. The band is mustering on the side of the road. A few members set off to look for Trevor and someone goes to talk to the organisers. Meanwhile, the now familiar procession files past. Given return visits, there is little variation and because of its added travel time to most parades, Castlederg is usually slotted in near the end.

9.45 p.m. As two new members of the colour party get last-minute instructions on decorum, Judy, the band's only female musician, comes over to chat and mentions that this will be the last parade for her and husband Gordie in the drum corps before they retire. She joined the Castlederg Young Loyalists in her mid-teens and spent five years as a flag-bearer in the colour party 'back when we were winning all the awards for the colour party'. Then she asked Trevor if she could join the fluters. 'I'd been in a band before, you see, a flute band in Sion Mills and I knew how to flute already.' So Judy became the sole female fluter and 'one of the boys'. Nobody ever made her feel different from the other fluters and she did not stand on ceremony just because she was a girl. When conversation became a bit colourful, she could hold her own. 'Even when we had to change our uniforms there recently, and there was nowhere else to go, I just went ahead and changed like everyone else. It was casual and nobody passed any remarks. So that was good. But this band was always like that. They made you feel welcome ...' Judy pauses as tears well in her eyes: 'I'll really miss this band, so I will. I'll never join another band because this is my band and it'll be my band forever.' Her tearful moment passes and she predicts the most difficult time will be when the band parades through the town and she will want to be part of it. Maybe she can join the Old Boys and change it to the Old Boys and Girls, I suggest. 'I'm not that oul yet,' Judy laughs as we are joined by her husband Gordie with flag-bearer Joanne and her partner Richard from the fluters who are also set for their final parade.

10.10 p.m. Trevor has come up from the village at last and is relaxed and smiling as he hikes up the road with the younger band members. At the signal of Trevor's drum roll, they are soon off and marching along in their signature formation – tight with short rapid steps. Along the route, bandsmen congregate on the footpaths, applauding as they identify the last band making a distinctive impression as it moves through Coagh in the penultimate spot before the Tamlaghtmore Tigers close their annual event.

10.35 p.m. The parade stalls opposite a garage forecourt as another band comes along on the return route. They compete for volume and the Castlederg crew more than holds its own. As the tune ends, I ask Neil how they keep it up. He says it helps to keep your eyes on the fluter in front and match finger movements to maintain tempo. If co-ordination is lost, the tune falters.

10.40 p.m. Up ahead, the colour party veers to the right to get around a road obstacle but risks collision with another band. Kenny hesitates, halts abruptly and then side-shuffles back into place. It is an atypical faux pas. Finally, a break and the band moves off again veering left into a side road where another band has paused to finish a tune. Then off again and within moments the reason for the delay is obvious. Marshals have cordoned off the road and are directing the parade through a narrow walkway. The band has started 'The Spirit of Ulster' and shows precisely that in a slick move. Starting with the colour party, they march smartly out of parade formation into single file and down the narrow path, before forming back into ranks on the other side. Not a single note is missed and each member of the band seems to know instinctively how to move. The reformed band finishes in a flourish and launches into the crowd-pleasing 'Killaloe' as it proceeds through a small estate adorned with Loyalist flags. Back on the main street, the parade heads down past the Orange Hall where members of the host Tamlaghtmore band applaud.

10.50 p.m. There is further acclaim for the Castlederg Young Loyalists when they pause at the bridge playing 'Lannigan's Ball'. The cheers are led by Trevor's friends who have come along for his last parade. Then it's off to the round-about junction and the formal dispersal, when the final notes are sounded and the band falls out on command. Judy, Gordie, Joanne and Richard assemble for a photo in full uniform be-fore they retire from the Castlederg Young Loyalists. Gordie notes he has been in the band for fifteen years. 'Don't know what I'll do with my weekends now,' he remarks. 'You can stay home with your wife,' laughs Judy. Richard says he, Gordie and Judy bowed out before but came back, while Joanne had also been out because of their baby. That prompts Joanne to say, 'I don't know if I'm even leaving the band. I haven't made up my mind yet.'

11.10 p.m. Trevor and young Davy are comparing notes, when Michaela comes bustling through to complain that the colour party was deeply embarrassed up in the village and she blames Kenny. 'I'm never parading with him again,' she declares. A few stern words from Trevor remind her that she is in a public place and any criticism of another band member should be saved for later. The wee tantrum has upset the bonhomie of the last parade in 2009. But all parades are charged with emotion and the loss of perfection is a matter of hurt pride for Michaela this time.

11.55 p.m. We are almost in Castlederg and Neil and young Davy Lowry, who is travelling home with us, have been talking of new tunes that the band might rehearse for next season. They talk of hymns and marches such as 'Black Watch', noting that other bands have played them and they will have to put the Castlederg stamp on them. They agree that their renditions are always played to a more suitable marching pace. They discuss the benefits of travelling widely to parades, if only to experience other styles and tunes. I ask Neil how many miles he has driven to parades since he bought the car almost exactly one year ago, just days before joining the Castlederg Young Loyalists. The dashboard shows 16,460 miles and, apart from the short round trip to work, this has been for band practice, parades and other band business. I say he must be cleaning up on mileage expenses and they both laugh. The conversation breaks off when Davy phones the Indian takeaway. 'I just have to tell them who I am and they know it'll be a kebab and chips,' he says.

12.05 a.m. We disembark at the Orange Hall and I head home while the two young bandsmen unload the flags and other gear, carrying them back into the Orange Hall for storage until the Castlederg Young Loyalists Flute Band is back on the road and once again marching to the beat of its own big drum.

POSTSCRIPT

Friday, 6 February 2010

The Loyalist flags that wafted proudly over the entrance of Millbrook Gardens in Castlederg last summer are now tattered rags clinging to the lamp-posts in the wind-driven rain of a dreary winter's day. Yet even in the depths of winter, the issue of parades is still generating a lot of heat. Northern Ireland's First and Deputy First Ministers, Peter Robinson and Martin McGuinness, today announced that they have concluded the longest negotiations of the peace process to date in an agreement over the pivotal issues of devolving policing and justice powers and dealing with contentious parades. While the agreement on policing is for local ministerial control, the second issue has been handed to a working group of Sinn Féin and DUP Assembly members to devise an alternative method of dealing with parades. The British and Irish governments favour the adoption of what is called the 'Derry model' whereby the Apprentice Boys talk directly to Nationalist residents. That is the suggestion also of the Ashdown Commission review, although its findings are still under wraps pending local agreement.

With the Orange Order in the wings, there is a clear desire

for a resolution. However, many marching bands resent being treated as the mere coat-tails of the Orange Order, fearing their concerns as independent local organisations will not be addressed in a formula designed to suit a hierarchical and centralised institution. For while the Orange still hosts many parades, these take place in two months of summer and overwhelmingly on a single day. Moreover, their major parades are popular spectacles not because of the dwindling ranks of men in sashes, but because of the bands, and in particular because of the energy and noise of the Blood and Thunder bands. In a more secular age, the bands represent a new cultural expression for Loyalist communities. But what of the general perception of Blood and Thunder bands outside their own constituency?

The English and Americans, it has been said, are two peoples divided by a common language. The same and much more could be said of the two traditions that make up the community now pursuing a shared future in Northern Ireland. Down the four centuries since the Plantation of Ulster, they have remained apart, yet locked together, worshipping the same God but in different houses, speaking the same language but with subtle nuances that differentiate one from the other, learning the same history but from opposite perspectives in different schools, and listening to the same tunes but calling them by different names. Their fraternal societies – born of a need for fellowship and mutual support as much as a desire for control of territory or economic power – have often been mirror images of each other. Their pageantry and folk memories are inextricably entwined, yet the heroes of one are the villains of the other and there has been a constant and abiding impulse to emphasise the difference.

Even after sixteen years of relative peace and the constant blurring of edges in an age of popular culture that revolves around British soccer, reality TV and soap operas, denial and open resentment linger in a society constructed on mutual suspicions and fed on the disparagement of what the other holds most dear. Nothing is beyond dismissal and disdain. While Protestant Loyalists regard the cultural energy of Gaelic games as an open affront because of the choice of club names and other trappings, Catholic Nationalists see Loyalist parades merely as assertions of Orange supremacy involving bands whose sole purpose is to provoke them. Any reference to Blood and Thunder bands is prefaced with pejorative references to 'coat-trailing' sectarianism and, invariably, the bands are seen as merely the bully-boys of the Orange movement or, worse, as the musical wing of Loyalist paramilitary groups. Their parades are resented and opposed as a matter of course.

Yet if understanding is the prelude to acceptance and trust, there must be recognition of the inherent value of all indigenous culture and tradition in such a small space. In the twenty-first century, this involves understanding and accepting the marching bands as the most vibrant aspect of Ulster Protestant culture. For although they emerged in the darkest days of the Troubles as an outlet for young Protestants to assert their place as the world of their fathers crumbled, the Blood and Thunder bands are now the embodiment of Protestant pride. In their muscular music, strident style and parade-ground choreography, they encapsulate the martial spirit of the past for the first generation of Ulster Protestants that has not taken up arms in defence of their own community ... and in defiance of their neighbours. By adapting the uniforms, parading and the musical legacy of their military forebears, they carry on traditions that have underscored generations before them that rallied to fife and drum. The heroes they proclaim are young men from their own communities who went off to fight the Great War, especially those who perished nobly. It is this Ulster heroism, rather than traditional images of Royal succession, that is honoured by the uniformed young men who step out along the highways and byways of every town and village in Northern Ireland over nine months of the year. It is their memory that is evoked at the growing number of indoor concerts that sustain them through the remaining three months of winter. It is their codes of conduct and their values that will increasingly inform the thousands of young Protestant boys that enlist in local bands each year.

Finding a place for that culture is as vital as the need for the bands to assuage the concerns of those Nationalists who oppose and dismiss Loyalist parades out of hand (just as this opposition is mutually dismissed in turn). Changing the

views of, and within, Blood and Thunder bands is a daunting
task, not least because of their 'congregational' organisation
as independent units. They do not have a unified view,
much less a united voice, yet the Ulster Bands Forum is a
vitally important and lively arena that is producing change,
particularly in the standards of music and decorum being
promoted to raise the profile and reputation of the bands.
An equally pressing catalyst for change is the very success
of the Blood and Thunder bands. Already, the calendar is
choc-a-bloc, and with limited time for parades, growing
membership, more bands and fewer resources, streamlined
arrangements are being considered, such as bands combining
for annual parades. That and other changes should make the
bands more accommodating to outside concerns, as will
the acceptance that the right to walk the Queen's Highway
is subject to licence, just as much as driving it. Finding a
community-based means of agreeing parade routes should
relieve pressure on an issue that is fraught with the impending
doom of the past. Yet never have the two extremes in Northern
Ireland seemed closer on pivotal issues that will underwrite
peace and mutual respect for difference. For if policing is
the essential bedrock of justice in Northern Ireland that has
never existed before for Nationalists, a year of Blood and
Thunder has convinced me that parading is at the very core
of Ulster Loyalist identity. Choosing to be entertained by it,
rather than offended, is the secret to a shared future.

APPENDIX A

(Parades Commission) Guidance for Anyone Participating in Parades

A   Behaviour

All participants in parades should:

- behave with due regard for the rights, traditions and feelings of others in the vicinity
- refrain from using words or behaviour which could reasonably be perceived as being intentionally sectarian, provocative, threatening, abusive, insulting or lewd
- obey the lawful directions of parade organisers and stewards at all times, from assembly to dispersal
- abide by the conditions of this code of conduct
- comply with police directions and in accordance with legislation

B   Dress

No paramilitary-style clothing is to be worn at any time during a parade.

C   Parade

Whenever possible, the parade should be positioned on one side of the carriageway so as to allow for the free flow of traffic, or as otherwise stipulated by police.

D   Route

Participants should keep to the designated route as directed by the police.

E   Alcohol

Alcohol should not be consumed immediately prior to, or during, a parade. An organiser or steward who believes a participant to be under the influence of alcohol, should take the necessary measures to remove that person from the parade.

F   Bands and Music

Each band must clearly display its name. Restrictions on the playing of music will be in accordance with the conditions as set out in Appendix B of this code. No musical instrument will bear any inscription or mark of a proscribed organisation.

G   Flags etc.

Flags and other displays often have a legitimate historical significance, but in no circumstances should such items relating to a proscribed organisation be displayed.

H   Stewards

The names of stewards will have been notified to the police and the Parades Commission at the time of notifying the proposed parade. Stewards should:
- be properly trained
- be briefed by the organisers prior to the parade

- carry proof of their status at all times during the event, and provide this information to police on request
- be fully aware of their responsibilities and role
- be highly visible by means of jackets, singlets, armbands, etc.
- not consume alcohol before or during the parade
- co-operate with the police
- be prepared to identify to the police any persons in the parade who may be committing any offence against criminal law

I   Policing

Organisers of parades must co-operate with the police from the time of submission of the notice of intention to parade until the parade disperses.

J   Dispersal

When a parade has concluded, all those taking part must disperse immediately. It will be the responsibility of the organisers to ensure compliance with instructions in this regard.

K   Abiding by Conditions

Organisers must ensure that all participants in any parade have been informed of any conditions imposed. As a general principle, the organiser is responsible for the behaviour of all participants and for ensuring compliance with the code of conduct.

APPENDIX B

Guidance for Anyone Participating in Parades in the Vicinity of Sensitive Locations.

A   Places of Worship

- Only hymn tunes should be played
- When church services are taking place, no music should be played
- There should be no irreverent behaviour
- Marching should be dignified

B   War Memorials and Cemeteries

- Only hymn tunes should be played
- Behaviour should be respectful
- Marching should be dignified

C   Where the Majority Population of the Vicinity are of a Different Tradition, and in Interface Areas.

- Behaviour should be respectful
- There should be no excessively loud drumming
- Participants should refrain from conduct, words, music or behaviour which could reasonably be perceived as intentionally sectarian, provocative, threatening, abusive, insulting or lewd
- Marching should be dignified

NOTES

1   There are very few if any 'Orange bands' now and they are usually pipe bands made up of Lodge members which only take part in Lodge parades a couple of times a year. Lodges usually hire bands – pipe, accordion, Blood and Thunder etc. – for parades. Many bands are loosely affiliated to Lodges and use their halls for practice, but they are independent secular bodies with almost no crossover memberships, while Orange lodges are a religious Protestant fraternity. These independent bands, especially Blood and Thunder bands take part in the competitive band parades that extend from March to October and in the winter concerts thereafter.

2   Jonathan Bardon, *A History of Ulster* (Blackstaff, Belfast, 2005), p. 803

3   Ronan McSherry, 'Derg Citizens to have their say on Regeneration', *Ulster Herald*, 8 October 2009, p. 16

4   Lord Byron, *Don Juan: Canto the Eight*, Verse I (1819–1824)

5   Tobias Smollett, *The Adventures of Peregrine Pickle* (London, 1751), p. 13

6   Gilbert K. Chesterton, *The Victorian Age in Literature* (London, 1913), p. 36

7   Desmond Bell, *Irish Times*, 15 August 1985

8   Desmond Bell, *Acts of Union: Youth Culture and Sectarianism in Northern Ireland* (Macmillan, London, 1990).

    The main paramilitary groups were:

    UDA – Ulster Defence Association, Loyalist

    UFF – Ulster Freedom Fighters, Loyalist, cover name used by
        UDA

    UVF – Ulster Volunteer Force, Loyalist, founded 1912 to resist
        Home Rule; A Loyalist paramilitary group formed in 1966
        named itself the UVF

    Red Hand Commando, Loyalist, cover name used by UVF

    LVF – Loyalist Volunteer Force, Loyalist, breakaway from UVF in
        1996

    IRA – Irish Republican Army, Republican, founded 1916; split

in 1922 into National Army and Irregulars, and in 1969 into
Official and Provisional wings

INLA – Irish National Liberation Army, Republican, 1974 split
from Official IRA

Dissident Republicans (active 2010) are Continuity IRA and the
Real IRA

9   Neil Jarman, *Material Conflicts: Parades and Visual Displays in
Northern Ireland* (Berg, Oxford and New York, 1997)

10   Ruth Dudley-Edwards, *The Faithful Tribe* (Harper Collins, London,
1999), p. 12

11   *Ibid.*, p. 41

12   Michael Ignatieff, *Blood and Belonging: Journeys into the New
Nationalism* (Viking, London, 1993), p. 178

13   Joseph Ruane and Jennifer Todd, *The Dynamics of Conflict in Northern
Ireland – Power, Conflict and Emancipation* (Cambridge University
Press, 1996), p. 179

14   Gary Hastings, *With Fife and Drum* (Blackstaff, Belfast, 2003), p. xi

15   Liam Clarke, 'Orange Order Ranks Drop to Record Low,' *The
Sunday Times*, 28 June 2009

16   Brian Feeney, 'Craven Commission Again Fails to Protect the Weak,'
The Wednesday Column, *Irish News*, 26 August 2009

17   Neil Jarman, 'Commemorating 1916, Celebrating Difference:
Parading and Painting in Belfast' in Adrian Forty & Susanne
Kuchler (eds), *The Art of Forgetting* (New York, 1999), p. 180

18   Hastings, *op. cit.*, pp. xiv–xv

19   The cutting has no newspaper name on it, but it may have been taken
from the Tyrone Constitution of that week in 1977.

20   David McKittrick, Seamus Kelters, Brian Feeney, Chris Thornton and
David McVea, *Lost Lives* (Mainstream, Edinburgh, 2004), p. 990

21   *Ibid.*, p. 974

22   *Ibid.*, p. 978

23   *Ibid.*, pp. 990–991

24   From a 1988 interview with Fergal Keane broadcast on BBC in 1988
and included in the DVD '30 Years of Marching', an anniversary
souvenir package from Castlederg Young Loyalists Flute Band, 2007.

25   McKittrick *et al.*, 2004, p. 1129

26 *Ibid.*

27 Fergal Keane, 'A Casualty of the Troubles is Simply a Dead Friend Now', *The Times*, 20 May 2000

28 McKittrick *et al.*, 2004, p. 1234

29 *Ibid.*, p. 1236

30 *Ibid.*, p. 1501

31 David Lister, 'It's Dishonouring Why They Died', *The Times*, London, 19 April 2003

32 cain.ulst.ac.uk/issues/parade/parade.htm

33 www.cylfb.co.uk/home.htm

34 http://www.youtube.com/profile?user=bandxparades#g/u

35 Claire Mitchell and James Tilley, 'Disaggregating Conservative Protestant Groups in Northern Ireland: Overlapping Categories and the Importance of a Born-again Self-identification', *Journal for the Scientific Study of Religion*, 2008, 47(4), pp. 734–748

36 Claire Mitchell, *Religion, Identity and Politics in Northern Ireland: Boundaries of Belonging and Belief* (Ashgate, Aldershot, 2006) p. 143

37 Bardon, *op. cit.*, p. 439

38 *Ibid.*, pp. 444–5

39 *Ibid.*, pp. 454–6

40 Martin Middlebrook, *The First Day on the Somme* (Pen and Sword, London, 2007), p. 223

41 Sam Allen, *To Ulster's Credit* (Killinchey, 1985), p. 118

42 Bardon, *op. cit.*, p. 455

43 Kevin Connolly, BBC Ireland Correspondent, 'The Somme: The Irish in Battle', posted on the BBC website (http://news.bbc.co.uk/1/hi/uk/5126128.stm), 28 June 2006

44 Bardon, *op. cit.*, pp. 555–7

45 *Ibid.*, p. 573

46 *Ibid.*, p. 572

47 *Ibid.*, pp. 574–7

48 All annual band parades are competitive and practically every band has an annual parade. The only non-competitive parades are those conducted under the aegis of the loyal orders such as 12 July, Relief of Derry, Last Saturday, church parades etc.). Each band organises judges for its own parade.

49   Full details of all Notifications of Parade are posted on the website of the Northern Ireland Parades Commission at www.paradescommission.org

50   *Annual Report and Financial Statements Parades Commission for the year ended 31 March 2008* (The Stationery Office, London, 2009)

51   'Police Federation Chief Slams Libya Fiasco', *Belfast Telegraph*, 25 September 2009

52   House of Commons Debates, *Hansard*, 21 January 2009, column 739

53   Rosetta Donnelly, 'Parades Commission Demands Explanation for Illegal Omagh Parade,' *Ulster Herald*, 9 April 2009

54   Quincey Dougan, 'Drumbeat' Column, *Newsletter*, 23 April 2009

55   *Ibid.* The battle of the bands is an overall prize for a the band judged to be the best at a number of venues.

56   *Ibid.*, 30 April 2009. William Savage was an RUC officer who was killed in a remote control landmine explosion near Forkhill, south Armagh, in 1984.

57   *Ibid.*, 7 May 2009

58   *Ibid.*

59   *Ibid.*, 14 May 2009

60   'Band Parade "provocative"', *Newry Democrat*, 20 May 2009

61   Dougan, 'Drumbeat', *Newsletter*, 14 May 2009

62   *Ibid.*, 22 May 2009

63   *Ibid.*

64   'Fresh Arrests Over Coleraine Murder', *Newsletter*, 26 May 2009

65   'Parade to be diverted away from murder site', *The Irish Times*, 28 May 2009

66   Lisa Smyth, 'Loyalist Parade Passes Peacefully but Tensions Still Simmer', *Sunday Life*, 31 May 2009

67   'Parade "dragged" into fallout over murder' *Newsletter*, 1 June 2009

68   Jim Gibney, 'Loyalist Ring of Steel Finally Penetrated by Rule of Law', *Irish News*, 4 June 2009

69   'Orange Hall and GAA club fired, robbed' *Belfast Telegraph*, 23 May 2009

70   A well-known annual event hosted by the Royal Black Preceptory in the village of Scarva, County Down, whose central feature is a pageant type re-enaction of a swordfight between costumed

characters representing King Billy and King James. King Billy always wins and it is portrayed in TV and other media coverage as a fun event after all the serious business of the Orange parades.

71   Dougan, 'Drumbeat', *Newsletter*, 18 June 2009

72   *Ibid.*

73   *Ibid.*

74   *Ibid.*, 25 June 2009

75   Maeve Connolly, 'Flute Band Says Sorry to Catholics', *Irish News*, 19 June 2009

76   Dougan, 'Drumbeat', *Newsletter*, 25 June 2009

77   Michael O'Regan, 'Orangemen Reject Call to Reroute all Contested Marches', *The Irish Times*, 22 June 2009. Kevin Lynch was an IRA hunger striker from Dungiven, County Derry.

78   Dougan, 'Drumbeat', *Newsletter*, 1 July 2009

79   *Ibid.*

80   *Ibid.*

81   *Ibid.*

82   Dominic Bryan, 'The Marching Season', *Orange Parades: The Politics of Ritual, Tradition and Control* (Pluto Press, London, 2000), p. 127

83   *Ibid.*, p. 128

84   'Flags at Centre of Parade Tension', *Impartial Reporter*, 9 July 2009

85   Dougan, 'Drumbeat', *Newsletter*, 9 July 2009

86   *Ibid.*, 16 July 2009

87   'Fear and Loathing in Antrim', *Belfast Telegraph*, 11 July 2009

88   'Castlederg "Still Sectarian" Claims McHugh', *Derry Journal*, 17 August 2007

89   Dougan, 'Drumbeat', *Newsletter*, 22 July 2009

90   *Ibid.*, 30 July 2009

91   *Ibid.*

92   *Ibid.*, 6 August 2009

93   *Ibid.*, 13 August 2009

94   Claire Simpson, 'Band is Trying to Shake Off Blood and Thunder Image', *Irish News*, 8 September 2008

95   Bobby Magreechan and George Holmes, *The Ulster Drum* (Ulster-Scots Agency, Belfast, 2009)

96   'Apprentice Boys Call for Screens', BBC Northern Ireland News

website, 21 July 2009

97 Jim Brownlee, 'Apprentice Boys are Working Towards a Better Future,' *Newsletter*, 7 August 2009

98 Brian Lacey, *Discover Derry* (O'Brien, Dublin, 1999), pp. 31–38

99 Mark Oliver, 'Operation Banner, 1969–2007', *The Guardian*, 31 July 2007

100 McKittrick *et al.*, 2004, p. 42

101 Lacey, *op. cit.*, p. 88

102 www.rathcoolekai.webs.com

103 'Apprentice Boys pass peacefully', BBC Northern Ireland News website, 10 August 2009

104 'Nine Charged as Trouble Breaks Out after Apprentice Boys Parade', *Belfast Telegraph*, 10 August 2009

105 'Republicans "Behind City Trouble"', BBC Northern Ireland News website, 10 August 2009

106 *Ibid.*

107 Dougan, 'Drumbeat', *Newsletter*, 20 August 2009

108 'Loyalist Band Leader Fined for Spitting at Nationalists', *Belfast Telegraph*, 13 August 2009

109 Alan Rodgers, 'Removal of Flags Stokes Tension in Derg Area', *Ulster Herald*, 13 August 2009

110 Dougan, 'Drumbeat', *Newsletter*, 20 August 2009

111 *Ibid.*

112 McKittrick *et al.*, 2004, pp. 1077–9

113 *Ibid.*, pp. 1227–9

114 Lesley-Anne Henry, 'Sinn Féin Accused of Hypocrisy Over Loyalist Parade', *Belfast Telegraph*, 21 August 2009

115 Dougan, 'Drumbeat', *Newsletter*, 27 August 2009

116 *Ibid.*

117 *Ibid.*, 3 September 2009

118 *Ibid.*, 10 September 2009

119 *Ibid.*

120 Off-licences put alcohol purchases into blue plastic bags in Northern Ireland. Blue Bag Brigade is a very well-known term for camp followers who walk along behind bands etc. with their alcoholic carry-outs.

121 'SF protests are "sham"', *Ulster Herald*, 24 September 2009

INDEX

Northern Ireland Police Federation 143

O

O'Donovan Rossa, J. 100
O'Hanlon, Fergal 297
O'Neill, Michelle 296
Ó Cúiv, Éamon 267
Omagh 17, 50, 53, 55, 65, 69, 102,
104, 108, 113, 114, 115, 118, 125,
126, 148, 149, 150, 151, 152, 153,
155, 156, 167, 172, 187, 206, 208,
224, 231, 243, 255, 256, 257, 258,
263, 270, 271, 274, 286, 306, 307,
308, 309, 312, 317, 322, 326
Omagh Protestant Boys 50, 54, 103,
119, 125, 153, 164, 172, 224, 242,
248, 311, 312, 317, 322
Operation Banner 51, 283
Orange Order 9, 19, 22, 23, 24, 26, 27,
30, 35, 36, 37, 38, 44, 53, 63, 98, 106,
131, 132, 140, 141, 142, 159, 160,
168, 180, 185, 186, 190, 215, 217,
219, 223, 229, 235, 236, 238, 239,
240, 244, 245, 246, 247, 248, 256,
257, 258, 260, 262, 263, 264, 265,
275, 280, 282, 306, 331, 332, 333
Orritor 215

P

Parades Commission 16, 43, 125, 128,
129, 130, 131, 132, 133, 134, 135,
138, 139, 140, 141, 142, 143, 155,
156, 160, 161, 162, 167, 168, 204,
244, 249, 250, 299, 300, 318, 336, 337
Plantation of Ulster 11, 332
Plumbridge 259, 309
Pomeroy 298
Portadown 10, 30, 122, 124, 126, 129,
142, 156, 175, 214, 289, 294, 318
Porter, Kenny 54, 104
Portrush 74, 88, 89, 93, 94, 270
Poyntzpass 271
Pride of Ballinran 21, 216, 275, 312, 317
Pride of the Derg 15, 17, 153, 160,
176, 182, 183, 253, 254, 259, 302,
303, 306, 308, 317

Pride of the Maine 213, 214, 288
PSNI 76, 155, 156, 170, 291, 292, 315

Q

Quiet Man, The 136

R

Rainey, Councillor Allan 258, 259
Randalstown 56, 157, 318, 319
Rasharkin 10, 37, 136, 300
Rathcoole 31, 32, 288, 295
Rathfriland 125, 210, 285, 314
Red Hand Defenders Flute Band 55,
125, 158, 177, 211, 227, 229, 259,
260, 288, 316, 317
Relief of Derry 273, 280, 282, 283
Robert Graham Memorial Flute Band
287, 301
Robinson, Peter 331
Roslea 206
Rossnowlagh 205, 245, 249
Roughan Silver Band 268
Royal Black Preceptory 9, 22, 38, 98,
141, 217, 223, 306, 308, 309
Royal Inniskilling Fusiliers 108, 114
Royal Irish Regiment (RIR) 46, 47,
69, 263, 307

S

Salvation Army 131
Sandy Row 137, 148, 276
Sash, The 54, 102, 119, 137, 154, 155,
316, 319, 320
Scarva 203, 277
Schomberg Ulster-Scots Association
274
Schwaben Redoubt 109, 110, 111
Scotland 17, 21, 25, 30, 38, 83, 98,
109, 130, 137, 160, 211, 225, 226,
227, 243, 274, 276, 313
Second World War 115, 116, 117
Seskinore 258
Shankill Road 83, 158, 163, 165, 211,
271, 276, 288, 303, 313
Sinn Féin 66, 68, 135, 140, 156, 159,
164, 168, 215, 232, 250, 252, 254,